# Revisioning Beckett

*Samuel Beckett (left) and S. E. Gontarski (back). In between is Rick Cluchey. Photograph by John Minihan. © University College Cork*

# Revisioning Beckett

## Samuel Beckett's Decadent Turn

### S. E. Gontarski

BLOOMSBURY ACADEMIC

NEW YORK · LONDON · OXFORD · NEW DELHI · SYDNEY

BLOOMSBURY ACADEMIC
Bloomsbury Publishing Inc
1385 Broadway, New York, NY 10018, USA

BLOOMSBURY, BLOOMSBURY ACADEMIC and the Diana logo
are trademarks of Bloomsbury Publishing Plc

First published in the United States of America 2018

Cover design: Anna Berzovan
Cover image © Getty Images

Library of Congress Cataloging-in-Publication Data
A catalog record for this book is available from the Library of Congress.

ISBN:     HB:     978-1-5013-3763-5
          PB:     978-1-5013-3762-8
          ePDF:   978-1-5013-3765-9
          eBook:  978-1-5013-3764-2

Typeset by Integra Software Services Pvt. Ltd.
Printed and bound in the United States of America

To find out more about our authors and books visit
www.bloomsbury.com and sign up for our newsletters.

*For Marsha,*

*Yet again,*

*For all*

*She is*

*Chance furnishes me what I need. I am like a man who stumbles along; my foot strikes something; I bend over, and it is exactly what I want.* James Joyce to Jacques Mercanton ("The Hours of James Joyce," 1962, 213)

*[…] here begins the freedom of the mind, or rather the possibility that in the course of time the mind will be free to write what it likes.* Virginia Woolf on Aphra Behn (A Room of One's Own, Ch. 4, 64)

# CONTENTS

# FOREWORD

Readers coming to the work of S. E. Gontarski for the first time should understand some of the context that surrounds his career, because so much of this context underlines that this work is no distant "academic" affair. As the old cliché has it, Stanley Gontarski has skin in the game. Indeed, Gontarski taught me firsthand that being a literary critic does not involve offering an overview, as if from Olympus, or authoritative ruminations on what one has read and others have done, as if in a comfortable armchair by the fireside. If pursing the former image (the critic as God) leads inevitably to bathos, pursing the latter (the critic as self-aggrandizing Ivy League or Oxbridge don) leads equally ineluctably to a crisis of interpretation, as no one, however privileged, occupies the seat of meaning. The critic is, rather, an actor, like anyone else.

While it has often been denied, and they have often been derided, critics are essential parts of the ecosystem that allowed Samuel Beckett's works to emerge, and critics continue to help those works thrive. One could put it another way: Beckett's relations with critics he knew personally, like Ruby Cohn, James Knowlson, Herbert Blau, Martha Fehsenfeld, and S. E. Gontarski (the list is quite long and I've left many people out), opened a dialogue that was two way. A whole critical milieu emerged out of the encounter, especially in theater studies, and in consequence the discipline itself changed around the world through the 1960s, 1970s, and 1980s. These changes would not have been possible in the same way without the exchanges between Beckett and the critics. Much the same could be said of Beckett's engagement with publishing and avant-garde writing through the come and go between Beckett and the milieus surrounding Editions de Minuit in Paris, Calder in London, and Grove Press in New York, and critical works also helped those scenes to grow. So too, Beckett's own work was affected, sometimes directly, by these encounters.

For an example of how Beckett was affected one does not have to look further than the genesis of Beckett's extraordinary late play *Ohio Impromptu*. A critic who wanted to be a part of the creative process as much as concerned with it, the young Stanley Gontarski wrote to Beckett and asked him if he might have a new play that could be performed at a conference Gontarski was planning to celebrate Beckett's seventy-fifth birthday, to take place at Ohio State University in 1981. Beckett initially replied that he had nothing to hand, but, just as invitations to offer new work would lead to other late plays (*Catastrophe* and both the theater and television versions of *What Where*, for example), the idea intrigued Beckett and so he wrote a play for the occasion.

Gontarski not only knew Beckett, but other actors on the scene. Beckett's New York publisher, the larger-than-life Barney Rosset, became a close friend. Gontarski was also close to Herbert Blau, who, not without attracting criticism, demonstrated how one might move between the theatrical and critical worlds, with, in Blau's view, the work of criticism as much a performance as a work of theater.

Having been very much on the scene as Beckett worked in the theater in his last years, Gontarski was crucial to the documentation of the process, editing *The Theatrical Notebooks of Samuel Beckett: The Shorter Plays* and *The Theatrical Notebooks of Samuel Beckett, Vol. II, Endgame*. His interests were not just in Beckett's theater, however, as he also edited *Samuel Beckett: The Complete Short Prose, 1928–1989*. In addition, over the years he has written and edited many major books on Beckett's works. Confirming his status as one of the preeminent critics in the field he took over the editorial responsibilities for *The Journal of Beckett Studies* from 1989 to 2008. In short, then, Gontarski's name has, for many years, been inextricably linked with Beckett's.

Yet he has not been content to rest in place. Rather than ever more quietly repeating ideas uncovered while Beckett was alive Gontarski has moved on in his own work, bringing literature into dialogue with philosophy, and the work of Henri Bergson and Gilles Deleuze in particular. Following Bergson, perhaps, Gontarski has seen that thought never ceases to move and that the work of the critic, of participating in creation, opening the way to it and from it, is ongoing.

It is not my intention to offer an introduction to the essays collected here. Rather, I simply mean to encourage readers to imagine these essays as part of something organic, an ecosystem of creative activity named Beckett that remains very much alive. In this collection, Gontarski, in returning to Beckett's works and those that surrounded them from a different perspective, sees things again, offering us new ways of understanding.

*Anthony Uhlmann*
*Western Sydney University*

# ACKNOWLEDGMENTS

Among the pleasures of publication the opportunity to acknowledge publicly the support and advice one receives from family, colleagues, and editors is especially gratifying. In this case I am happy to thank Haaris Naqvi, editorial director at Bloomsbury Academic, not only for his guidance in shaping this current book, *Revisioning Beckett: Samuel Beckett's Decadent Turn*, but, over the past several years, for his help on and support of the book series that I coedit (with professors Paul Ardoin and Laci Mattison) for Bloomsbury called *Understanding Philosophy, Understanding Modernism*, two volumes of which, those on Henri Bergson and on Gilles Deleuze, my general coeditors and I edited to launch the series. Such a fruitful and personal editorial relationship has, unfortunately, grown all too rare in our current climate of corporate publishing. Happily, my coeditors and I have found such nurturing at Bloomsbury. I am grateful as well that my longtime collaborators and coauthors have supported this volume. Anthony Uhlmann, who wrote its "Preface" and with whom I share philosophical and theoretical sympathies, has been a stalwart ally for many years now. And the encyclopedic-minded annotator par excellence, Chris Ackerley has brought his "eye of prey" to bear on these essays and in the process has saved me from any number of blunders. And, of course, few things are possible in my world without home-front support, and for that I thank my wife, Marsha, who has been on this crazy adventure with me for over fifty years now, and to whom this book is, once again, *come sempre*, dedicated.

Earlier versions of the essays that comprise *Revisioning Beckett: Samuel Beckett's Decadent Turn* have been generated initially by a variety of speaking invitations, *Festschriften* requests, and other occasional presentations and publications. I am indebted to the conveners of those meetings and to the editors of those publications for permission to reprint the essays here collected, with appropriate acknowledgments and, in most cases, in considerably revised, altered, and expanded versions.

Introduction: "Demonology, Sade-ism, and Samuel Beckett's Decadent Turn" was first presented as "Of Vices and Virtues: Samuel Beckett's Offenses 'against all sense of [...] decency'" as the keynote address at the "Beckett and Vice" conference, Harrah's Resort, Southern California, February 22, 2016.

Chapter 1: "Samuel Beckett and *Lace Curtain* Irish Modernisms" was presented as "Sweeney among the Moderns: *The Lace Curtain* of Irish Modernisms" as a keynote address at the "Acting Out: IV International Flann O'Brien Society" conference, Salzburg, Austria, July 17–21, 2017.

Chapter 2: "Publishing in America: Sam and Barney" was published as "The Business of Being Beckett: Beckett's Reception in the USA," *The International Reception of Samuel Beckett*, edited by Mark Nixon and Matthew Feldman (London: Continuum International Publishing, 2009, 2011): 21–49.

Chapter 3: "*Eleutheria*: Samuel Beckett's Suppressed Bohemian Manifesto" was published as "*Eleutheria*: Samuel Beckett's Suppressed Play: An Introduction" in *Eleutheria*, by Samuel Beckett, translated from the French by Michael Brodsky (New York: Foxrock, Inc., 1995), vii–xxii.

Chapter 4: "Textual Aberrations, Ghost Texts, and the British *Godot*: A Saga of Censorship" was first presented as "Of Vices and Virtues: Samuel Beckett's Offenses 'Against All Sense of [...] Decency'" as the keynote address at the "Beckett and Vice" conference, Harrah's Resort, Southern California, February 22, 2016, and subsequently expanded and published as "Ballocksed, Banjaxed or Banjoed: Textual Aberrations, Ghost Texts, and the British *Godot*," *Journal of Modern Literature*, 41.4 (summer 2018).

Chapter 5: "'nothingness/in words enclose?': *Waiting for Godot*" was published under that title in the *Festschrift, Surprised by Scenes: Essays in Honour of Professor Yasunari Takahashi*, edited by Yasunari Takada (Tokyo, Japan: Kenkyusha, Ltd., 1994), 375–92.

Chapter 6: "An End to Endings: Samuel Beckett's End Game(s)" was presented as a keynote address at the Setagaya Public Theater Setagaya, Tokyo, on September 29, 2006, as part of the "Borderless Beckett: International Samuel Beckett" symposium. It was published under that title in a collection of conference papers, *Borderless Beckett: International Samuel Beckett Symposium Papers* (Tokyo:

Tokyo Press Co., Ltd., 2007), 69–79, and subsequently in an expanded form as "An End to Endings: Samuel Beckett's End Game(s)" in *Borderless Beckett/Beckett sans frontiers* (*Samuel Beckett Today/Aujourd'hui*), edited by Minako Okamuro, Naoya Mori, Bruno Clément, Sjef Houppermans, Angela Moorjani, and Anthony Uhlmann, No. 19 (2008): 419–29.

Chapter 7: "Samuel Beckett's Art of Self-collaboration" was written originally as "Rewriting Himself: Samuel Beckett in the Theatre," an invited lecture for the Third Annual Samuel Beckett lecture series at Trinity College, Dublin, April 2, 1998. It was revised and subsequently published in 2009 as "Revising Himself: Samuel Beckett and the Art of Self-collaboration," in *Reflections on Beckett: A Centenary Celebration*, edited by Anna McMullan and S. E. Wilmer (Ann Arbor: University of Michigan Press), 153–72.

Chapter 8: "Beckett's Keyhole Art: Voyeurism, *Schaulust,* and the Perversions of Theater" was delivered at the "Samuel Beckett: Textual Genesis and Reception" conference sponsored by IASIL (International Association for the Study of Irish Literature), Charles University, Prague, Czech Republic, July 27, 2005. It was subsequently published as "Beckett through the Keyhole: Voyeurism, the Scopophilic Drive, and the Appeal of Theatre" in *Litteraria Pragensia: Studies in Literature and Culture*, special issue edited by Ondrej Pliny and Louis Armand, XVII.33 (July 2007): 63–72.

Chapter 9: An earlier version of "'He wants to know if it hurts!': The Body as Text in Samuel Beckett's Theater" was delivered as "The Body in the Body of Beckett's Theater," at the "Beckett in Berlin 2000" conference at Humboldt University, Berlin, September 21, 2000, and was subsequently published under that title in the collection of conference papers entitled *Endlessness in the Year 2000* in *Samuel Beckett Today/Aujourd'hui*, guest eds. Angela Moorjani and Carola Veit, 11 (December 2001): 169–77.

Chapter 10: "Theoretical and Theatrical Intersections: Samuel Beckett, Herbert Blau, Civil Rights, and the Politics of *Godot*" was delivered as a plenary address, "Thinking Samuel Beckett through Herbert Blau," at the "Chaos and Form: Echoes of Beckett in Literature, Theatre and the Arts" conference sponsored by the Department of Analytic Philosophy, Institute of Philosophy, Czech Academy of Sciences, Charles University, Prague, Czech Republic on April 12, 2016. A shorter, revised version was delivered at the

ACKNOWLEDGMENTS xvii

"Beckett and Modernism" conference at the University of Antwerp on April 29, 2016. The latter version was subsequently expanded and published in the conference papers, *Beckett and Modernism*, edited by Dirk Van Hulle, Verhulst Pim, and Olga Beloborodova (London: Palgrave, 2018).

Chapter 11: "Beckett and the Revisioning of Modernism(s): *Molloy*" was published as "*Molloy* and the Reiterated Novel" for the *Festschrift*, "*As no other dare Fail*": *Essays in Honor of Samuel Beckett's Eightieth Birthday*, edited by John Calder (London: John Calder [Publishers] Ltd., 1986), 57–65.

Chapter 12: "A Sense of Unending: Fictions for the End of Time" was published as "A Sense of Unending: Samuel Beckett's Eschatological Turn," *Samuel Beckett Today/Aujourd'hui*, edited by Matthijs Engelberts and Sjef Houppermans No. 21 (2010): 135–49.

Chapter 13: "The Death of Style: Samuel Beckett's Art of Repetition, Pastiche, and Cutups" was published as "Style and the Man: Samuel Beckett and the Art of Pastiche," *Pastiches, Parodies & Other Imitations. Pastiches, Parodies & Autres Imitations (Samuel Beckett Today/Aujourd'hui)*, edited by Marius Buning, Matthijs Engelberts, and Sjef Houppermans, 12.1 (December 2002): 11–20.

# Demonology, Sade-ism, and Samuel Beckett's Decadent Turn: An Introduction

*To decompose is to live too.* Molloy, 25

*What we call literature (not belles-lettres or poetry) implies that license is given to the writer to say everything he wants to or everything he can, while remaining shielded, safe from all censorship, be it religious or political. Jacques Derrida, "This Strange Institution We Call Literature" (1989)*

## *Le demimonde*

Amid a prudish, self-confident if not smug nineteenth-century Europe, undercurrents of seismic cultural change were already irreversible, its rumblings eroding presumptive cultural stability, an assumed natural order, its inhabitants sliding, by degrees, toward ideological uncertainties—as Freud dismantled childhood innocence and exposed the depths and conflicts of human desire, as John Ruskin became Walter Pater, as *The Shropshire Lad* (1896) grew into *The Ballad of Reading Gaol* (1898), and as realism developed into naturalism, Ibsen mutating into Zola or Gorky, *An Enemy of the People* (1882) transforming into *The Lower Depths* (1901, Kurosawa film 1957). Naturalism itself subsequently developed at first into forms of expressive, distortive figuration on canvas, stage, and page with Expressionism, Futurism, post-Impressionism, and Cubism, and then, abandoning figuration entirely, into pure abstraction and Abstract Expressionism. The emerging field of art photography quickly deserted figuration as well, as in Man Ray's *Dust Breeding* (1920), a photograph of accumulated dust on Marcel Duchamp's *The Large Glass* (1915–23). Even as formal portraiture grew unrecognizable (viz. Picasso, Matisse et al.), however, the Surrealists returned to automated figuration through emerging technology and produced playful self-portraits, with the usual mugging, using the near-instantaneous process of photo booths in the Paris of 1929.[1] The ten-minute process, then, produced a string of black-and-white images without human intervention (see Jones). The Polaroid portraiture of Warhol and Mapplethorpe would follow on half a century later.

Such revolutionary, formal shifts in the arts fractured not only art's images but time as well, disrupting the comfort and flow of orderly, linear time, replacing, overlaying, or cross-cutting it with the simultaneity of multiple moments or its acceleration. Time grew less an objective sequence of measurement than psychological (Bergson) and relative (Einstein) instantiations. In the interlude to Virginia Woolf's *To the Lighthouse* (1927), for example, "Time Passes" and, somehow, narratologically at least, stands still, while in Marcel Duchamp's *Nude Descending A Staircase, No 2* (1912), the fractured multiplicity of a figure moves: in the frozen moment of art time passes. Even in her sheltered life, which was effected only tangentially by the Great War, and amid the narrative's parallel plot lines and multiple, overlapping voices, Virginia Woolf's Clarissa Dalloway reflects such doubts amid her domesticity: "To see her own sister killed by a falling tree [...] before your eyes [...] was enough to turn one bitter [...] she thought there were no gods; no one was to blame." Amid such personal crisis and a general enfeeblement of religion, Clarissa developed an alternative, personal humanism in response to her skepticism: "she evolved this atheist's religion of doing good for the sake of goodness" (Woolf 1925, 78).

Of the aftermath of the Great War, such calamities not yet numbered, Peter Thompson writes in *The Guardian* that "The Weimar Republic was essentially a shell-shocked society in which many of the old certainties had been smashed to pieces. Worse than that, nothing had arisen from the ruins to give anyone any hope for the future." Weimar's crisis remained apposite for if not emblematic of the greater part of Europe as well, and it held implications for the remainder of the century, from the rise of National Socialism in response to the Weimar crises, to the defeat of democracy in Spain, to the next Great War and its pogroms and genocide, and to the subsequent Cold War with its looming threat of human annihilation amid a nuclear winter.

Such artistic upheaval was alarming to some cultural critics, most notably, perhaps, because his work was so influential, German eugenicist Max Nordeau (1849–1923) whose *Degeneration* (1895) was celebrated and quickly translated into English. By 1898, its American edition (New York: D. Appleton and Company) was in its ninth edition. Nordeau assailed the Modernists, the Symbolist poets and their celebration of synesthesia in particular, for a level of degeneracy that approached or was tantamount to criminal behavior. In his dedication to the book Nordeau praises Italian criminologist Professor Caesar Lombroso effusively, and Nordeau's work would extend Lombroso's notions of profiling, that inherited bodily traits, especially abnormalities, were reliable indicators of character, particularly an individual's propensity for crime. The transformation of Robert Louis Stevenson's Dr. Jekyll into the criminal, Mr. Hyde (1895), for instance, was accompanied by pronounced changes in physiognomy. Nordeau, then, would use scientific and evolutionary language to condemn much of the experimental art of the nineteenth century: "Degenerates are not always criminals, prostitutes and lunatics; they are often authors and artists. These, however, manifest the same mental characteristics, and for the most part the same somatic features, as members of the above mentioned anthropological family, who satisfy their unhealthy impulses with the knife of the assassin or the bomb of the dynamiter, instead of with pen and pencil." And in a bout of self-pity, Nordeau notes, "grievous is the fate of him who has the audacity to characterize aesthetic fashions as forms of mental decay" (vii–viii). Nordeau's particular target of such abandonment of traditional discipline and disciplines, such rejection of logic and order in the arts, was mysticism, and in

Book II of *Degeneration* he assails the Pre-Raphaelites (Chapter II), Symbolism (Chapter III), Tolstoy (or "Tolstoism," Chapter IV), and Wagner ("The Richard Wagner Cult," Chapter V). In Book III he targets the "Ego-mania" of those who see and use language as a non-referential medium, and Nordeau attacks Baudelaire ("Parnassians and Diabolists"), among others, for his mystical and antisocial leanings. In "Parnassians and Diabolists," Nordeau moves from Théophile Gautier to the "diabolist" Baudelaire, as among those who reject sense and meaning and finally celebrate evil, citing Gautier's dictum: "For the poet, words have in themselves, and outside the sense they express, a beauty and value of their own, like precious stones as yet uncut [...] they charm the connoisseur who looks at them [...]. Gustave Flaubert, another worshipper of words, takes entirely this view of his subject when he exclaims: 'A beautiful verse meaning nothing, is superior to a verse less beautiful meaning something'" (Nordeau 1895, 267). Furthermore, "Baudelaire hates life and movement. [...] He abhors the natural as much as he loves the artificial," his poems expressing a "desperate cry towards the 'new'" (Nordeau 1895, 286–8).

Nordeau's appeal for a language and art that reflect reality as we think we already know it might be dismissed as so much uninformed positivism, like similar attacks against Henri Bergson, in whose intuition critics noted leanings toward mysticism, but despite such excoriation of what are movements and thoughts in the throes of becoming Modernism, via aestheticism and decadence, perhaps, Nordeau would have considerable influence on twentieth-century artists, either directly or via secondary commentators on eugenics, T. S. Eliot, the Woolfs, Virginia and Leonard, Djuna Barnes, Eugene O'Neill, and William Butler Yeats, among them: "In 1915, Virginia Woolf described a walk on which she met 'a long line of imbeciles.' She wrote that 'everyone in that long line was a miserable ineffective shuffling idiotic creature, with no forehead or no chin & [sic] and an imbecile grin, or a wild, suspicious stare. It was perfectly horrible. They should certainly be killed'" (Woolf cited in Glover). Woolf here seems to be echoing Dr. W. Duncan McKim who published *Heredity and Human Progress* in 1900:

> The roll, then, of those whom our plan would eliminate, consists of the following classes of individuals coming under the absolute control of the State:—idiots, imbeciles, epileptics, habitual

drunkards and insane criminals, the large number of murderers, nocturnal house-breakers, such criminals whatever their offence as might through their constitutional organization appear very dangerous, and finally, criminals who might be adjudged incorrigible. Each individual of these classes would undergo thorough examination, and only by due process of law would his life be taken from him.

The painless extinction of these lives would present no practical difficulty—in carbonic acid gas we have an agent which would instantaneously fulfill the need. (McKim, 265)

Samuel Beckett had no sympathy for eugenics, of course, but he would take extensive notes from *Degeneration* as he was writing what he thought would be his first published novel, *Dream of Fair to Middling Women*. He was at least intrigued with Nordeau's vocabulary if not his assault on, among other things, mysticism and the experimental arts in general. Beckett noted and would use in his early writing, particularly *Dream of Fair to Middling Women* (to which the first numbers refer in what follows), such words and phrases from Nordeau as "corprolalia" (7, *DN* 671), "cicisbei" (13, *DN* 612), "logorrhea" (14, *DN* 636), "obsidional" (16, *DN* 624), "siege-crazy" (26, *DN* 624), "coenaesthesis" (32, *DN* 666), "inchoate liminal presentations" (33, *DN* 626), "Gedankenflucht" (thought flight) (45, *DN* 628), "aboulia" (46, *DN* 616), "echolalia" (168, *DN* 629), "gigerls" (89, 90, *DN* 623), "precarious ipsissmosity" (113, *DN* 670), "troglodyse" (123, *DN* 657), and "arithmomaniac" (220, *DN* 662); these were copied into his *Dream Notebook* (*DN*) of the 1930s (*DN*, 89–97) as he was reading *Degeneration* (Pilling 1999, 2004). In particular Beckett noted Nordeau's analysis of the world's largest flower in Sumatra, one that smells like a rotting corpse, using the image in the early poem "Enueg I" and in *The Unnamable*: "bloodied rafflesia in sombre Sumatra."[2] Amid such degeneracy, Beckett's aesthetic comments would be fodder for Nordeau's attacks as he proclaims, in his review of the poetry of Denis Devlin, proffering "the vile suggestion [to the likes of Nordeau, certainly] that art has nothing to do with clarity, does not dabble in the clear and does not make clear." Nordeau's ideas would finally take a nefarious ideological swerve with the National Socialist government of Germany as it conducted its campaign against what it deemed "degenerate art" at first and then directly in pogroms against those whom authorities deemed "degenerate." As Jonathan Glover writes in *The Guardian*: "Revulsion against Nazi eugenics is deep and uncontroversial. It involved coercive sterilisation of whole groups of people with disorders such as schizophrenia. In a grim rehearsal of the later genocide, it led to the murder by gassing of 70,000 psychiatric patients" (Glover).

With its rejection of neoclassicism in the *fin de siècle* and the erosion of Enlightenment values, and despite the condemnation of critics like Nordeau, innovative, advanced, experimental art and decoration turned to sensuality in style and subject as in the Art Nouveau of Alfonse Mucha,[3] art that took a decidedly decadent if not sinister swerve from middle to under class, toward what Verdi would depict as "the woman who went astray," *La Traviata* (1853, after *La Dame aux Caméllias*, 1852, itself an adaptation of the Alexandre Dumas, fils, novel of that title and whose title character, Marguerite Gautier, reappears as late as Tennessee Williams's *Camino Real* [1953]). Georges Bizet would celebrate the anti-bourgeois, Romani spirit in *Carmen*, after the Prosper Mérimée novel of that title, in 1875, and Puccini would follow suit with *La Bohème* in 1896, based on the Henri Murger collection of short stories "Scènes de la Vie de Bohème" ("Scenes of Bohemian Life"), published in 1845.

In 1928 Radcliff Hall published *The Well of Loneliness*, often called "the archetypal lesbian novel," which was heavily influenced by the work of her friend, Havelock Ellis, particularly his very influential *Sexual Inversion* (1897) in which he argued that gender identification was not necessarily aligned with anatomy but with sexual preferences. The novel's publisher, Jonathan Cape, was prosecuted under the Obscene Publications Act (1857), after which the novel was banned until 1949 in the UK,[4] although it was published in English in Paris in 1933. In the Anglo-Saxon world, at least, such topics risked official censure, but, as Louis Menand notes, publisher Jack Kahane would move his publishing operation across the Channel, open business as Obelisk Press, publishing in English in Paris, and make such risqué works available for, essentially, British tourists: "In 1929, Kahane published *Sleeveless Errand*, by Norah James, a novel that had been banned in Britain solely because its characters lead bohemian lives." Such abstention from and rejection of middle-class standards were thus associated with or could lead to a slide into unacceptable or deviant social and personal behavior.

In 1933, Kahane published Radclyffe Hall's *The Well of Loneliness*, which had been banned in a notorious trial, and after its first Paris publisher, Pegasus, went out of business. The most risqué words in that novel are: "And that night they were not divided." But it is the story of a lesbian relationship, and what made it obscene, according to the presiding magistrate, was that lesbian sex "is described as giving these women extraordinary rest, contentment, and pleasure; and not merely that, but it is actually put forward that it improves their mental balance and capacity." (Menand 2016, 79)

Even more overtly, the swerve exploded into decadence and eroticism depicted in Aubrey Beardsley's illustrations for Oscar Wilde's *Salomé* (1894) and in his covers for *The Yellow Book* (1894–1897),[5] of which Beardsley was art editor. While Wilde was much inspired by the sensuality and spirituality of Gustav Moreau's depiction of Salomé's dance and John the Baptist's floating head in *The Apparition*, Beardsley would redraft, or rather blend or overlay, his images with strains of demonology like those in Gustave Doré's illustrations to Dante's *Inferno* (from 1855, but popularized in the folio editions of the 1860s) and John Milton's *Paradise Lost* (1868), or those in Jacques Auguste Simon Collin de Plancy's *Dictionnaire Infernal* (1818, especially the edition of 1863 with the Louis Le Breton illustrations). Beardsley's innovation was to combine such depictions of imagined demons with the sensuality in the *art nouveau* of Mucha (among others). S. L. MacGregor Mather's translation of *The Lesser Key of Solomon* would reprint many of Le Breton's illustrations, and *The Lesser Key of Solomon* became a staple text for the Hermetic Order of the Golden Dawn, of which Mather[6] was a founding member, William Butler Yeats and Maude Gonne enthusiastic advocates and practitioners, for a time. Yeats was, furthermore, a contributor to *The Yellow Book*, as well. Samuel Beckett was particularly drawn not to the magic of the Golden Dawn but to the demonic images in Doré's illustrations to Dante's *Purgatorio* (Canto IV), of the slothful Belacqua in particular. One Belacqua Shuah, who "conceives of himself first as an artist" as critic Jerri Kroll puts it, and who is "a student of the bohemian pose" (Kroll 1993, 35), is the conflicted, featured figure and authorial stand-in in Beckett's early fiction. In "Sanies II," the narrator will remember Becky Cooper's brothel in the underside of

Dublin, on Railroad Street, and Belacqua will make his way there
at the end of the story "Ding-Dong," as, according to John Pilling,
Beckett himself had on October 3, 1931, as he recently translated
René Crevel's, "The Negress in the Brothel" for Nancy Cunard's
*Negro* (Pilling 2006, 33).

Beardsley's single, initial drawing for *Salomé* was rejected by its
commissioning British publisher, but he subsequently developed
a suite of ten full-page, erotic drawings that alone could stand as
an emblem of this tectonic slide, exposing in the process culture's
recesses and underside, Beardsley and Wilde, at least, entranced by
the nether depths of culture and humanity, the hedonistic world of
the *demimonde*, in something, after Nietzsche, of a transvaluation
of values already substantially transvalued. Wilde published his
philosophical novel, *The Picture of Dorian Gray*, in July 1890 in
*Lippincott's Monthly Magazine,* and despite J. M. Stoddart, the
magazine's editor, removing some 500 words from Wilde's novel
(without Wilde's knowledge), readers were offended, and bookseller
W. H. Smith refused to stock the magazine at all. Although Wilde
never contributed to *The Yellow Book, The Picture of Dorian Gray*
features "the yellow book" that Lord Henry sends Dorian Gray
after the suicide of his first love; it is a major corrupting influence
on Dorian. Gray's "yellow book" is generally considered to be
*À rebours* by Joris-Karl Huysmans, a signature work of Parisian
decadence that heavily influenced British aesthetes like Beardsley.
The uncensored version of the novel, with a new, aphoristic
"Preface" by Wilde, which not only defended the work against
calls for censorship but functioned as something of a manifesto of
decadence, was published by Ward, Lock and Company in 1891,
but in his revisions Wilde grew more circumspect and downplayed
the homosexual references in favor of aesthetic ones. The original
*Lippincott* version of the novel, then, is more overt despite its
censorship, and would subsequently feature prominently in
Wilde's trial in 1895, in which he was finally convicted of "acts
of gross indecency" (*Gay UK*). While the decadence of Wilde
would essentially die with him in a Paris hotel room in 1900,[7] its
afterimages, a broader bohemianism, associated in one form or
another with the avant-garde, persisted through the remainder of
the twentieth century.

James Joyce, rather the Dublin bohemian, Stephen Dedalus,
would enter the *demimonde* through "The Mabbot Street entrance

to nighttown" in a drift toward Bella Cohen's brothel in "Circe," the theatrically structured fifteenth episode of *Ulysses* (1922), the chapter technic, hallucination, the encounter a fusion, a mash-up of another closet drama, Goethe's *Faust,* its "Walpurgisnacht" revels merged with *Venus in Furs,* the 1870 novel by Leopold von Sacher-Masoch, art, like Stephen, detouring from the high street toward culture's underbelly, a turn from day to night thoughts and so to Molly Bloom's erotic, late-night musings that conclude, if that is the word, *Ulysses.* The publication of *Ulysses* in Paris by Shakespeare & Co in 1922 served as inspiration for Jack Kahane to begin Obelisk Press that would launch Henry Miller with his *Tropic of Cancer* in 1934, its postwar reprints, a measure of popularity among soldiers and the Lost Generation, as Gertrude Stein dubbed the group of Parisian expatriates (the book was reprinted in 1950, 1952, 1959, 1960, and 1962). Kahane would also publish *Lady Chatterley's Lover* two years later, in 1936. The first American edition of *Tropic of Cancer* was pirated in 1940 by Medvsa [*sic*] Press. Printed in Mexico but with a New York colophon, the book distributed illegally in the United States twenty-one years before the sensational, ground-breaking Grove Press edition, dated 1961 but released only in 1964 after innumerable local court battles, Grove's *Tropic of Cancer* preceded by its unexpurgated *Lady Chatterley* in 1959. Grove Press would then be the American press Samuel Beckett would be associated with, and it would champion his work in the United States.

The shift, then, was toward an anti-bourgeois, countercultural art, artists themselves engaging the *demimondaine* overtly, as outsider, absinthe-sipping artists embraced their doomed, cursed, marginal, even criminal status, poets and would-be poets succumbing to the siren call of "*la fée verte*," the green fairy: "Kevin Egan rolls gunpowder cigarettes through fingers smeared with printer's ink, sipping his green fairy" (*Ulysses* 1986, 36). At the end of "Oxen in the Sun," Stephen shouts, "Absinthe for me, savvy?" and then, "Landlord, landlord, have you good wine, staboo? Hoots, mon, a wee drap to pree. Cut and come again. Right. Boniface! [that is, 'about face,' a reversal of his order.] Absinthe the lot. *Nos omnes biberimus viridum toxicum diabolus capiat posteriora nostria*" (*Ulysses* 1986, 348) ["We will all drink green poison, and the devil take the hindmost" (Gifford and Seidman 2008, 446)]. In *Circe,* Bloom intervenes with the

soldiers to explain Stephen's belligerence: "He doesn't know what
he's saying. Taken a little more than is good for him. Absinthe.
Greeneyed monster" (*Ulysses* 1986, 483). Stephen was among
those (at least would be) artists for whom the green fairy was
thought to be poetic inspiration and through which apparent evil
might generate its own beauties, flowers, say—*Les Fleurs du mal*
(1857, revised and expanded 1861), as Baudelaire phrased it, or in
the image Baudelaire used for his dedication to these poems, "Ces
fleurs maladives" ("These sickly flowers"), the poems dedicated
to the "degenerate" Théophile Gautier, as it turns out. Baudelaire
and Verlaine were her prophets; Rimbaud—whose 1871 poem
*Le Bateau ivre* (*The Drunken Boat*), Beckett would translate in
early 1932 (Beckett 2012, 415) and which translation, done for
Edward Titus, was lost for a time, rediscovered only in 1984
(Beckett *Letters* 2016, 638); any number of critics have deemed
the translation a discrete poem in and of itself[8]—their offspring
with Verlaine, perhaps, playing the role of Rimbaud's demon lover
as well. These are precisely the features that Nordeau would attack
as not only degenerate but criminal as well, and the poems of *Les
Fleurs du m*al were a particular target of Nordeau, who notes, "We
then find ourselves in the presence of the literary phases called
Diabolism and Decadentism. 'Diaboliques' and 'décadents' are
distinguished from ordinary criminals merely in that the former
content themselves with dreaming and writing, while the latter
have the resolution and strength to act. But they have this bond
in common, of being both of them 'antisocial beings'" (Nordeau
1895, 260–1).

As an "antisocial being," then, Baudelaire would celebrate
not industry, duty, or social responsibility, but aimlessness,
meandering, and boredom, spleen he called it in the posthumously
published *Le Spleen de Paris* in 1869, fifty-one prose poems
with which he blurred distinctions between prose and poetry,
hybridizing creative discourse. Its preface, "To the Reader,"
concludes with an acknowledgment of "this delicate monster"
of boredom:

> It's Boredom!—eye brimming with involuntary tears
> He dreams of gallows while smoking his hookah.
> You know him, reader, this delicate monster,
> Hypocritical reader, my likeness, my brother!

T. S. Eliot would retain the final line in its original French as one of the cultural shards to bolster "The Burial of the Dead" in *The Waste Land* (1922): "*Hypocrite lecteur,—mon semblable,— mon frère!*" Christopher Isherwood would return to the decadent, ominous spirit of Bella Cohen, in the Kit Kat Klub set in 1931 Berlin on the eve of a fascist ascent to power in *Goodbye to Berlin*, one of *The Berlin Stories* (1945). Its spirit would become popular entertainment after the Second World War, first in John Van Druten's adaptation, *I am A Camera* in 1951, then as *Cabaret* in 1966. Both transformations of the Isherwood novel became catchy musicals, and both plays were subsequently produced as popular films.

Guillaume Apollinaire would take up Baudelaire's call for urban meandering in his long poem, *Zone* (1913), which Samuel Beckett translated in 1948–9 (Beckett 2012, 414), and Apollinaire would revitalize Baudelaire in 1917 with new anthologies, *L'Oeuvre poétique de Charles Baudelaire* (Paris: Bibliothèque des Curieux reissued in 1924). A separate edition of *Les Fleurs du Mal* in a "text definitive avec les variantes de la premiere edition" was republished almost a decade after Apollinaire's death at the Front. His anthology of 1927 (Paris: Bibliothèque des Curieux) presented Baudelaire to a new generation, both poets thus anthologists themselves and unrepentant cosmopolitans, wandering city poets. In August of 1857, a French court objected to thirteen of the most erotic of the 100 poems that made up *Les Fleurs du Mal*, six of which were banned: "Lesbos," "Femmes damnés," "Le Léthé," "À celle qui est trop gaie," "Les Bijoux," and "Les Métamorphoses du Vampire." The offense that the French court cited was their "realism," rather that the poems "necessarily lead to the excitement of the senses by a crude realism offensive to public decency."[9] In 1955, such phraseology would be echoed by British censors in their condemnation of Beckett's *Waiting for Godot*. The complaint to the Lord Chamberlain by one Lady Howitt cited the play's displays of "lavatory necessities [ ... ,] offensive and against all sense of British decency" (see Chapter 5 for details). Baudelaire would call such a turn of mind, such an embrace of a rejected, essentially seldom-seen world, such offences against "public decency," modern or Modernist, even as he simultaneously decried urban modernization, the loss of *his* Paris. A series of poems added to his expanded 1861 edition contained thirty-five new poems including the "Tableux Parisienne," a sequence of eighteen poems in which he mourned urban renewal, the Haussmannization of central Paris. The six excluded poems of the 1857 edition, however, remained banned in the 1861 expanded edition, published, finally, as *Les Épaves* (i.e., scraps) only in 1866. As Louis Menand put it, "The French may have felt embarrassed that, in 1857, the government had prosecuted two of the country's most famous writers, Gustave Flaubert and Charles Baudelaire. Flaubert got off, but six of Baudelaire's poems were banned, a prohibition not officially lifted until 1949" (Menand 2012, 79) but the two would both be condemned again as degenerates if not criminals by Nordeau in 1892 (1895 in English). The American edition from New Directions Press in 1955 timidly printed only three of the six poems banned in 1857.

# Art and pornography

In the 1880s, Henri de Toulouse-Lautrec (1864–1901) would bring to the fore the bohemian quarter of the city of light, and so celebrate the nightlife of La Butte, Montmartre, and its red windmill, the Moulin Rouge, with paintings and posters that featured the celebrated dancer, La Goulou. Such images, scandalous for their time, have since become fashion accessories for handbags and parasols. Egon Schiele's portraits, especially those of young women, on the other hand, were intimate to the point of being deemed pornographic in his time, as they often are in ours. The subtitle to scholar Simon Schama's *New Yorker* (November 10, 1997) review of a Schiele retrospective at the Museum of Modern Art noted that "Egon Schiele's demonstrative sex art made painting and pornography inseparable" (98), part of what Schama calls Schiele's "pudenda parade" (105). As late as November 2017, in preparation for the centenary year of his death, Schiele's paintings still generate public resistance, as Kimberly Bradley writes in *The New York Times*:

> Vienna's Tourist Board has also been working on a campaign celebrating these [Klimpt and Scheile, both of whom died in 1918] and other big-draw exhibitions, and Viennese modernism in general. But the campaign ran into an unusual glitch —the office's originally planned posters, featuring large Schiele nudes, turned out to be too racy.

According to a Vienna Tourist Board spokeswoman, Helena Hartlauer, Transport for London rejected the original images, citing trepidation about depicting genitals in public space. Ms. Hartlauer said that modified advertisements with pixelated genitals were also declined. Ultimately approved were versions using the same artworks (Schiele's "Seated Male Nude (Self-Portrait)," 1910, and "Girl With Orange Stockings," 1914, and other paintings by the artist, all from the Leopold Museum collection), but with certain bits covered by a banner. (Bradley)

And the religious and mythically inflected Symbolism of Gustave Moreau, teacher of Henri Matisse and Georges Rouault, his *La Poète et la Sirène* (1893), and Emannuel Hannaux's starkly white Belle Époque sculpture of that title (1903), for instance, or Moreau's own *Autumn* or *Dejanira* (1872–3) with its hidden Hercules about to reclaim his wife, the abducted Dejanira, would blossom alongside Baudelaire's evil flowers. The Dadaist and Surrealist, Francis Picabia, would produce stunningly realistic, eroticized nudes as he returned to figurative painting in the 1920s, and he would parody academic nude painting in the 1940s. Such decadent or "degenerate" art, however, such public ventilation of private secrets, emotions, dreams, fantasies and the conflicted ambiguities of desire, an art of the margins, was much of the driving impetus for Samuel Beckett's six-month tour of Germany between 1935 and 1936 to see, before much of it was removed, hidden or simply destroyed, German modernism, art that flourished under Weimar Germany, the work of Max Beckmann, Otto Dix and Georg Grosz, among others, art deemed, after Nordeau, culturally undesirable and so decadent by Weimar's successors, the regime in power during Beckett's tour, headed by Adolf Hitler. Such art was shown, when it was at all, in sequestered portions of public museums or in private galleries like the Gurlitt Gallery, which Beckett visited in 1936. The forward-looking art dealer Hilderbrand Gurlitt was, for instance, the first to exhibit French impressionist painters in Germany.[10] Recent revelations, however, have documented not only Gurlitt's secreting some 1,500 Nazi-looted artworks for his personal benefit, mostly from (fellow) Jewish owners, but his additional complicity in offering looted works for sale on international markets to support the Nazi war effort (Eddy, C1). The newly discovered "collection was hailed by art historians as 'the most important discovery of

Nazi looted art since the allies discovered the hoards in the salt mines and the castles,'" according to *The New York Times* (Eddy C6).

Beckett also met Will Grohmann, sometimes called "the godfather of modernism": "Here [Dresden] I have met all kinds of friends and interesting people, especially an art historian called Grohmann who knew them all, from Picasso to Salkeld, and he has done a big catalogue of Klee, Kandinsky, Kirchner & Baumeister [...]. He has Picassos & Klees & Kandinskys & Modrians [for Mondrians] and a lot of Germans. He was removed from his post in the Real Gymnasium, here at the Gallery in 1933, like all the others of his kidney. Through him I was able to visit one of the best collections of modern art in Germany, the Ida Beinert collection [...]. Including a Kokoschka portrait of Nancy Cunard!!! Painted in Paris 1924" (Beckett *Letters* 2009, 446). Discomfited by a series of persistent illnesses, Beckett deemed his German tour decidedly disappointing, however: "The trip is a failure. Germany is horrible. Money is scarce. I am tired all the time. All the modern pictures are in the cellars," the journey, he notes, "turned out indeed to be a journey from and not to, as I knew it was, before I began it" (Beckett *Letters* 2009, 397).[11]

Shortly after Beckett's tour, German officials opened the Degenerate Art (*Entartete Kunst*) exhibition of Dada and Expressionist art in Munich in 1937 as Hitler spoke nationally to denounce such degeneration.[12] Nordeau's critique had become part of the Nazi campaign for racial purity as the denounced art was deemed to have been produced by Jewish, Communist, and other un-German artists, even as many of the condemned artists were not Jewish, Communist, or anti-German, after which public condemnation, however, many works disappeared or were publicly destroyed or secreted away, but the creation of decadent art was in and of itself deemed criminal. Franz Marc's *Tower of Blue Horses* (1913), an iconic work of the Blaue Reiter[13] group, was at first part of the Degenerate Art exhibition but was removed and thence mysteriously disappeared and so may still exist. Much of that assault was against the reformulation of aesthetic and cultural values we call Modernism, deemed, post-1933, not only an insult to the German temperament and soul but criminal behavior.

Such a modern turn in the arts, a Modernist frame of mind, a way of thinking more than a series of techniques, and one not necessarily restricted to a period but developing aggressively during the end of the nineteenth and the first third of the twentieth centuries, fired the imagination of a young Samuel Beckett and helped shape his understanding of what art is, what art does or what it might do. In February of 1938, trying to live from translations in Paris, Beckett contemplated an offer from Jack Kahane of Obelisk Press to translate the marquis de Sade's *120 Days of Sodom*, but Beckett admitted to reservations about associating himself so directly with the *demimonde*, still stinging, perhaps, from the banning of *More Pricks than Kicks* in Ireland in 1934, which actually put him in good intellectual company. He wrote to his sometime literary agent and full-time confidant, George Reavey, in 1938:

> I wish very much you were here to advise me about translation (of Sade[']s 128 Days for Jack Kahane). I should like very much to do it, & the terms are moderately satisfactory, but don't know what effect it wd. have on my lit. situation in England or how it might prejudice future publication of my work there. The surface is of an unheard of obscenity & not 1 in 100 will find literature in the pornography, or beneath the pornography, let alone one of the capital works of the 18th century [i.e., 1785], which it is for me. [ ....] Anyhow it can't be a rational decision, the consequences are unforeseeable [ ....] 150,000 words at 150 francs per 1000 [words] is better than a poem by AE [the Irish mystic, George Russell], but doesn't really enter as an element into the problem. (Beckett *Letters* 2009, 604–5)

Writing to Thomas MacGreevey some nine days before seeking Reavey's advice, a vacillating Beckett seems already to have decided against accepting the commission: "I said it was unlikely but that I would go & talk it over. I went & said I was interested en principe [...]. Though I am interested in Sade & have been for a long time, and want the money badly, I would really rather not" (Beckett *Letters* 2009, 605n4). But to Reavey, again on 8 March, Beckett wrote, "I have accepted the Sade translation at 150 francs per 1,000 [words]. He wants to postpone for 3 or 4 months. I have written that I can't guarantee being of the same mind then, or having the time to spare. No contract therefore yet" (Beckett *Letters* 2009, 610). The work finally would appear only in 1954, translated by Austrin Wainhouse, and then from the imprint of Kahane's son,

Maurice Girodias, and his Olympia Press, which imprint would, almost simultaneously, also publish Beckett's, *Watt* (1953), *Molloy* (1955), and the three French novels (1955), as *Waiting for Godot* was making its London debut.

# "the Sade Boom"

The serious philosophical and literary interest in Sade, despite his "unheard of obscenity," was an intellectual touchstone of advanced thinking of the times, at least on the continent, and was thus part of Beckett's sensibility dating at least from his 1930 monograph on Marcel Proust in which he notes what has become one of the work's more frequently cited passages: "Tragedy is the statement of an expiation, but not the miserable expiation of a codified breach of a local arrangement, organised by the knaves for the fools. The tragic figure represents the expiation of original sin, of the original and eternal sin of him and all his 'soci malorum',[14] the sin of having been born," or, that is, procreation generally for Schopenhauer. But the excerpt that directly precedes the above passage is seldom cited, yet it speaks to Beckett's willingness to take on the Sade translation: "Here, as always, Proust is completely detached from all moral considerations. There is no right and wrong in Proust nor in his world. (Except possibly in those passages dealing with the war, when for a space he ceases to be an artist and raises his voice with the plebs, mob, rabble, canaille.)" (Beckett 1957c, 49). Beckett's willingness to bracket key features of art, to re-value literature, suggests something of a Modernist ethics and something of an elitist separation from the "plebs, mob, rabble, canaille." And recollecting this period, Beckett wrote to George Reavey on August 28, 1972, that, "I think I know the Apollinaire Sade you mention [see below], in a series entitled 'Les Maître de l'Amour' (Bibliothèque des Curieux). I once had it and find that I still have, in the same collection, his Divine Aretino [*sic*] in 2 vols. He must have been the initiator of the Sade Boom" (Beckett *Letters* 2016, 306; see also Seán Lawlor and John Pilling [Beckett 2012, 414]).

As Beckett suggests with his reference to the "Sade boom," Sade was already very much in the air as Beckett was contemplating this translation commitment, and he refers directly in 1972 to the 1909 volumes once in his personal library, *L'oeuvre du Marquis de Sade: Zoloé, Justine, Juliette, la Philosophie dans le boudoir, Oxtiern ou Les malheurs du libertinage: pages choisies, comprenant des morceaux inédits*, Introd., essai bibliographique et notes par Guillaume Apollinaire. In its preface Apollinaire outlines Sade's appeal:

> It strikes me that the time has come for these ideas that have been ripening in the unspeakable atmosphere of the restricted sections of libraries, and this man who was completely forgotten throughout the nineteenth century might well assume a dominant position in the course of the twentieth.
>
> The marquis de Sade, the freest spirit that ever lived, also had very special ideas about women, whom he wanted to see as free as men. (cited in Seaver 2012, 354, see also pp. 351–9)

Georges Bataille's "The Use Value of D. A. F. de Sade (An Open Letter to My Current Comrades)" would then appear in 1930 to regenerate "the Sade boom" (Bataille 1986, 91–104). Pierre Klossowski's *Sade mon prochain* (*Sade My Neighbor*, 1991) was originally published in 1947. Furthermore, as Richard Seaver notes in his memoire, *The Tender Hour of Twilight*:

> By 1948, having read all there was to read by and about the man, [Jean-Jaques] Pauvert made up his young mind; he would devote himself to resuscitating Sade, would publish all his works, no matter how long it took, or whatever obstacles, including the threat of confiscation, even prison. And, most daring of all, he intended to publish Sade not clandestinely, as others had before him, with his imprint and address openly and proudly affixed to the cover. When he made this life-altering decision, Jean-Jaques Pauvert was all of twenty-two. (Seaver 2012, 355)

The young publisher's "pig-headed courage," as Seaver put it (Seaver 2012, 355), generated a corresponding intellectual commitment. Maurice Blanchot published *Lautréamont et Sade* in 1949 (the "Sade's Reason" chapter in part included Blanchot review of Klossowski's *Sade mon prochain*). In 1951, asked to write an "Introduction" to Sade's *Justine*, Simone de Beauvoir produced

*Must We Burn Sade?: An Essay by Simone de Bouvoir* in which she followed up Apollinaire and explored the ethical relationship between freedom and intimacy, as she notes, "[Sade] posed the problem of the *Other* in its most extreme terms" (cited in the *Stanford Encyclopedia of Philosophy*).[15] Both, moreover, extend Baudelaire's 1909 call: "Il faut toujours en revenir à de Sade, c'est dire à l'homme naturel, pour expliquer le mal. Débuter par une conversation, sur l'amour, entre gens difficiles," used as an epigraph to Bouvoir's essay. Gilles Deleuze will see in both Leopold von Sacher-Masoch's *Venus in Furs* and Sade's *oeuvre* what he calls in *Proust and Signs* (1964) a "symptomatological semiotics," which finally develops into his "schizoanalysis" or "schizoanalytic de-oedipalization" in *Anti-Oedipus* (1972) and into the "becoming, after Bergson" of *A Thousand Plateaus* (1980). Part of the enterprise is that at which Beckett hints but does not or will not act, at least in 1938, to "find literature in the pornography, or beneath the pornography," a bracketing of fantasy and "unheard of obscenity" from literary and philosophical values, and hence a devaluation of literature's visceral, primary, immediate appeal. For de Beauvoir, beyond his "unheard of obscenity," de Sade signifies a recalibration of freedom, for Deleuze a debunking of Freud, or at least of Freudian desire, and particularly of sadomasochism. What appears to be Beckett's cultural or professional timidity of 1938, his uncharacteristic careerism, his fears of "the effect it [his translation] wd. have on my lit. situation in England," which he apparently saw as his primary market before his shift to writing primarily in French, stands in contrast to his commitment to his own work in the face of cultural resistance and restrictions of the artist's freedom amid the still-timid ethos of postwar, 1950s England and Ireland, his own "pig-headed courage."

Pauvert, French publisher of Sade, would establish a substantial if temporary liaison with Maurice Girodias, with whom he shared an office for a time. Both would publish in 1954 the notorious, contemporary, neo-Sadean *L'Histoire d'O*, by one Pauline Réage (later disclosed to be Anne Desclos). Girodias then quickly if not overly hastily published its first English translation as *The Story of O*. Almost immediately thereafter, Girodias would publish Beckett, through the intervention of Richard Seaver and what was called the *Merlin* group, after the magazine they edited for a time in Paris,

*Molloy* in 1955, *Watt* in 1958, and the *Three Novels: A Trilogy* in 1959, all under his Olympia Press imprint (in conjunction with *Merlin*). All of these, including the complete Sade and *The Story of O*, retranslated for Grove Press in 1965 by Seaver himself under the coded name of Sabine d'Estrée, Beckett's American publisher, Barney Rosset, would subsequently publish and celebrate (Seaver 2012, 357).

Beckett's interest in so-called decadent art, in the *demimonde* and bohemia, for convenience, and his praise and deep study of Sade suggest a thinker willing if not eager to look beyond accepted values and not only to critique those values, as everyone of his age and milieu was engaged in as something of a Modernist enterprise, but to search out, design, and express alternative values, literary and ethical, even (or especially) the value(s) of language itself, the issues or limits of its own possibilities, that is, to debunk the expectation of a neutral language expressing a stable reality, a reality prior to its linguistic expression. For Beckett there may be no "reality" separate from an artistic expression. When T. S. Eliot detailed his defense of "obscurity" in modern and Modernist art in his 1933 Harvard lectures, "The Use of Poetry and the Use of Criticism," he noted in particular: "there is the difficulty of the author's having left out something which the reader is used to finding; so that the reader, bewildered, gropes about for what is absent, and puzzles his head for a kind of 'meaning' which is not there and is not meant to be there" (Eliot 1986, 143–4). Beckett showed little interest in bridging the chasm between literary culture and the academy, as Eliot did, and showed even less interest in meeting reader or spectator expectations, in providing what might be thought of as something perceived as missing, in whether or not the emotional, affective response of the reader or spectator, that is, the impact of the artwork, was or is coeval with that which generated the images in the first place. Or, further, whether or not the experience of perception and thought produces either pleasure or displeasure; in this regard, authorial intention is not part of the artistic equation. The experience is not a matter of psychological, physiological, or conceptual matching. What matters are flows of thought and the impact of, often scarcely definable, affect, even as the dominant strain of much early Beckett criticism was to pursue lines of thought that assumed the "author's having left out something which the reader is used to finding."

# "We are part of the same story"

In the 1950s and 1960s, then, Beckett's reputation would grow through overt association with the *demimonde*, precisely the association he resisted in 1938 as potentially damaging to his reputation, through three English language publishers, three promoters of decadence and the *demimondaine*: Maurice Girodias of Olympia Press, Paris; John Calder (Publishers) Ltd., of London; and Barney Rosset of Grove Press, New York, conspirators all in something of a crusade against middle-class values, and all three would publish, or distribute, finally, de Sade and Réage/Desclos, among others. It was Girodias, a self-described publisher of what he called "dirty books" who would outline that association in an open letter[16] of desperation sent to Beckett (among others) on September 17, 1986. As he admitted: "It would be idle for me to ignore my reputation as a pornographer since I myself coined the term 'dirty books' (dbs for short) to describe that meat and potatoes part of my production." Girodias went on to note—to Beckett directly:

> We're all part of the same story; we were all engaged in this long-winded battle against censorship, Joyce and yourself, my father and myself, Rosset, Calder, and a few more of that ilk dispersed in various countries—Miller, Bataille, Nabokov, writers and artists who were concerned not so much about sexual freedom as about intellectual freedom. It seems hard to explain to the younger generation that Samuel Beckett's work might have been affected by the existence of censorship in those days; but in fact it was. Not just the bans in Ireland and the minor quibbles with censors over words[17]; but the overall ostracism dictated by the "spirit of censorship" which prevailed in the middle class public and which therefore caused so many publishers to reject it [*Watt* in particular]. You made a good choice when you gave me *Watt* to publish simply because Olympia was fighting at the forefront of the battle, and victory was in sight; you knew it then, and I hope that you have not quite forgotten the nature of that struggle ... And would it be impertinent to suggest that you owe your next [English language] publishers, Rosset and Calder, to the fact that I had published you in the first place? (Rosset 2017, 354–5)

Girodias may be overstating his case some since the censurable incidents in *Watt* are decidedly minimal. In one section Arthur recommends to Mr. Graves a "marital aid" called Bando, apparently an aphrodisiac, itself banned (as the product's name suggests) in the Republic (170), but otherwise filth and depravity seem less at issue than the flux of narration, a perceived incoherence, yet this work, too, was banned in Ireland on publication. In response to a letter from Rosset of March 26, 1956, to the effect that Hamish Hamilton had refused *Malone Dies* the publisher expecting "a censorship problem" (Beckett *Letters* 2011, 615n3), Beckett responded on April 7, 1956 that "The books as they stand in English are I think unpublishable in the UK, where there is some kind of official Public Morals organization that has all the publishers terrified with the threat of action for obscenity" (Beckett *Letters* 2011, 614).

In his 1986 appeal to Beckett, Girodias is particularly bitter toward the treatment he received at the hands of Beckett's first biographer, Deirdre Bair, with whom he had cooperated but who finally excoriated him. He cites Bair's claim that he, Girodias, went on to "sign a contract for *Watt* with Samuel Beckett despite his [Beckett's] revulsion for 'any publishing venture the least bit immoral or unsavory'; and then [she] proceeds to heap more sneaky derogatory remarks on my father [for whom Beckett was ready to translate Sade in 1938] and myself." Bair's statement of Beckett's prudishness seems risible given his substantial interest in Sade in the 1930s and 1950s, and his run-ins with British censors in the 1950s which put the lie to Bair's assertion. James Knowlson's 1996 "authorized" biography, *Damned to Fame: The Life of Samuel Beckett*, continues the theme of Beckett unease that *Watt* was advertised along with Henry Miller's *Plexus*: "As someone who in the end had declined to translate the Marquis de Sade for Maurice Girodias's father in the 1930s because he did not wish to be too closely associated with the predominantly pornographic publishing house, Beckett *may have* been a little uncomfortable with this" (Knowlson 357, emphasis added). While technically accurate, although who declined whom in 1938 may be of some issue, Knowlson's comment, too, may overstate Beckett's squeamishness since he remained fully immersed in and was translating not only Sade for Georges Duthuit in 1950 and '51 but French theorists writing about and so promoting the work of Sade as well, namely Maurice Blanchot, Pierre Klossowski, and Maurice Heine, Beckett sounding in the process like something of a Sade scholar (see also Beckett *Letters* 2011, 224). As he wrote to Duthuit in December of 1950: "I have read Blanchot's *Sade*. There are some very good things in it. A few tremendous quotations that I did not know, in the style that I knocked up for you from *120 Days*. Hard to single out one passage to translate, but I managed to and started on it" (Beckett *Letters* 2011, 211). Beckett picks up the thread a fortnight or so later, on January 3, 1951, sounding quite like the French theorists he so often decried:

> I have finished the Blanchot. It makes 12 pages of text. Some excellent ideas, or rather starting points for ideas, and a fair bit of verbiage, to be read quickly, not as a translator does. What emerges from it though is a truly gigantic Sade, jealous of Satan and his eternal torments, and confronting nature more than human kind. I do not find it any trouble at all, although my English is going off noticeably. I am only comfortable now with a pastiche of 18th-century style—which does not come amiss as it happens. We can put in too the end of the text that I read you, about the disappearance of the body. (Beckett *Letters* 2011, 219)

On January 8, Beckett continued his progress report: "I have translated 4 letters by Sade (one of them extremely beautiful), cutting down as far as possible the rubbish [that Sade editor and biographer Gilbert] Lely writes as linking material. All the rest of the work he has given you seems pointless and unusable. The so-called notes on the death penalty make no mention of it. For that you would have to go back to Sade himself, probably *Philosophy of the Bedroom*" (Beckett *Letters* 2011, 222).

Furthermore, Beckett was well aware of the reputation of his American publisher since Grove Press was publishing and promoting Sade, among other socially unacceptable writers, along with his books, and advertisements for them often appeared in the same publication, *The Evergreen Review*, chiefly, even on the same page. *Oh! Calcutta*, for instance, as it turned out, included Beckett's "Breath" as the lead "entertainment." Beckett objected to the publication but less because of its overt sexuality than the fact that producer Kenneth Tynan altered Beckett's text significantly. Amid Beckett's detritus, Tynan added "including naked bodies." The *Oh! Calcutta* volume would feature prominently in the press's Evergreen

Book Club promotions amid material that made Beardsley's erotic illustrations seem timid. Moreover, in April of 1970, as Grove Press ran afoul of the nascent women's movement which protested Grove Press's depiction of women, the *New York Times* described his American publisher as "a pioneer publisher of erotic literature," and further that "Grove's sado-masochistic literature and pornographic films dehumanize and degrade women."[18] One participant of what was an occupation and takeover of the sixth floor executive suites of the Grove Press building on Mercer Street noted of Rosset's work space: "He has the most obscene office I've ever seen" (April 14, 1970, p. 55). Rosset and his Grove Press were not only Beckett's exclusive American publishers, and so the generator of the bulk of his income, but after *Godot*, Rosset would assume the role of Beckett's American theatrical agent, at least for works written in English, so that Beckett was doubly bound to Grove Press and its public image. The paradox is captured succinctly by Paris bookseller Adrienne Monnier: "He [Beckett] is a man of extreme modesty, in spite of the obscenities with which he freely sprinkles his books" (Monnier 1976).

# "minor quibbles with censors over words"

What Girodias denigrates as "minor quibbles with censors over words" were in fact major battles in Ireland and the United Kingdom over restrictions imposed by official censoring agencies, the office of the Lord Chamberlain in the United Kingdom in particular, whose sanitizing efforts threatened the possibilities of British performances of Beckett's first two plays. Chapter 4, "Textual Aberrations, Ghost Texts, and the British *Godot*," details the extent and the seriousness of such "minor quibbles" in relation to London performances in 1956 and 1964 and surprisingly with the publication in Britain of *Waiting for Godot* (1956) by Faber and Faber; moreover, the censorship conflicts surrounding *Godot* were reprised some eight years later with *Endgame*. Writing to Rosset on January 20, 1958, Beckett noted, "I had lunch a week ago with [George] Devine and confirmed to him that I could not allow the prayer passage [in *Endgame*] to be either suppressed or mutilated by the Lord Chamberlain. He was very understanding and did not press me. He went back to London very warlike. He may present the play at the Arts," the London Theatre Club where *Godot* had to be performed before receiving its commercial approval from the Lord Chamberlain (letter not included in Beckett *Letters* 2014). These conflicts in the United Kingdom, then, parallel, inform, and are informed by Beckett's work on Sade for Duthuit and the revived, postwar *transition* magazine even as the publication of *Watt* in Paris in English by the Olympia Press was banned in Ireland in 1954 under the Censorship of Publications Acts of 1929, which banning was followed by that of *Molloy* in 1956 from the same Paris publisher (*More Pricks than Kicks* having been banned on publication in 1934 received its imprimatur in 1952) (see further details in Chapter 1). Beckett was, moreover, in the process of simultaneously withdrawing his work from the Dublin Theater Festival that had banned a Ulysses adaptation and an O'Casey play, *The Drums of Father Ned*, although the O'Casey play, but not the *Ulysses* adaptation, received a reprieve shortly thereafter (see letter to Brendan Smith, January 20, 1958 [Beckett *Letters* 2014, 99n1]). Each of these interlaced encounters is fuller and more comprehensible seen in relation to the others, and such re-contextualization, re-viewing Beckett and his milieu, generates (or re-generates) a *Revisioning [of] Beckett.*

Beckett's professional relations on the other side of the Atlantic are, moreover, detailed in Chapters 2 and 3 as well, culminating with former Grove Press editor-in-chief, Barney Rosset's publication of Beckett's first full-length play, *Eleutheria*, in 1998, in defiance of prohibitions imposed by Beckett's own Estate, then headed by French publisher Jérôme Lindon. That bitter dispute led to Rosset's dismissal as Beckett's theatrical agent in America, a position that Beckett thought would secure Rosset's economic future in the face of his having lost control of Grove Press in 1986. On February 1 of that year Beckett wrote to reaffirm his commitment to and confidence in Rosset as his American theatrical agent and to offer a gesture he thought would insure Rosset an income stream, but that agreement was voided by the Beckett Estate as Rosset staged a public reading of the play in New York. When he finally published the play in 1995, however, it was with permission of the Estate, but he was economically devastated and the punishing termination of his function as Beckett's theatrical agent was never rescinded (see Chapter 3 for additional details).

Rosset's impact on Beckett's career is rarely credited fully. He was not only Beckett's long-time American publisher and theatrical agent/producer but also the driving force behind Beckett's return to writing in English, the prime instigator of his strategic move from the overly commercial Broadway stage to the little theaters off-Broadway in New York's bohemian enclave, Greenwich Village, where Grove had its offices, and of his direct engagement with film, and so, finally, Rosset was instrumental in Beckett's becoming a visual artist (see also Chapter 2). Beckett's direct oversight of and revisions to what became simply *Film*, a Grove Press generated and financed project, was, in turn, made possible by Beckett's one and only trip to the United States in 1964, during which he stayed with Rosset. While *Film* has never received wide distribution, it has had considerable and recurrent residual influence as it became central to Gilles Deleuze's film theories as he crowned it "the greatest Irish film."[19] It has, furthermore, inspired filmmakers like Dora Garcia to revision it with a parallel work that embraces and engulfs Beckett's own visual achievement. Her 2007, black and white, 11' 35" *Film (Hôtel Wolfers)* is a video tour of the decaying Brussels hotel, itself an image of decadence, as a narrator summarizes and critiques *not* the hotel on view but Beckett's *Film*.[20] *Film (Hôtel Wolfers)*, then, not only details the degeneration of a storied Brussels landmark, designed by Henry van de Velde in 1812, and, except for its elegant, minimalist, Bauhaus furniture, its ambiance echoes or revisions that of *Film*, although only visual suggestions connect the space filmed and the narration. That is, the narration relies on the spectator's having some residual memory of Beckett's work since no direct visual parallels are drawn; no images from *Film* are intercut. Moreover, like *Film* itself, *Film (Hôtel Wolfers)* is most stunning in its very ordinariness, its unexceptionality strikingly highlighted in Garcia's revisioning, which is thus a recontextualization. Furthermore, Garcia treats *Film (Hôtel Wolfers)*, shot, like *Film*, in 35 mm then transferred, like *Film*, to video, and so indirectly Beckett's *Film*, as something of a crime scene, the slow inspection of which is conducted by the camera, and so its connection to a filmic genre, or to the genre of film itself, is as strong if not dominant as it is in Beckett's work from its title onward to its closing credits. The process of close inspection (of the ordinary), moreover, implicates the viewer, creating something of the mood of film noir or period horror films as Garcia, like Beckett, exploits the camera's first-person point of view and appeals to the viewer's scopophilic drive. *Film (Hôtel Wolfers)* is thus already familiar to us as it invokes an anticipation that it will finally, perhaps, disappoint. As Garcia notes, "we read the house as a crime set, the camera reads as an evil presence." The voice-over narration, however, explains and critiques O's action in Beckett's *Film*, concluding that O's movements are a cover-up, an attempt to eliminate potential witnesses, to his behavior, yes, but also, or primarily, to his existence. Over a slow-motion pan of the abandoned and now decaying Hôtel Wolfers, the narrator critiques the camera in Beckett's *Film* as "an evil presence" that has a terrible effect on the figures it confronts, the couple on the street, the elderly woman on the stairs, even the cat and dog, and we, spectators, audience, are looking through that camera: we are the camera and so the narrator concludes, "I am the monster."

Any number of visual artists have thus revisioned Beckett's art and/ or his images and thereby have recontextualized it, most famously, perhaps, Bruce Nauman's 1968 "Slow Angle Walk (Beckett Walk)," the video for which reinforces the very ordinariness of the activity, walking. Spanish artist Juan Muñoz's 1999 drawings and sculptures like the "Conversation Piece, NY" of 1992, in which human figures are partially enclosed or entrapped in jars or urns, call up, without overt reference, Beckett's entombed creatures in *Play* and *Happy Days*, and, likewise, shift the experience, as does Winnie, from the extraordinary and inexplicable to the quotidian. Ross Lipman's restoration of *Film*, furthermore, developed into an ancillary or parallel video essay called *Not Film* (2015), which makes much of the designated time frame of *Film*, noted in *Hôtel Wolfers* as well, to see Beckett's *Film* in conjunction with the introduction of sound in film, the development of "talkies," which it, predominantly silent, emphasizes with its shocking single sound, "Shhhh." *Not Film* has, in turn, (re)generated interest in *Film* itself, both now available in Blu-ray format (2017), and the two works are often shown in tandem or in conjunction with each other, almost as a single entity, something like *Film Not Film*, perhaps.

Against such a background, such recontextualizing, a spirit of rethinking and revisioning, the essays of *Revisioning Beckett* enfold, play with, play against, recontextualize, reassess, and so revision

Beckett's thought, theater, and prose, in something of an historical, theoretical, and aesthetic loop. As Boris Groys suggests in his critique called "anti-philosophy," which Groys associates with anti-art: "Any object or text can be put in the limited context of the cultural field in which it was 'originally' produced and situated. But it can also be taken out of this limited context, and placed in a universal context of philosophical or artistic comparison, where other criteria of evidence are at work" (Groys 2012, xiii). These "other criteria of evidence" are part of a shift away from the *production* of texts to their *curation*, whereby "experiences would become universally evident" (Groys 2012, xiii). Such is a shift away from what might be called the "truth value" of art. As Pozzo reminds Vladimir and Estragon, for instance, "Forgive all I said [...] I don't remember exactly what it was, but you may be sure that there wasn't a word of truth in it" (Beckett 1954, 23); or as Beckett makes even more explicit in his aesthetic caveat at the opening to the script of *Film*: "No truth value attaches to above, regarded as of merely structural and dramatic convenience" (Beckett 1971, 11).

Gilles Deleuze will see Beckett's *Film* in Bergsonian terms as the fulfilment of three aspects of what he calls the "movement-image" in his study of silent cinema *Cinema 1: The Movement-image* in which he offers a taxonomy of development through Beckett's work: the "action-image" as O is fleeing down a street trying to merge with a wall, then proceeding up the stairs of a building pursued by E (or the camera[man], actually). Once inside, we see the room as O and E (or Deleuze's OE) see it. For Deleuze this is the "perception-image," as "O perceives (subjectively) the room, the things and the animals which are there, whilst OE perceives (objectively) O himself, the room, and its contents: this is the perception of perception, or the perception-image, considered under a double regime, in a double system of reference" (Deleuze 1986, 67). While O rocks in his chair, reviewing photos then nodding, OE, the camera, O's perceiving self, violates the "angle of immunity." With that angle increased to ninety from forty-five degrees in the room, we have the perception of affect, "the affection-image": "The character O is thus now seen from the front, at the same time as the new and last convention is revealed: the camera OE is the double of O, the same face, a patch over one eye (monocular vision), with the single difference that O has an anguished expression and OE has an attentive expression: the impotent motor effort of the one, the sensitive surface of the other" (Deleuze 1986, 67). As a denouement, Deleuze notes that this final image is "the most terrifying, that which still survives when all the others have been destroyed: it is the perception of self by self" (Deleuze 1986, 67). Deleuze thus localizes the 1964 film within the techniques of silent film, at the end of that era since Beckett's *Film* "introduces" sound, the single "Shhhh" and so reinforces its liminal 1929 period setting. But for Deleuze the film finally supersedes the "time-image" initiated in post–Second World War, New Wave French Cinema, Beckett's work thus situated within a specific historical moment, the development of sound in cinema, and the French New Wave, and recontextualized, revisioned in terms of a regenerated avant-garde (Uhlmann 2015, 23).

Neither philosophy, cultural history nor sociology, however, this is art, an entity without function or utility, an object or event without "truth value" and hence thus, perhaps, decadent, and Beckett's ties to decadence and bohemianism reach back at least to his university days. In editor Michael Smith's interview with Mervyn Wall in *The Lace Curtain*, 4, mostly about poets of the 1930s at University College, Dublin, Smith asked Wall about "highly experimental artists" of the period and mentions *At Swim-Two-Birds* and *Echo's Bones* as particular examples. Wall essentially ignores *At Swim-Two-Birds* (regrettably one might observe) and responds about "Those who looked to Paris, did not wish to remain in, or be influenced by the already thoroughly plowed four fields of Ireland" (83). Discussing his meetings with Beckett "in the early thirties in his rooms at Trinity when he was a lecturer in French there" (85), Wall goes on to say that they also met "at a bohemian-type party in the Wicklow Mountains" (85). Such bohemian inclinations, directly manifest in Beckett's Trinity College days, permeate *Dream of Fair to Middling Women, Echo's Bones and Other Precipitates, More Pricks than Kicks* and, yes, the first full-length play, written in French, *Eleutheria*, if not in the entirety of the Beckett *oeuvre*. In his "Preface" to Beckett's *Selected Poems—1930–1989*, David Wheatley makes the case for rethinking Beckett outside of or beyond Ireland, or for taking him "out of this limited context, and [ ... placing him] in a universal context of philosophical or artistic comparison" as he emphasizes Beckett's interest in and connections to European intellectual currents and avant-gardes. For Beckett, as acknowledged in his "Homage to Jack B. Yeats," "The artist who stakes his being is from nowhere, has no kith." Beckett, furthermore, goes on to gloss his comment, which turns out to be an anti-gloss, Beckett evoking the traditional terms of critique, even his own, only to sweep them away, "None of this final mastery which submits in trembling to the unmasterable. No. Merely bow in wonder" (Beckett 1984, 149). Such proclamation, for Wheatley, "renders the concept of Irish poetic *Modernism as a shared front* null and void. Beckett's poetry might just as fruitfully be compared to the Objectivist poetics of George Oppen, Lorine Niedecker and the later W. S. Graham. It is also important to keep a sense of French poetics such as Éluard, Char, Michaux as no less Beckett's contemporaries" (Beckett 2009a, xviii, emphasis added). This "Introduction" places its emphasis on "French poetics" and details the depth of Beckett's involvement with international avant-gardism, an ethos that ran counter to a nationalist aesthetics and theocratic politics of an early, semi-independent Ireland. The following chapter continues to assess that relationship in further detail, including Beckett's late-life rapprochement with the land of his birth, but the spirit of his work as it runs counter to received wisdom, to both cultural and social expectations, to bourgeois and commercial values remained, to the very end, what is here called decadent.

# Notes

1 Shown as part of the exhibition "ISelf Collection: Self-Portrait as the Billy Goat" at Whitechapel Gallery, London, April 27–August 20. Exhibition catalogue: *Creating Ourselves: The Self in Art*, ed. Emily Butler with Candy Stobbs. http://www.artbook.com/9780854882571. html (December 8, 2017).

2 For more analysis on Beckett and Nordeau, see Ackerley, C. J., 2006, 167–76.

3 See, for example, Mucha's *Salon des Cent* posters of 1897 at which exhibition the likes of Albert André, Pierre Bonnard, Frédéric-August Cazals, Edgas Degas, Henri, Evenepoel, Henri-Gabriel Ibeis, Gustave-Henri Jossot, René Lalique, Henri Matisse, Gustave Moreau, and Louis Valtat exhibited.

4 Details from the British Library exhibition, "Gay UK: Love, Law & Liberty," June 2–September 19, 2017: https://www.bl.uk/events/gay-uk-love-law-liberty (July 14, 2017).

5  See also https://en.wikipedia.org/wiki/The_Yellow_Book
   (July 29, 2017).

6  His wife, Moina Mathers, born Moina Bergson, was the sister of
   the French metaphysician, Henri Bergson, who himself had mystical
   leanings even as he saw himself as a materialist scientist, but then
   again, so did Sir Arthur Conan Doyle whose interest in Spiritualism
   was profound.

7  The Buggery Act of 1533 made homosexuality illegal with penalties
   that included death. Although the death penalty was eliminated in
   1861, anti-homosexual laws grew stricter with the Criminal Law
   Amendment Act of 1885 that made homosexuality, even acts carried
   out in private, illegal. Wilde was found guilty of "gross indecency"
   under the act in 1895. Details from the British Library exhibition,
   "Gay UK: Love, Law & Liberty," June 2–September 19, 2017: https://
   www.bl.uk/events/gay-uk-love-law-liberty. (July 14, 2017).

8  See, for example, Macklin 2003.

9  Cited in Broder, Melissa. "On Charles Baudelaire's *Les Fleurs du
   Mal*" at https://pen.org/on-charles-baudelaires-les-fleurs-del-mal/
   (October 24, 2012).

10 See also https://www.moma.org/collection_ge/artist.php?artist_
   id=12283&role=3

11 See also Ewald Dülberg's (1888–1933), *Das Abendmahl* (*The Last
   Supper*), a painting once owned by Beckett's uncle, William Abraham
   "Boss" Sinclair. It hung in the Boss's home in Kassel. It appears briefly
   in the 1930 poem, "Casket of Pralinen for a Daughter of a Dissipated
   Mandarin" and features in *Dream of Fair to Middling Women*
   (Beckett 1992a, 76–77). The painting was evidently destroyed in the
   purge of decadent art. A photographic image survived, however, and,
   through the good offices of James Knowlson, was made available and
   used for a wraparound cover to Pilling 2004. (See also Ackerley and
   Gontarski 2004, 157.)

12 On the murky ethical issue of how some of this "degenerate" art,
   with the sanction of the Nazi government, was sold to Western
   collectors to help fund the German war effort, see William D. Cohan,
   "MoMA's Problematic Provenances," *Art News,* November 17,
   2011: http://www.artnews.com/2011/11/17/momas-problematic-
   provenances/; and MoMA's institutional response: https://www.
   moma.org/collection/provenance
      See also MoMA's usefully detailed German Expressionism timeline:
   https://www.moma.org/s/ge/curated_ge/chronology.html

13 Compare to, rather contrast with Henri Matisse's *The Blue Window* painted the same year as *Tower of Blue Horses* and also part of the Degenerate Art exhibition, the former lush and curvaceously sensuous, in keeping with Matisse's odalisques of this period, the latter striving for ascension, spirituality—in their own ways decadent both. "Matisse's *The Blue Window* was removed from the Folkwang Museum in Essen. It had originally been acquired by the German arts patron Karl Ernst Osthaus, who assembled a collection of avant-garde art, one of the first in Germany to include many works by contemporary French artists" (see link in note 11 above. See also *Degenerate Art: The Fate of the Avant-garde in Nazi Germany* [1991], digitalized edition at https://archive.org/details/degenerateartfa00barr.)
  Marc's painting is visible far right (so to speak) in a photo from the ongoing Degenerate Art exhibition: scroll down at https://www.moma.org/calendar/exhibitions/3868?locale=en

14 "Compagnon des miserere" completes the phrase from the final paragraph on "The Suffering of the World" from Schopenhauer's *Studies in Pessimism (Parerga and Paralipomena)* of 1851). It's the proper form of address to one's fellow sufferers (Schopenhauer 2010). This Edition is part of the Cambridge Edition of *The Works of Schopenhauer*. http://assets.cambridge.org/97805218/71389/frontmatter/9780521871389_frontmatter.pdf

15 Of further interest here is Max Horkheimer and Theodor Adorno's "*Juliette* or Enlightenment and Morality." *Dialectic of Enlightenment*, pp. 63–93. "The work of the Marquis de Sade exhibits 'understanding without direction from another' [as Adorno and Horkheimer cite Kant's *Critique of Pure Reason*]—that is to say, the bourgeois subject freed from all [cultural, or conformist] tutelage" (Adorno 2002, 70). See also Jamieson Webster's useful critique of Adorno and Horkheimer's critique of Kant's *Critique of Pure Reason*: http://www.publicseminar.org/2016/03/a-short-lecture-on-adornos-juliette-or-enlightenment-and-morality/ (December 9, 2017) and Pier Paolo Pasolini's *Salo, Or The 120 Days of Sodom* (1975).

16 A copy of the letter was given to the present author, along with copies of other publishing correspondence, for the Grove Press issue of *The Review of Contemporary Fiction* (Gontarski 1990). The letters between Girodias and Rosset on the American publication of Henry Miller were included in that special edition, 72–8, as was the author's interview with Girodias, 124–8; the letter of September 1986 was not, however, used in its entirety in the *Review of Contemporary Fiction*, although it is discussed in the interview with Girodias. The letter is reproduced in full in Rosset (2017, 351–60).

17  See, for example, "'I think this does call for a firm stand': Beckett at the
    Royal Court," (Gontarski 2016, 23–40) and Chapter 4 in the current
    volume, "Textual Aberrations, Ghost Texts, and the British *Godot*."

18  Further details of the 1970 conflict between Grove Press and its
    feminist employees can be found in my "Introduction" to *The Grove
    Press Reader: 1951–2001* (Gontarski 2001, xxv–xxx) and in Rosset
    2016, 249–52.

19  See, for example, "The Greatest Irish Film": https://engl328.files.
    wordpress.com/2012/02/deleuze-on-film.pdf

20  Available on Vimeo at https://vimeo.com/70588378

# PART ONE

# A Professional Life

# 1

# Samuel Beckett and *Lace Curtain* Irish Modernisms

*Lacking traditions one must make them; having traditions one must break through them.* Brian Coffey, *"Extracts from 'Concerning Making,'"* The Lace Curtain 6, p. 31.

*Dublin is as ever only more so. You ask for a fish &* *they give you a piece of bog oak.* SB 1935.

*This particular state, Ireland, is no longer young [ ....]* *It is time we grew up, forgot about Cathleen and all* *her hang-ups and hangovers. Time to forget about the* *Celts, time to face the reality that Irish unification may* *never happen, and it does not matter much anyway.* *Time to embrace a post-nationalist Ireland in a post* *nation-state Europe. Dennis Kennedy, October 2010.*

In August of 1934, *The Bookman*, a London literary monthly, published an essay called, innocently enough, "Recent Irish Poetry" (86.515 [August 1934] 235–44). It turned out to be a provocative if not pugnacious assault on Ireland's literary patrimony, its national,

artistic endowment, if not on nationalism itself. It drew a line in the
turf for the relatively new, postcolonial Irish Free State delineating
what the essay's author saw as a parochial preoccupation with place,
established alternatives, rather antitheses to a received nationalist
narrative, and challenged its ethos and aesthetics. Terence Brown
put the matter in broadly general terms thus: "the 1930s would
certainly give the cultural historian apparently sufficient ground
for concluding that modernism and post-colonial nationalism [...]
are antithetical in their particular manifestations" (Coughlan and
Davis, 25). J. C. C. Mays concurs, "the thesis of the Revival [which]
focused on the myth and folklore of the Irish countryside produced
an antithetical interest in the modern urban world" (Coughlan
and Davis 104). The line that marked out that divide between the
"Irish countryside" and "the modern urban world" was the one
delineated in "Recent Irish Poetry," written by one "Andrew Belis,"
pseudonym, it turned out, of a recent Trinity College alumnus
(1923–7) and acolyte of James Joyce. Samuel Beckett had already
produced a witty if, to the few intimates who read it, baffling
critique of Dublin's intellectual life in his academic novel, *Dream
of Fair to Middling Women* (1932), which became something of
a dead-end for its author as it failed to find a publisher. Beckett
rewrote that autobiographical, Trinity College send-up into a
collection of shorter, less experimental pieces and called it, in a
biblical echo that itself doomed the book, finally, *More Pricks than
Kicks* (1934). It quickly ran afoul of the new nation's Censorship
of Publications Acts (of July 16, 1929). Beckett's persistent attacks
on his homeland's politics and aesthetics–in the 1932 novel,
*Dream of Fair to Middling Women,* and the 1934 collection of
stories extracted from it, *More Pricks than Kicks*–culminate in
the 1934 essay; they were and would continue to be pervasive
and trenchant, particularly his denunciation of that Censorship of
Publications Acts, which went hand in glove, according to Beckett,
with Catholic Ireland's total ban on contraception to express the
Free State's stifling ultraconservatism, what Beckett wittily called
in 1934 the "sterile nation of the mind and apotheosis of the litter"
(*Disjecta* 87, see also *Letters* 2009, 176). Not long after, in 1935,
Beckett would write a more direct critique called "Censorship in
the Saorstat" (i.e., Saorstát Eireann, the official name in Irish of
the Irish Free State) also commissioned by *The Bookman*, but the
journal ceased publication before it could print Beckett's attack

which he concluded, finally, by citing his own censorship registry number, 465.[1] Although the "Saorstat" would lift its ban on *More Pricks than Kicks* in 1952, it went on to ban *Watt* in 1954 and *Molloy* in 1956 (both published in Paris). Beckett's troubles with his homeland would continue further into the 1950s and 1960s, as John Banville outlines the issues of Irish provincialism and theocracy in *The Irish Times*:

> [...] in 1958 the egregious Archbishop John Charles McQuaid refused to offer votive Mass at the opening of Dublin Theatre Festival because he disapproved of a play by Sean O'Casey and an adaptation of James Joyce's *Ulysses* that were due to be staged in the festival. Beckett was furious, and wrote to [American publisher] Barney Rosset, "The Roman Catholic bastards in Ireland yelped Joyce and O'Casey out of their 'Festival', so I withdrew my mimes and the reading of *All That Fall* to be given at the Pike [theatre]" [Beckett *Letters* 2014, 106, to Alan Simpson; the quotation to Rosset cited only in a note, 107n2]. The following year he wrote to his agent: "I do not wish my plays to be performed in Eire whether by amateurs or by professionals" [Beckett *Letters* 2014, 224, 225n3]. [...] and in the summer of 1960 a half-dozen copies of the trilogy were seized from Hanna's bookshop by the Garda. Beckett's friend Robert Pinget recorded, "We talk about the duplicity of the Irish, all niceness outside and enemies within. Sam takes all this very badly." (Banville 2014)

In "Recent Irish Poetry" Beckett's target was less the affront of censorship than the national literary revival that contributed to The Rising and to Ireland's at least partial independence, as a Dominion of the British Commonwealth of Nations (complete with Oath of Allegiance to the Crown), and simultaneously to an atmosphere that stifled innovation for a new generation of Irish writers, according to Beckett, of which Beckett felt himself or was trying to be a part. As John Harrington outlines the issues,

> If the Yeats-Synge vision of Ireland was the single object of ridicule in *More Pricks than Kicks*, Beckett's stories would, in effect, endorse the obvious alternative in local literary culture, that of the contemporary stories of O'Faolain, O'Connor, and

others. That alternative to Celtic twilight centered on escape from restrictive affiliations and allegiances previously constructed as a means to cultural identity and autonomy. [...] The literary models for this view were Joycean, especially *Dubliners*. (Harrington, 64)

*The Bookman* would simultaneously publish Beckett's very curious, mystical short story, "A Case in a Thousand," and he may have adopted a pseudonym for the essay less to mask his identity (few were fooled by it, and, moreover, he and his "lace curtain," Dublin 4 family had already been humiliated by his literary efforts when *More Pricks than Kicks* wound up on the "Index of Forbidden Books in Ireland") than to differentiate his twin efforts, diminishing the possibility that the Dublin-based story would be seen as an exemplum of the critique. Outlined in "Recent Irish Poetry," in a brash, even superior sort of way, then, is a set of reservations, something of an argument for what will come to be called Modernism, and it segregates Irish writers, at least Irish poets of the 1930s, on either side of that marshy, shifting demarcation, parochial, bog-bound on one side and urban-cosmopolitan on the other, a demarcation between western and eastern, between archipelago and continental, between Romanticism and Modernism, perhaps, and finally between exiles and homebodies.

But Beckett's demesne is neither so easily geographical nor national, and so not overtly binary. The pseudonymous author proposes as his principle of individuation or segregation (which he applies consistently) the degree to which Irish writers are aware of "the breakdown of the object," a theme in the fore of his own critical and creative writing. He accuses the majority, those whom he calls "antiquarians," of "delivering with the altitudinous complacency of the Victorian Gaels the Ossianic goods," and further condemns the mysticism, what he calls the "iridescence of themes" of such poetic *luminaries* as George Russell (pen name AE, short for Aeon), James Stephens, Austin Clarke (unmistakably lampooned as Austin Ticklepenny in *Murphy*), and poetic patriarch, William Butler Yeats. Among those approved, on the other hand, are most notably friends, Denis Devlin, one of the few, for example, who is "aware of the vacuum which exists between the perceiver and the thing perceived," and Beckett's epistolary confidant, Thomas MacGreevy, praised for his clear elucidations, "the vision without the dip," that is, insights without aid of a candle.

Beckett's imagery here denegrates *The Candle of Vision* (1918),[2] George Russell's essays on Celtic mysticism to which Miss Carriage of *Murphy* will allude shortly thereafter (102, 155). The narrator of *Murphy* will acknowledge, moreover, that Murphy shared Neary's greatest fear, to "fall among Gaels" (*Murphy* 6).

Despite such harsh treatment of Irish literary patrimony, especially in a nation fully secure in neither its tentative independence nor its national identity, the essay turned out to have staying power, a certain longevity, or at least it was resurrected, reprinted anyway, in the summer of 1971 in the fourth issue (of six) of another short-lived literary venture, *The Lace Curtain: A Magazine of Poetry and Criticism*,[3] part of an ongoing attempt to situate a new and younger generation of Irish writers within a larger, less provincial Modern urban world, the journal's editorials and selections suggesting something of a second generation of Modernism, a post-1930s Irish Modernism, or what the editors of the 1995 critical anthology, *Modernism and Ireland: The Poetry of the 1930s* (Cork University Press), Patricia Coughlan and Alex Davis, call an "exploration of the fate of modernism in Irish literature." In a retrospective essay in that volume, one of the founders of that journal and its associated New Writers' Press, Trevor Joyce, notes of the Beckett reprint, "This was, to the best of my knowledge, the first time he allowed his piece on Devlin to come out under his own name" (Joyce, 293). Joyce's memory is only partially accurate. He seems to confuse the essays reprinted in *The Lace Curtain* nos. 3 and 4, since the Beleis/Beckett effort in issue 4 featured Devlin so little, and Joyce continues his confusion: "It had originally appeared anonymously in *The Bookman* in the 1930s" (Joyce 293)—well, "pseudonymously" anyway. The poetic heir to Brian Coffey in some senses and one of the leaders in this postcolonial redefinition of Irish Modernism, if not Irish nationalism, Joyce offered his own treatment or redrafting of the received Irish literary patrimony with his translation or reworking of the *Buile Suibhne*, edited by his *Lace Curtain* cohort Michael Smith and published in 1976 by their own New Writers' Press as *The Poems of Sweeney Peregrine: A Working of the Corrupt Irish Text*,[4] which, as the subtitle suggests, offers a satirical reworking of the tale, particularly "The Man of the Wood" segment, and so shares some characteristics with the Finn MacCool rendering of *Buile Suibhne*, itself redrafted as St. Ronan's curse on Sweeney-Trellis in Orlick's assault on his own patrimony in *At*

*Swim-Two-Birds* (Plume, 246–7), these, perhaps, in consort with Beckett's lampoon of Cuchulain in *Murphy*. The fourth number of *The Lace Curtain*, then, took a decidedly defiant stand against the Celtic Twilight, even out Becketting Beckett's 1934 attack into which Flann O'Brien's antiquarian lampoons, his own *Working of the Corrupt Irish Text*, might have fit nicely, had the editors chosen to use them.

*The Lace Curtain* republication of "Recent Irish Poetry," now under Beckett's own name, was simultaneously something of a repatriation as well, suggesting at least a postwar or post-Nobel rapprochement between the apostate, Beckett, and his homeland as Smith and Joyce used Beckett's stinging critique of at least certain forms of hermetic Irishness to develop and legitimize their own realignments. The 1934 essay was then embraced in an attempt to carve out a native Irish Modernism and simultaneously to introduce to the Irish reading public more non-Irish writing, Beckett, perhaps, straddling those categories.

As early as its second issue (spring 1970), Smith and Joyce took the "criticism" subtitle of their journal's title seriously and opened their "Editorial" with a look behind the genteel "lace curtain" of Irish literary respectability: "The awarding of the Nobel Prize to Samuel Beckett affords the Irish literary Establishment another occasion for publishing the lie that Ireland is an incorrigibly literary country and that Dublin is an *internationally important* centre of literary activity" (2). The editors dispute that "lie" since most of its internationally noted writers had fled the land of their birth in order to develop creatively, and the editors take on the political issues of the day as well, noting that "Mr [Charles] Haughey's tax concessions are irrelevant to the Irish artist who must work full time at some mundane livelihood job or else never earn enough to be taxed away" (2). The editors cite their most prominent examples:

> It was only through an almost miraculous moral tenacity and integrity that such writers as Patrick Kavanagh[5] and Brian O Nualain (Flann O'Brien) survived (even if somewhat scarred).[6] [Both had been closely associated with the Pre-*Lace Curtain* journal, *Envoy: A Review of Literature and Art*, 1949–51.] Their survival was their own individual achievement; they were wise enough and great enough not to care for the plaudits and "respect" of uncivilized and hypocritical "educated" Dublin

society. *The Lace Curtain* salutes the living spirit of these two great writers [both dead by then, we might add, O'Brien on April Fool's Day in 1966, Kavanagh a year later], and while it admires the work of Mr Beckett, it should have been happy—and now especially since he hardly needs the money—to see him—like Mr Sartre, reject that soiled prize. (2)

In the following issue, No. 3, Michael Smith offers a longish editorial/review, contrasting "Irish Poetry and Penguin Verse," which editorTrevor Joyce called, "a rebarbative attack on Brendan Kennelly's *Penguin Book of Irish Verse*"[7] that Smith characterizes as one that features "a nostalgic backward look" (Coughlan and Davis, 8, 281). Much of the editorial half of the review is an all-out attack on the patriarch of Irish poetry, William Butler Yeats, and Smith suggests that "Even a superficial look at the Literary Revival reveals Yeats as the arch-manipulator, encouraging here, criticizing there, always suppressing, hoisting, punishing" (4). In a gesture of inclusion if not appropriation, perhaps, Kennelly includes a single Beckett poem translated from the French and retitled generically as "Poem," that is, "I would like my love to die," and a single poem by Denis Devlin, "The Colours of Love," who, Kennelly says, in the "Contents" not in the "Introduction," "Deserves more attention" (20); both are poems of failed love. Smith's editorial, then, retraces the battle lines set out in Beckett's 1934 essay on Irish poetry, Kennelly subsuming it all under a grand meta-narrative of native Irish myth around which Irish poetry is seen to be unified and so defined. And Smith lays out Kennelly's biases (while deflecting his own): "In all the reviews of the anthology I have read, none has failed to comment on the ludicrously unjustified preponderance of space allotted to Frank O'Connor [22 poems and whom Kennelly calls 'Ireland's Ezra pound' (30)], James Clarence Mangan [of 'Dark Rosaleen' fame (q.v.), 18 poems[8]] and Sir Samuel Ferguson [of *Lays of the Western Gael* (1865) fame, 11 poems]," translators, real or fake, all (8).

Smith's pointed response to Kennelly's highly influential, defining anthology (which is published in a second, expanded edition in 1981 and which adds a second Devlin poem, the associated comment now "His work has begun to attract the critical attention it deserves" [18], the "Introduction," however, is essentially unchanged) is, furthermore, taken up more fully in its subsequent

issue that reprints Samuel Beckett's review of Denis Devlin's
poems, *Intercessions* (41–4), in which Beckett praised Devlin for
creating a poetry "free to be derided (or not) on its own terms
and not in those terms of the politicians, antiquaries (*Geleerte*)
[*sic*, exhausted or depleted] and zealots." Beckett's critique here
is used to resist the likes of Kennelly's grand narrative of Irish
aesthetic (and so, presumably, political) unity (41).[9] The poetically
inclined Good Fairy in *At Swim-Two-Birds* might have been
cited in support; the shape-shifting Pooka, himself a concocted
figment of Irish imagination, is a fan not of antiquarians but of
cosmopolitans, "I always make a point of following the works of
Mr Eliot and Mr Lewis and Mr Devlin" (170). Within Kennelly's
structure, moreover, in something of a canonization, almost all
of translations of Irish poetry or song from Old Irish are those
of the prolific Frank O'Connor, to whose preponderance in this
anthology Smith repeatedly objects.

The expanded issue, No. 4 (summer 1971), now edited by Smith
alone as Trevor Joyce withdrew to concentrate on writing his own
poetry, returns to the battle as it took on the look of a Beckett
tribute with a portrait of Ireland's latest Nobel laureate dominating
its cover, and an opening "Editorial" that resumed the assault on
received literary wisdom: "Conventionally, the tradition of Modern
Irish Poetry is described as having its source and existence in W. B.
Yeats and his survivors in the Twilight" (3). The counterexample
that follows immediately thereafter is a suite of Beckett poems
reprinted from his first poetry collection, *Echo's Bones and Other
Precipitates* (Europa Press, 1935),[10] suggesting the sort of poetry
Beckett was writing as he was simultaneously critiquing his
homeland's poetic patrimony: "Alba," "Serena I," "Da Tagte Es,"
"Malacoda," and "Gnome" (5–7). The issue reprinted as well two
more of Beckett's early essays, the aforementioned "Recent Irish
Poetry" (58–63) and "Humanistic Quietism[11]" (70–1), the latter a
brief appraisal of Thomas MacGreevy's *Poems* of 1934 (London:
William Heinemann; New York, Viking Press), the review written
originally for *The Dublin Magazine* and signed simply S. B. Denis
Devlin himself would rereview MacGreevy's *Poems* in 1972 for
*Hibernia Review of Books* (February 4, p. 10) just as MacGreevy's
*Collected Poems* was being issued from New Writers' Press, which
was simultaneously publishing Devlin's poems.[12] Beckett opens his
MacGreevy review with the now-famous incantation, "All poetry,

as discriminated from the various paradigms of prosody, is prayer," an acknowledgment at least of if not a tribute, perhaps, to Tom MacGreevy's piety (70). Beckett's praise for MacGreevy is even more direct in "Recent Irish Poetry" where he calls MacGreevy's poetry "the most important contribution to post-War Irish poetry" (74). In *The Lace Curtain* 6, the journal's final issue and with MacGreevy's portrait dominating its cover, Anthony Cronin[13] will call Beckett's review "the only decent review that MacGreevy ever got" (58) as he would call "the cosmopolitan" MacGreevy, "the first modern Irish poet," refer to him as "not a dealer in local color" (58), and cite, from Beckett's attack in "Recent Irish Poetry" on "the true Gael," Irish anti-cosmopolitanism as the cause of MacGreevy's neglect (56, 59).

Cronin himself puts MacGreevy among the cosmopolitans in the Eliot tradition: "Whether from Eliot or otherwise," Cronin notes, "he had learned […] that the liberation from rhyme had in fact created new possibilities for the enjoyment of rhyme" (58).[14] Cronin's comments thus complement or augment Beckett's of 1934: "What is badly needed at the present moment is some small Malherbe of free verse to sit on the sonnet and put it out of action for two hundred years at least. Perhaps Mr Pound … ?" (74). MacGreevy's *Collected Poems*, also from New Writers' Press in 1971 and edited by Thomas Dillon Redshaw, would reprint Beckett's review, "Humanistic Quietism," yet again, "the only decent review that MacGreevy ever got," as a "Foreword" and the issue ends by declaring its continental allegiances, reprinting a *transition* magazine manifesto, "Poetry is Vertical" (73–74), to which Beckett (reluctantly) and MacGreevy (clearly eagerly) were signatories. In his summation of the period Mervyn Wall would note: "these urban poets, Coffey, Devlin and Beckett, had no wish to write of battles long ago, nor were they mesmerized by the Irish countryside. 'I hate scenery' was a constant saying of Devlin's" (85), or as Estragon suggests in *Waiting for Godot*, "You and your landscapes! Tell me about the worms!"

Issue 4, then, includes as well two essays by Niall Montgomery, the second of which is a belated tribute to, if not a gesture of recuperation for, Flann O'Brien, complete with an editing redundancy that may be intended to recall the metatextuality of *At Swim-Two-Birds*, if it is not simply a blunder; that is, rather than editing out the (apparent) error, the editors include a footnote to call attention to it, a gesture worthy of O'Brien while also perhaps a nod to Beckett's *Watt*, two novels that Cronin and Montgomery consider not only distinctly Irish, but Dublin novels.[15] As Montgomery notes (75), "Brian Ó Nualláin was a fantastic and wonderful fellow and to say *nach mbeidh a leitheid aris ann* is putting it mildly; there was never the like of him, certainly not in U. C. D. in the 'thirties, where he descended, like a shower of paratroopers, deploying a myriad of pseudonymous personalities in the interest of pure destruction" (74). Montgomery's Irishism, "*nach mbeidh a leitheid aris ann*" (or, *Ní bheidh a leithéid arís ann*), is not only a staple of Irish obituaries, but it recurs throughout *An Béal Bocht* (1941), *The Poor Mouth*, translated and published as such only in 1973. "Most dazzling," Montgomery continues, "was his consistent presentation of uncommon ideas as common sense: the delirium on which he imposed order was very real to him—he hypnotized a generation into believing that it [presumably the 'delirium'] was Ireland. Maybe it was, then.

His satire, when he was young, seemed to spring up not out of bitterness but from helplessness, disbelieving enjoyment of the perverse fantasy of conventional behavior" (74).

If Montgomery's essay was a gesture to embrace O'Brien among the writers of a new Irish Modernism, the choice of representative work is something less than a compelling argument, limited, presumably, by the journal's emphasis on the genre of poetry. The issue prints another side of Ó Nualláin, neither satires nor the "pure destruction" cited by Montgomery or even the *Buile Suibhne* translations and recastings prominently on display in *At Swim-Two-Birds* to which Montgomery refers, but three tender, even sentimental translations from Old Irish, songs perhaps, a mode that Beckett excoriates in his essay; isolated thus the poems, the airs would bring an approving nod from those "antiquarians" of the Celtic Twilight, Brendan Kennelly included, but derided in the issue: "*Three Poems from the Irish*," translated by one Myles na gCopaleen[16]: "AOIBHINN, A LEABHRÁIN, DO THRIALL" ["To the Lady with a Book"], "Domfarcai fidbaidæ fál" ["A hedge [of trees] before [surrounds or fenced] me"],[17] and, the most famous of them (since it appears in the first volume of the *Field Day Anthology* there not in Ó Nualláin's translation, however), "Scél lem dúib" ["Brief Account" or rather "Here's a song"] (46–7), the first and third of these reprinted in the *Flann O'Brien Reader* in

1978, not long after their appearance in *The Lace Curtain*.[18] [http://
www.archipelago.org/vol7-3/ScelLemDuib.html.][19]

Montgomery ends his tribute to Ó Nualláin with a look
backwards to O'Nolan's UCD days, which the poems apparently
celebrate: "last evening [and presumably this would be four years
earlier] the posters said 'Death of Famous Irish Writer' and there
was snow in April for a man who did his M. A. thesis on nature
in Irish poetry." In his tribute to O'Brien shortly after his death,
John Montague, on the other hand, also offers a translation of one
of Sweeney's laments from the *Buile Suibhne* in a poem entitled
"Sweetness (from the Irish)" and subtitled "I. M. Flann O'Brien,
who skipped it" (the "it" suggesting that this lament is excluded
from *At Swim-Two-Birds*). A prose introduction to the poem evokes
the novel by locating Sweeney at "the church of Swim-Two-Birds,
opposite Clonmacnoise" [cf. 1976, p. 95] and Montague's tribute
ends, without irony, as follows:

> O hear me, Christ
> Without stain, never
> Let me be severed
> Oh Christ, from your sweetness! (65)

And yet, even as the poems, selected for *The Lace Curtain* by
O'Brien's widow a note tells us, seem almost out of character if not
out of place in so politically charged a journal, they invoke books
and writing and come out of a tradition of monkish meditation and
song, essentially prayer, like all good poetry according to Beckett,
and they are not Frank O'Connor translations.

Perhaps a more appropriate entry for *The Lace Curtain*, at
least one more in keeping with Montgomery's assessment and the
politics of the journal, although it is not poetry per se, might have
been O'Brien's treatment of "antiquarians," of Irish nostalgia for its
past, the Sea Cat episode from his Gaeltacht novel, *The Poor Mouth*
(although only available in Patrick C. Power's English translation in
1973), a satire of cosmopolitan urbanites getting in touch with their
authentic Irish roots, the language of which, as the Dublin folklorist
notes, "He understood that good Gaelic is difficult but that the best
Gaelic of all is well-nigh unintelligible"; the Sea Cat herself gave
off "an ancient smell of putridity which set the skin of my nose
humming and dancing." Eminent historian Dennis Kennedy opened

his lecture at Trinity College, Dublin, in October of 2010 by invoking the Sea Cat encounter: "Bonaparte O'Coonassa, wandering among the rocks of Donegal, feels menaced by something evil pursuing him. He smells it and hears it snorting and barking, and then he sees it—'a large quadruped—a great hairy object, grey haired with prickly red eyes'" (Kennedy 2010). For Kennedy,

> The people of Ireland, like O'Coonassa, it seems, are being pursued and terrified by a creature, possibly of their own imagining—and it is Ireland, "the pleasant little land which is our own" as O'Brien has it.
>
> And that, it seems to me, is Ireland in a nutshell, a nightmare hangover resulting from too much bad history and an obsession with the physical island itself.
>
> History, like alcohol, is highly intoxicating, and bad history, like bad drink, can cause serious hangovers. Nationalism is one of these. It can leave those who have over-indulged incapable of thinking clearly, possessed of strange notions, in a general state of hostility towards any who do not share their views. (Kennedy 2010)

Kennedy goes on to note that "One British commentator and writer, the gloomy Dean Inge of St Paul's, acidly described a nation as 'a society united by a common delusion about its ancestry and by a common hatred of its neighbours'. He was probably thinking of Germany, but the definition applied as aptly to Ireland" (Kennedy 2010). Kennedy's essay would have fit neatly into *The Lace Curtain* campaign, particularly the issue of 1971, and could serve as a companion piece to Beckett's critique of 1934. But this is not the O'Brien that *The Lace Curtain* shows us.

Writing in *The Irish Times* on the centenary of O'Brien's birth, furthermore, Fintan O'Toole extends the comparison and draws a direct parallel to Beckett thus:

> The ancient smell of putridity that emanates from this half-comic, half-terrifying embodiment of Ireland is not unrelated to the stink of "history's ancient faeces" that, according to the narrator of Samuel Beckett's *First Love* (written five years after *The Poor Mouth* in 1946) largely constitutes "the charm of our country". If Beckett and O'Brien shared a great deal besides

their belief that something was rotten in the state of Ireland, the overwhelming difference between them is that Beckett, like the majority of their literary contemporaries, managed to flee from the Sea-cat. O'Brien, almost alone among the great writers of 20th century Ireland, fell into its clutches. He stayed in Ireland and paid a fearful price in frustration and neglect. (O'Toole 2011)

Beckett, too, might have yielded to the Sea Cat and paid that "fearful price." As the typescript for *Murphy* was floundering and being rejected by a sequence of publishers, he toured Germany and wrote to Mary Manning on January 18, 1937, "No, I have not written at all and have no plans. Mother writes why don't I contribute to the papers, I write at least as well as the Irishman Diarist." "The Irishman Diarist" was written mostly by then-editor R. M. Smyllie, who soon after would be interested in a series of letters from Brian O'Nolan that would themselves soon develop into "Cruiskeen Lawn," the first appearing in October of 1940. And Beckett would comment in the letter to Manning cited above on something of the strange smell of Ireland: "I know the smell you describe. The decay ingredient you omit, what you get in a cemetery. You like it because it is associated with your innocence. I dislike it for the same reason. It is part of the home poison. A swamp smell" (Beckett *Letters* I 2009c, 423–4).

Much of what Beckett and O'Brien shared, "swamp smell" or "The ancient smell of putridity" aside, is apparent in their first published novels: *Murphy* (1938) was Beckett's novel of flight, although his past pursues him into and throughout London, *At Swim-Two-Birds* (1939), O'Brien's novel of imaginative flight but physical resignation, and both, as John P. Harrington notes, share "a parodic deflation of the contemporary power of Celtic myth—for O'Brien the Finn legend of the Leinster cycle as for Beckett the Cuchulain legend of the Ulster cycle" (Harrington 105). They were published within a year of each other; James Joyce read and loved them both, quoting portions of *Murphy* by heart and recommending both to Paris bookseller Adrienne Monnier in 1940 (Harrington 105). According to another Irish poet/civil servant, Mervyn Wall, in an interview with Smith in *Lace Curtain* 4, "Some Questions about the Thirties" (77–86), "Joyce was delighted with *At Swim-Two-Birds* and sent a copy to

O'Nolan [Flann O'Brien] to be autographed" (83).[20] And in one
of the curiosities of Modernist literature, stores of both would be
destroyed in the blitz of 1940. O'Brien/O'Nolan could be as sharp
a critic of the antiquarians as Beckett or Smith, such invoked, for
instance, in Shanahan's assessment of Finn Macool's Sweeney tale
in *At Swim-Two-Birds*:

> Now take that stuff your man was giving us a while ago [...]
> about green hills and the bloody swords and the bird giving
> out the pay from the top of the tree. Now that's good stuff,
> it's bloody nice. [...] You can't beat it, of course [...] the real
> old stuff of the native land, you know, the stuff that brought
> scholars to our shore when your men on the other side were on
> the flat of their bellies before the calf of gold with a sheepskin
> around their man. It's the stuff that put our country where she
> stands today, Mr. Furriskey, and I'd have my tongue out of my
> head by the bloody roots before I'd be heard saying a word
> against it. (106)

Of the original publication of "Recent Irish Poetry," Denis
Devlin had written to Thomas MacGreevy on August 31, 1934 that
Beckett's essay had "raised a storm" and that "It appears that Yeats
was furious; it appears that Austin Clark [...] will pursue Sam to his
grave; it appears Seamas [for Seumas] O'Sullivan thought he might
have been mentioned at least"; while Higgins was "glad he got off
so lightly" (cited in Beckett *Letters* I, 224n3), Beckett admiring "the
sweet smell of dung" in Higgins's poetry. The reissue of "Recent Irish
Poetry" in *The Lace Curtain*, on the other hand, generated no such
response and even went unmentioned in subsequent editorials. *The
Lace Curtain* translations did little to enhance O'Brien's reputation,
even as the 1970s saw his work printed in important journals like
*Antaeus*; issues 16 and 19, both of 1975, included excerpts from
O'Brien's forthcoming novel, *The Poor Mouth*, although the editors
identify one of O'Brien's books as *The Salkey Archive*. The first of
these was a translation issue so it's the Patrick C. Power translation
that is printed. The Irish return to Beckett in the 1970s, on the
other hand, did effect, or at least sped his repatriation. In 1984
he was elected to the Aosdána as Saoi, a Charles Haughey created
honorific, a state sponsored association, with stipend, of some 250
Irish artists (200 at the time), poets Anthony Cronin (Haughey's

culture advisor), John Montague, and Trevor Joyce among them. The repatriation culminated, or was completed perhaps, just weeks before Beckett's death in 1989 as Montague, after a poetry reading in Paris, visited the infirm Beckett and solicited from him a contribution to *The Great Book of Ireland*, a monumental project, finally completed and published in 1991. The volume included some 143 poets, the single, handcrafted volume held at University College Cork. Beckett's contribution written in his shaky, failing hand directly onto velum was a poem he had written originally on the occasion of the death of his father, "Da Tagte Es," reprising his contribution to *The Lace Curtain* 4 and doing so, as it turned out, on the eve of his own death. Montague's recollection of the scene is his own farewell not surrogate:

> The scroll will not stay put. Baffled, Beckett wrestles with the vellum, whilst I set up the small black ink bottle, with the skinny nib to dip in it. Finally, I have to hold down the curling corners, as he strives to write what may be his last lines [ ....] The lines are not new: he has chosen a quatrain written after his father's death, and the implications for his own demise, so long attended, are all too clear.

> Redeem the surrogate goodbyes
> the sheet astream in your hand
> who have no more for the land
> and the glass unmisted above your eyes.

> The sheet is not astream, but bucking and bounding, and his hands are shaking. Twice he has to stroke out lines, but he still goes on, with that near ferocity I associate with him, until the four lines are copied, in the center of a page. He looks at me, I look down to check, and murmur appropriate approval. He rolls the vellum, and with due ceremony hands it over to me, with the carton. Then, with a gesture of finality, he sweeps the lot, ink bottle, long black pen and spare pages of vellum, into the wastepaper bin. (*The New York Times*, April 17, 1994)

For Beckett both exiled and at home in Paris, the gesture may have again been some compensation for the paternal good-by undelivered in person, the farewell scene revisioned, the sentiment disguised in a foreign tongue. For Ireland, as a new millennium approached, Beckett, it appears, received a death-bed redemption as an Irish poet. His attitude may have been best summed up, however, in the "Addenda" to *Watt*: "for all the good that frequent departures out of Ireland had done him, he might just as well stayed there" (*Watt*, 248). Beckett returns to the sentiment in his first radio play in 1957, *All That Fall*, as Maddy Rooney notes: "It is suicide to be abroad. But what is it to be at home, Mr. Tyler, what is it to be at home? A lingering dissolution." Others had heeded such advice to their detriment.

Niall Montgomery, Dublin architects and friend to artists, Beckett and Flann O'Brien not the least among them, and in whose house the two met in 1939 just after the publication of *At Swim-Two-Birds* but of which Beckett is reported to have said of their discussion of James Joyce that the meeting "is better forgotten" (Harrington, 105), wrote one of the earliest appreciations, what he, like Molloy, Moran and Malone call a "report" on Beckett's fiction[21] for *New World Writing* # 5 in 1954. The title, "No Symbols Where None Intended," cites the closing of *Watt*, which Montgomery calls "the definitive Irish peasant novel," and further that it "is accurate Dublin, as first noticed by Joyce,[22] [that is, James in this case] and subsequently orchestrated in *At Swim-Two-Birds*, by Flann O'Brien, a homebased exile whose only other points of community with Beckett are bicycles, scatology, and plenary literary powers" (326), to which list we might add at least a distaste for provincialism, nationalism, and theocracy coupled with an embrace of at least certain forms of worldliness if not cosmopolitanism. Both had treated Ireland's mythic patrimony with something short of respect in major novels written only a year apart. Both at least acknowledged the climate of parochial Irish censorship in those novels as well, the dissolute narrator of *At Swim-Two-Birds* secreting all mention of questionable subjects, "Hastily I covered such sheets as contained references to the forbidden question of sexual relations" (Plume, 128). In *Murphy*, published the year before *At Swim-Two-Birds*, Beckett's narrator retreats into metaphor and is yet more direct: "Murphy knew what that meant. No more music [i.e., sex with Celia]. The phrase is chosen with care, lest the filthy censors should lack an occasion to commit their filthy synecdoche" (*Murphy* 46). And the narrator describes Celia's kiss as "the slow-motion osmosis of love's spittle," then adds, "the above passage is carefully calculated to deprave the cultivated [i.e., lace curtain] reader" (*Murphy*, 69). As Donal Ó Drisceoil notes in the *Irish Examiner*,

Censorship in Ireland, which was largely overturned 50 years ago, meant the public couldn't easily get their eyes on work by our best writers, making it a badge of honour [ ....] The mere suggestion of homosexuality, promiscuity, or prostitution was enough to ban a book. Most of the leading writers of modern fiction fell victim, leading cynics to dub the Irish Register of Prohibited Publications 'The Everyman's Guide to the Modern Classics.'

What Beckett tried to take on in 1934, in personal retribution in some respects, was something like home-grown Modernism, a category just shy of home-grown avant-gardism, and into which he tried to fit MacGreevy even as the category seems gerrymandered and exclusionary. In 1970 the ideological and aesthetic contrasts between *The Penguin Book of Irish Verse* and the literary journal *The Lace Curtain* reignited the issues, the latter rearmed with the award to Ireland of its third Nobel Prize for Literature creating something like dueling laureates, the neo or belated Romantic, Yeats, and the neo or belated Modernist, Beckett. Into that climate Patrick C. Power's translation of *The Poor Mouth* and Viking's publication of *Stories and Plays* appeared, both in 1973, and the Penguin group and Viking Press (or Richard Seaver) followed with reissues of two of Flann O'Brien's most important novels, *At Swim-Two-Birds* (1939 Longmans, 1950 Pantheon, rereleased in 1961 and 1968, reissued 1975 by Penguin) and *The Third Policeman* (1967), both Plume editions in 1976, and followed up with a major anthology, *The Flann O'Brien Reader*, edited by Stephen Jones in 1978. O'Brien's reputation would spike amid this flurry of publication, peaking about 1986, falling off considerably shortly thereafter, however. Beckett's and Joyce's would continue, and continue to rise, as O'Brien's, after periods of stagnation, is on the ascent as well. O'Brien remains, however, in a league with (or in league with) Beckett and Joyce once we attend to his mastery of deflationary comedy, his narrative dislocations, and his assaults on certain forms of "lace curtain" Irish pretensions. All three had rapier wit and a tendency toward parody and hoax, Beckett in his faux Trinity College lectures in French to the Modern Languages Society on "Le Concentrisme" and "Jean du Chas" (1930), the closing letters of complaint to "Mr. Germs Choice," often attributed to Joyce himself but written evidently by Vladimir Dixon (with Joyce's approval) for *Our Exagmination 'Round His Factification for Incamination of Work in Progress*, and Flann O'Brien, writing as Brother Barnabus, as early as the short-lived 6-issue UCD journal, *Blather* (August 1934–January 1935) and the series of letters to the *Irish Times* that developed into the "Cruiskeen Lawn" column. For a time Joyce was left out in the cold, at least by the lace curtain Irish, because of perceived decadent and continental qualities of his most Dublin novel, *Ulysses*, and Beckett likewise if more aggressively anti-lace curtain, while O'Brien was never fully in because of his modernity and never fully out as a stay-at-home writer and civil servant still flirting with antiquarian Ireland, he then neither, but it is precisely such neitherness, resistance to what Beckett called, in reference to Joyce, "the neatness of identifications," an aesthetics and technique suited to neither camp, that at present is regenerating critical and theoretical interest in renewed thinking about Irish Modernism.

# Notes

1  Reprinted in Julia Carlson (published for "Article 19: International Centre on Censorship," a watchdog organization named for Article 19 of the 1948 Universal Declaration of Human Rights); further discussed in Donal Ó Drisceoil, 2011.

2  One of Russell's epigraphs is from "Proverbs" 20:27: "The Spirit of man is the candle [or a lamp] of the Lord [searching all the inward parts of the belly]." The book is dedicated to James Stephens, "Best of companions."

3  This issue also contained poems by three of Beckett's associates, A. J. "Con" Leventhal, longtime confidant Thomas MacGreevy, and sometime literary agent George Reavey, as well as poets Beckett had praised in reviews, Denis Devlin and Brian Coffey. MacGreevy's and Coffey's collections of poetry are reviewed in the issue. The essay was collected again in 1984 in Beckett's own *Disjecta*, or "throwaways" as James Joyce, rather Leopold Bloom, might have called them, ed. Ruby Cohn (Grove Press 1984, pp. 70–6).

4  *The Poems of Sweeney Peregrine* are reprinted in the *First Dream of Fire They Hunt the Cold* (Shearsman Books, Exeter/New Writers' Press, 2001; 2nd edition, 2003), and in the volume of translations, *Courts of Air and Earth* (Shearsman Books, Exeter 2008). In her

"Foreword" to *Courts of Air and Earth*, American poet Fanny Howe notes of Trevor Joyce's translations that "They mediate between tradition and modernity," the former "music [that] expresses a single culture's necessity" and so develops community, the latter "abandons the community in favor of a plurality of interpretations." Seamus Heaney's version of the *Buile Shuibhne* was published in 1983 as *Sweeney Astray: A Version from the Irish*.

5   Kavanagh had thirteen poems published in *Lace Curtain* 4 (21–6), three of them nature poems under the general rubric of "Four Birds!"

6   On their falling out, over potatoes as it turns out, see Joseph Brooker. "Ploughmen without Land: Flann O'Brien and Patrick Kavanagh." *Flann O'Brien and Modernism*, ed. Julian Murphet, Rónán McDonald, and Sasha Morrell. London: Bloomsbury Academic, 2014, pp. 93–106. Brooker also deals with the issue at hand in this essay, the relationship between poets of the land, early Kavanagh, at least, and their mockers, sincerity versus satire, say, in this case an O'Nolan still a UCD wag. See *The Bog of Allen* as well as something of a precursor of *The Poor Mouth*.

7   As a measure of its popularity, hence a gauge of its influence, the 1970 volume was reprinted in 1971, 1974, 1976, 1979, and the second edition appeared in 1981.

8   A favorite with James Joyce, the poem is cited in "Araby," and Joyce wrote two essays on Mangan, whose literary hoaxes and fake translations (dubbed "reverse plagiarism") are occasionally cited as anticipations of Flann O'Brien. See *Poems* by Clarence Mangan (2004), ed. David Wheatley. Loughcrew, Oldcastle, Co. Meath, Ireland: Gallery Press. See also John Redmond's *Guardian* review, "The Man in the Cloak" (February 7, 2004), where he points out that

Mangan was camp. He is an incessant "play-actor" and self-mythologiser, at the beginning, in this respect, of a long line of Irish writers, including George Moore, Oscar Wilde, Yeats himself and Brendan Behan. [Flann O'Brien's omission here is curious.] In early life, for instance, Mangan was known as "The man in the cloak"; his middle name, Clarence, was his own adoption; and his translations, real and fake, from Gaelic, German and Arabic, bespeak a willed exoticism. David Wheatley, the editor of this selection, speaks, with no little understatement, of Mangan's "natural instinct for display."
https://www.theguardian.com/books/2004/feb/07/featuresreviews.guardianreview8

9   Beckett's review appeared originally in the Eurocentric *transition* magazine, April–May 1938.

10  The Europa Press became something of a club for these new, urban Irish Modernists, like New Writers' Press in the 1970s. Denis Devlin's poetry collection *Intercessions* (1934) and Brian Coffey's *Third Person* (1938) were also published by Europa Press, as was Beckett's translations of Paul Éluard's love poetry, *Thorns of Thunder* (1939).

11  Cited also in Stan Smith's assessment of MacGreevy, "From a Great Distance: Thomas MacGreevy's Frame of Reference," *The Lace Curtain* 6 (autumn 1978), 50. This would be the journal's final issue.

12  Beckett's own *Collected Poems: 1930–1978* would first appear from John Calder, Ltd., in 1982.

13  One of those reviews hostile to MacGreevy was written by Richard Thoma, associate editor of what was essentially an anti-Modernist, anti-Joyce, anti-*transition* literary journal, *The New Review*, ed. Samuel Putnam. Entitled "Island without Serpents," the review attacked MacGreevy's Catholicism and his "rambling, pedantic, speculative, dilettantish" style. George Reavey of Europa Press, publisher of the poems, would write a defense in the following issue, "Letter to Richard Thoma," *The New Review* 1.4 [winter 1931–31]: 397 (cited in Beckett *Letters* 2009c, 89n1).

14  See J. C. C. Mays, "How Is MacGreevy a Modernist." *Modernism and Ireland: The Poetry of the 1930s,* ed. Patricia Coughlan and Alex Davis. Cork: Cork University Press, 1995, 103–28.

15  The journal had its share of typographical blunders over its six publications, including in issue 3, "Then Icarus fell at out feet" in Gottfried Benn's poem, "Icarus" (38), and in issue 4, "wnown" for known, as in "not to have ever really wnown him," in Smith's interview with Mervyn Wall as Wall is speaking of meeting Beckett "in the early thirties in his rooms at Trinity" (85).

16  Probably from his 1934 MA thesis, University College, Dublin, *Nádúir-Fhilíocht na Gaedhilge* ['Irish Nature Poetry'], to which Montgomery refers.

17  An alternate translation of the first stanza of these verses written by an Irish scribe in the margins of St. Gall Priscian's *Institutiones Grammatice*:

> Domfarcai fidbaidæ fál:
> fomchain loíd luin,
> lúad nad cél
> huas mo lebrán ind línech fomchain trírech inna n-én
> [A hedge of trees surrounds me:
> a blackbird's song sings to me

praise which I will not hide
above my lined book,
the trilling of the birds sings to me]
(Whitley Stokes and John Strachan (ed.), *Thesaurus palaeohibernicus* ii [Cambridge 1903] 290.6–7).

18  Ed. Stephen Jones. New York: Viking Press (A Richard Seaver Book), 1978. The first appeared in *The Oxford Book of Irish Verse.*

19  "Scel Lem Duib" (A Ninth Century Irish Poem)

Here's a song —
stags give tongue
winter snows
summer goes
High cold blow
sun is low
brief his day
seas give spray
Fern clumps redden
shapes are hidden
wildgeese raise
wonted cries
Cold now girds
wings of birds
icy time—
that's my rime.

Translated by Flann O'Brien and cited in full by J. C. C. Mays in "Literalist of the Imagination," *Alive Alive O: Flann O'Brien's "At Swim Two-Birds."* Dublin: Woolfhound Press, 1985, 85, of which he says: "Brian O'Nolan translates literally and without mockery from the *Buile Suibhne* here, and the lay that Sweeny sang there is at the centre of the positive values in the book" (85).

20  See Brian Fallon in *The Irish Times*:

The death of Mervyn Wall a few years ago received less attention than it deserved, since he was a central figure in the Dublin literary world of the 1940s and 1950s. *Fursey*, a medieval Irish monk tormented by the devil, has a place in the Irish comic pantheon along with Brian O'Nolan's [Flann O'Brien's] Pooka MacPhelimey, or James Stephens' two Philosophers in *The Crock of Gold*. The book first appeared in 1946 (it is dedicated, incidentally, to Denis Devlin, one of Wall's many gifted contemporaries in UCD) and Wall added a sequel, *The Return of Fursey*. Though the book is occasionally marred by the kind of garrulous whimsy which was a common fault of the period, it wears its age well and fully deserves resurrection. It might, incidentally, make an excellent film for TV, given an imaginative producer with flair.

21  Montgomery's essay on Beckett, "No symbols where none intended," appeared in *New World Writing: Fifth Mentor Selection* (New American Library, 1954), which billed itself as "A New Adventure in Modern Reading." The essay title derives from the very last words to the "Addenda" of Beckett's novel, *Watt*. Beckett recited the passage in a chatty letter to Montgomery of November 1955 as, apparently, an acknowledgment of, if not an homage to, Montgomery and the essay (Beckett *Letters* 2011, 561), an essay for which Montgomery had asked permission to write. Beckett approved and of which he said, "I learned a lot about myself I didn't know & hadn't suspected. I emerged more organized than I am" (Beckett *Letters* 2011, 426, 427n1).

22  For more on the O'Brien/James Joyce affinity, see the John Ryan, editor of *Envoy* (something of a precursor to *The Lace Curtain*), memoir:

In 1951, whilst I was editor of the Irish literary periodical *Envoy*, I decided that it would be a fitting thing to commemorate the tenth anniversary of the death of James Joyce by bringing out a special number dedicated to him which would reflect the attitudes and opinions of his fellow countrymen towards their illustrious compatriot. To this end I began by inviting Brian Nolan [Flann O'Brien] to act as honorary editor for this particular issue. His own genius closely matched, without in any way resembling or attempting to counterfeit, Joyce's. But if the mantle of Joyce (or should we say the waistcoat?) were ever to be passed on, nobody would be half so deserving of it as the man whom under his other guises as Flann O'Brien and Myles na gCopaleen, proved himself incontestably to be the most creative writer and mordant wit that Ireland had given us since Shem the Penman himself." John Ryan, "Introduction" to *A Bash in the Tunnel* (Brighton: Clifton Books, 1970). *Envoy* also published "An extract from *Watt*," the first sighting of Watt, in volume 1, number 2, 1950: 11–19, and Beckett was less than pleased with the editorial emendations the journal made: "An extract from *Watt*, massacred by the compositor, appeared in that filthy new Irish rag *Envoy*" (Beckett *Letters* 2011, 202).

# 2

# Publishing in America: Sam and Barney

*[L]et me hasten before all else to say that few things
would give me more pleasure than to see you in Paris
next month, this month or any month, with I hope
Loly on your arm, and with my ill-gottens to buy for us
spirals of apéritifs and bring you to Bobino and supper
with buckets of Beaujolais and Sancerre at the ever
satisfactory Marquesas. SB to BR, May 26, 1956*

*Gratitude is a poor word for the beautiful set of 13
and the affection it brings me from you all and the way
it says how good things always were between us and
always will be. SB to BR and all at Grove,
April 16, 1966*

*I am always in touch with you, Barney, even without
writing or hearing. SB to BR October 12, 1978*

On June 18, 1953, Barnet Lee Rosset, Jr., the thirty-one-year-old
owner and sole employee of the fledgling Grove Press, took on a
new author, Samuel Beckett, a little known Irish émigré living in

Paris and writing (then) primarily in French: "It is about time that I write a letter to you—now that agents, publishers, friends, etc., have all acted as go-betweens. A copy of our catalogue has already been mailed to you, so you will be able to see what kind of publisher you have been latched onto. I hope that you won't be too disappointed. We are very happy to have the contract back from Minuit, and, believe me, we will do what we can to make your work known in this country" (Rosset 2016, 110). That initial letter began one of the most extraordinary relationships in publishing that lasted until Beckett's death on December 22, 1989. Its origins were modest: a little known writer (unknown in the United States) publishing arcane, experimental poems, plays, and novels with little prospect of commercial success championed by a neophyte American publishing house struggling to find its niche. Samuel Beckett went on, of course, to become one of the most influential writers of the twentieth century, his reputation solidified internationally by the award first of the *Prix International de Littérature* in 1961, which he shared with Jorge Luis Borges, and subsequently, of course, the Nobel Prize for Literature in 1969. Rosset, in turn, would guide what began as a small reprint house that he bought in 1951 for $3,000 into the most aggressive, innovative, audacious, politically active, and so sometimes reckless publishing concern in the United States for over three decades. Through the turbulence, the successes and failures of the press, Beckett remained a featured, signature author.

In these early years Grove Press was a decidedly amateurish concern. Rosset was operating it from his 57 W. 9th Street flat in New York's Greenwich Village, filling orders himself, wheeling parcels of books to the local post office in a shopping trolley. As business increased Rosset took on an assistant editor, Don Allen,[1] whom he had met at a night class "Editorial Practices and Principles of Book Publishing" offered at Columbia University by legendary Random House editor Saxe Commins (1892–1958).[2] Allen then took the basement flat next door to Rosset at 59 W. 9th Street, and Rosset finally moved his editorial offices out of his home and into the apartment just above Allen's basement residence, "Grove's first home away from home," as Rosset phrased it (Rosset 2016, 97). For a time Rosset sublet part of his expanded office space to a pair of new publishers, Arthur Cohen (1928–1986) and Cecil Hemley (1914–1966), founders of Noonday Press, but the mix of personalities was less than ideal, and Noonday soon moved to other offices. Even with the separation of business from living quarters, the Grove operation remained modest. *Newsweek* magazine described the enterprise on March 30, 1953, thus: "the Grove Press is housed on the ground floor of a Greenwich Village dwelling, with the shipping room in what used to be the dining room [. ... The office] overlooks one of those fine old Greenwich Village back yards of struggling trees, spare grass, spite-wall fences, clotheslines, and expanses of brick wall. Since the staff of the Grove Press consists only of a publicity man [John Gruen], a charming young German girl newly arrived in the United States [Hannelore (Loly) Eckert (born August 29, 1923) whom Rosset would marry on August 21, 1953], and a part time assistant who plays in bit parts in Broadway shows [Howard Turner], the overhead is not high." What the *Newsweek* profile intimated was that the Grove staff lacked publishing experience. Debutantes all, Rosset and his staff were fully engaged in professional development. Even as Rosset was making his first, extended European business trip to acquire books and to meet authors, Beckett included, his staff was arranging night classes for them all to take to learn the business of publishing. Grove's office manager, Howard Turner, wrote to Rosset in London a near-daily summary of business activities and offered the following update:

> After fifty-thousand man hours of standing in line and barking at inept, amateur student-clerks, I registered you and Marilyn [Meeker] in the Editorial Procedures course at NYU and me in Marshall Lee's[3] course in Book Design, also at NYU; and today I registered you and Loly in the [Wallace] Fowlie course at New School, and John [Gruen] in Hilda Livingston's course there. Descriptions of your courses are enclosed; they sound good. I went ahead with this without waiting for confirmation from you, because I was afraid the courses might fill up. I did not in any case ask for official Academic Credit (which costs extra); if you wish it let me know at once. (Stanley Gontarski Grove Press Research Archive, Florida State University)

What the staff lacked in experience, it more than made up for with enthusiasm and dedication.

Rosset and Beckett seemed, at the outset, an odd match: a classically educated Irishman with a master's degree in modern languages from the venerable Trinity College, Dublin, transplanted to France, and a scrappy Chicagoan from a middle-class banking family who had failed to complete degree requirements at three major American universities[4] transplanted to New York; a shy, bookish, taciturn artist with impeccable European (if not nineteenth-century) manners, on the one hand, and a brash, volatile, street-smart American more comfortable in the jazz clubs of Chicago than in any library or university. They were a generation apart in age as well; Samuel Barclay Beckett was born in Foxrock, County Dublin, on April 13, 1906, and Barnet Lee Rosset, Jr., in Chicago on May 28, 1922. But over a thirty-five-year period, a professional as well as spiritual bond developed between the upstart American publisher bent on challenging traditional restrictions on American publishing and the upstart Irish writer bent on challenging the literary traditions not only of his homeland but of Western literature as a whole. The two actually had a great deal in common. Rosset had Irish roots on his mother's side, Mary E. Tansey (b. 1899), who married the son of Russian Jewish immigrants, Barnet Lee Rosset (b. 1899); as Rosset describes them: "My father was a Jewish republican, my mother an Irish Democrat" (Rosset 2011). Rosset and Beckett were finally children of privilege, sons of the upper middle class, raised in posh suburbs (Rosset on Chicago's Lakeshore Drive; Beckett in Foxrock) and products of English public (Beckett) or American private (Rosset) schools. Both had a strong interest in sport(s): Rosset for (American) football and track; Beckett for cricket and golf. They shared an interest in tennis as well, Rosset having private courts built at each of his successive summer residences in East Hampton, N. Y. Sport "of all sorts" was part of their meetings in Paris, as Rosset remembers:

> We had found a common ground in games. I tried my hand at Beckett's favorite pastimes, chess and billiards, but found them too maddeningly demanding of precision for me to cope with.[5] Beckett, on the other hand, enjoyed playing my more slapdash table tennis. As a spectator sport we settled on tennis, which we both had once played, and we attended matches at Roland Garros stadium outside Paris.[6] Once we saw a match between the great American player Pancho Gonzales and the Australian champion, Lew Hoad, at a time when professionals could not compete against amateurs. The umpire was a Basque and an admirer of

Beckett. He waved enthusiastically at Sam as he mounted his tall chair courtside. The stadium was jammed. A couple of sets later, before a booing crowd, he was ejected at Gonzales' request after making a number of calls against him. He paused to chat for a moment with Sam in the midst of his forced exit. (Rosset 2011)

Both sought refuge in physical labor at their country homes, although Beckett's at Ussy was monastic compared with those that Rosset owned in East Hampton. Each was nearly obsessed with planting trees to surround his retreat. And each had a passion for music, even as their musical tastes differed. Rosset was committed to the jazz he grew up with and listened to in South Chicago nightclubs: "Soon after my return from China [where Rosset served during W. W. II] I again dropped into my favorite bar, Tin Pan Alley. Huddled in one corner, playing wonderfully, were the blind pianist and singer, Laura Rucker, and a great old jazz drummer named Baby Dodds (whose memoir of coming up the river from New Orleans I would later publish in *Evergreen Review* (Rosset 2016, 77). "It's by no accident," Rosset noted, "that Baby Dodds is in the first *Evergreen Review*. That's one of those things that went in a circle, where I think Don Allen got hold of the tapes or manuscript of Baby Dodds's memories of coming up the river [to Chicago]. But anyway, there he was. A strange, narrow long bar with these two people huddled in one corner. You had to fall over them to get past them, the blind pianist and the old drummer. But they were wonderful" (Rosset 2016, 77). Greenwich Village in the 1950s had a similar atmosphere and was, in fact, with San Francisco's North Beach, one of the bohemian enclaves of the United States.

Turning east from our narrow entrance lane [of his first Village residence at 267 ½ West 11th Street] you not only got West 4th St. but also the Village Vanguard, if that was where you wanted to go. Max Gordon was its great proprietor[7] and we got to know him and his wife, Lorraine, very well. Over a period of time, including when we no longer lived there on 11th St, we spent hours at the Vanguard with the likes of Pete Seeger and his folk group, The Weavers. Often they had come over to our place during breaks. One night, Marian Makeba came on stage, fresh from the Shabeens of South Africa and Johannesburg. And there could be seen Lenny Bruce fingering a cop in a trench coat in the audience, who really was a cop. Miles Davis playing his horn facing the wall because the listeners annoyed him. Jack Kerouac in a bizarre, more than slightly drunk, monologue, and Heddy Ledbetter, Leadbelly himself, fresh out of a Southern prison, escorted by Allan Lomax, singing his new, soon to be famous song *Goodnight Irene*. It was nice, even when Lenny told Max, from the stage, that the waiters were robbing him. Who cared? But success overruneth, The Weavers were attacked, people were blacklisted, those who had risen up were put back down.

One night Max came into the 55 [Bar, a jazz club] on Christopher St., which had become our bar of preference next door to the sort of literary Lion's Head [Tavern], to tell me that [Charlie] Mingus had not shown up that night. He had closed the place, refunded the money, and, totally calm, strolled over to the 55. Charlie was indisposed, a little bit, might be tomorrow too. So would I walk with him to another bar, Spike's, where Sun Ra had a gig. We did, and there Max signed up Sun Ra for the next night. Max spoke to Charlie's wife, and it was another uneventful evening for Max, but not for me. (Rosset 2011)

The first issue of *Evergreen Review* would then juxtapose the life story of legendary New Orleans drummer Baby Dodds with Beckett's poetry. Nearly all subsequent issues of the house literary journal contained essays on or reviews of jazz.

Beckett, on the other hand, was a proficient pianist who, throughout his life, could be moved to tears by Schubert. He had a piano in his Paris flat and another in his country house in Ussy-sur-Marne, the latter a Schimmel on which he played sonatas from Haydn, Beethoven, and Mozart, or accompanied himself with Schubert lieder. Both also had a strong distaste for authority, tended toward bohemian lives, and both developed a taste for revolutionary literature and avant-garde visual art. Central to Rosset's sensibility was his reading (as a Swarthmore undergraduate in 1940) of fellow countryman Henry Miller's banned novel, *Tropic of Cancer*, and his anti-American diatribe, *The Air-Conditioned Nightmare*. Central to Beckett's sensibility was his reading of fellow countryman James Joyce's banned novel, *Ulysses*, and his *Work in Progress*, published as *Finnegans Wake*, the latter of which Beckett, with Alfred Peron, began to translate into French. Both had strong, early attachments to women who would eventually marry their best friends and subsequently die early deaths of cancer. In Rosset's life the woman was fellow student at the Parker School in Chicago, Nancy Ashenhurst, who married his best friend, cinematographer Haskell Wexler. In Beckett's case fellow Trinity College student Ethna McCarthy married A. J. "Con" Leventhal in 1956 and died in May of 1959. She is immortalized as the "feminine incarnate" in Beckett's poem "Alba," the character based on her in *Dream of Fair to Middling Women*, as well. But Rosset found Beckett's relationship with another failed love even more poignant, formative, and persistent, that was between Beckett and his first cousin, Peggy Sinclair, who died early of tuberculosis and who appears as the Smeraldina in his early work:

> In 1958 Sam wrote a major piece in English. It was *Krapp's Last Tape*. The texture is almost wildly emotional. The chess playing atmosphere in *Endgame* is less evident; the fabric provides a sort of a sudden oasis of piercingly romantic fulfilment followed by desperate loss. The prose becomes suffused with sensuality and then with tears. Krapp, now an old man, plays and replays tapes from his younger days, trying to find some meaning or hope in his life. One passage is excruciatingly passionate. His/their love has now been destroyed beyond retrieval.
>
> "We drifted in among the flags and stuck. The way they went down, sighing, before the stem! (*Pause.*) I lay down across her with my face in her breasts and my hand on her. We lay there without moving. But under us all moved, and moved us, gently, up and down, and from side to side" (Beckett 2009b, 9).
>
> Then the previous tape is replayed [that is, "Scalded the eyes out of me reading *Effie* again, a page a day, with tears again. Effie ... (*Pause.*) Could have been happy with her, up there on the Baltic, and the pines, and the dunes" (Beckett 2009b, 11).]

Led to it by Beckett, I searched for the nineteenth-century German novelist Theodor Fontane's *Effi Briest* for clues to this passage. Finally Beckett told me that it related to a summer with his cousin Peggy Sinclair, in 1929, at a small resort on the Baltic Sea, where Peggy was engrossed in Fontane's novel about a young girl's calamitous life that ended with her death from tuberculosis. Although Beckett was only twenty-three at the time, his feeling for Peggy and the memory of their being together survived her engagement to another man and her death in 1933, coincidentally also of tuberculosis. (Rosset 2016, 127)[8] The story struck an incredibly strong chord in me. I had also suffered the loss of a young love, my Nancy, who went to high school with me in Chicago. During World War II, she married my best friend, and not much later died of cancer. I still grieve for Nancy and have dreams about her. (Rosset 2011)

Unlikely as it seemed, their relationship would grow to be mutually influential. Beckett would become one of Grove's most respected and, finally, profitable authors, a mainstay of Grove Press through its financially successful years as well as its near bankruptcies. Rosset in turn would have a significant impact on Beckett's career as he made good the promise of his initial letter, "Believe me, we will do what we can to make your work known in this country" (Gontarski 1990a, 65). Grove would go on to market the avant-garde writer aggressively, almost obsessively in the United States.[9]

Rosset's relationship with Beckett would grow well beyond that of author and publisher as Rosset took on the added responsibility of formally acting as American theatrical agent in 1957, after the first production of *Godot*, until Beckett's death in December of 1989, and in addition Rosset became the producer of a number of American productions. Rosset had been intimately involved in productions from the first, championing Beckett's appearance not in the more commercial Broadway theaters, but in the smaller, more intimate theaters of New York's bohemian Greenwich Village and its off-Broadway theaters. Beckett first broached the matter of Rosset's becoming his sole American theatrical agent in a letter of April 6, 1957, as preparations for an American production of *Endgame* were taking final shape. Rather than a formal contract between the two, Beckett offered a letter in which he expressed his general confidence in Rosset even as the decision might "bring down, from Covent Garden [i.e., Curtis Brown] and I suppose from [Michael] Myerberg [producer of the New York *Waiting for Godot*], thunderbolts upon my head, but the bloodiness and bowedness of that perishing appendix can hardly be augmented. [...] Let me know if you would be disposed to take it on" (Beckett *Letters* 2014, 39).[10] Beckett had already raised the issue with his American director, Alan Schneider, two days earlier, on April 4:

"I shall probably take control of U. S. A. performance rights away from Curtis Brown and give it to Rosset," a decision he confirmed in his subsequent letter to Schneider of 30 April (Harmon, 13–14). In a letter of March 26, 1961, to the producer of *Krapp's Last Tape*, Harry Joe Brown, Beckett outlined what became his standard position about productions in the United States: "All decisions with regard to productions rest with Grove Press and will be approved by me" (letter not included in Beckett *Letters* 2014), the statement essentially repeated to producer/director Richard Barr on September 25, 1963: "There can be no question of my ever accepting arrangements for any of my plays in the USA that are not approved both by Barney Rosset and Alan Schneider" (letter not included in Beckett *Letters* 2014). And as late as February 1, 1986, Beckett reaffirmed his commitment to and confidence in Rosset as his theatrical agent (see Chapter 3 for further details).

Between the 1957 Cherry Lane Theater *Endgame* and Beckett's death in 1989, Rosset would help make Beckett an off-Broadway fixture, most performances taking place in Rosset's beloved Greenwich Village. Born in Chicago, Rosset would finally call home not New York City per se but its bohemian enclave, Greenwich Village, or what locals simply call "The Village":

In Greenwich Village … [I] had arrived at the center of the universe. The Irish, the Jews, the Italians. It was a community, a culture. There were the artists, the writers, the theater people. Books, curtains, canvases were in the air. Eugene O'Neill's plays were put on here, the Communists, the anti-Communists, gathered in Union Square [see the film *Reds*]. Joan [Mitchell] and I had found [it] home. We found disparate souls now joined. Location is important. The hub of my existence was just uptown of Washington Square and it stayed that way. With some deviation of course. My psychoanalyst [Clifford Sagar], who was that for more than fifteen years, asked me once if I noticed that each time I moved I seemed to be getting closer to the Bowery [then an area for derelicts and the homeless]. I was, but I hadn't noticed. It was where my rough tough and drunk Uncle Barney would have been found hanging out—but I don't think the hobos like him ever rode the Pere Marquette railroad beyond Chicago, if they ever got that far. But they got close to the Bowery of the mind. So did I. (Rosset 2011)

The Village, then, was an American echo of left-bank Paris, and Rosset's sensibility, like Beckett's, favored its ethos and the inhabitants it attracted, particularly the dispossessed and the culturally marginal. A child of the Great Depression, Rosset was attracted by hobo figures like his "rough tough and drunk Uncle Barney," particularly if they were artists and/or political activists.

Albert Bein, the delinquent uncle of my friend Joe Bein from Chicago, was not only a hobo but also a playwright of no small caliber. Albert had been imprisoned in a Midwest prison during the Depression thirties. When he was released he hit the rails to California. The first trip, he fell off a freight car and lost half a leg.

Albert became a well-known playwright in the American theater. One play of his, "Heavenly Express" [Broadway opening, April 1940], old the stories of the hobos going west and stopping at a restaurant run by a mother whose son was a hobo and who had disappeared from a freight train. She took care of all the hobos who made it to her place and one day, she knew, her son would come through on the heavenly express. The New York production started the careers of John Garfield and Burl Ives. Albert Bein was blacklisted by the McCarthy contingent. On election night in 1948, I literally huddled in the middle of the very small living room at Albert's 1 Christopher Street apartment with Albert and his wife and listened to the election results of the presidential race. Truman, Dewey, Wallace. We had thought that Wallace might actually have a chance, especially in New York. He did have a chance, only it was a chance to make Dewey president! As this realization grew on me, black mud replaced my blood. I left the Beins and staggered home. Joan was in France [and Rosset was soon to follow], all was well with the world. The man who had given the order to drop the atom bomb was still our president. (Rosset 2011)

For Rosset, then, Beckett and Greenwich Village were a perfect match, and he drummed that message to Beckett on January 27, 1956 and so frequently that he risked "being thought of as the village crank by you and [British producer Donald] Albery because I have conducted this monotonous diatribe about off-Broadway" (cited in Gontarski 2010, 27).

Politically and culturally, then, Rosset and Beckett had much in common, and through their thirty-six-year relationship, Rosset would exert considerable influence on Beckett's professional career. As he noted in his initial letter, "*En attendant Godot* [*Waiting for Godot*] should burst upon us as an entity in my opinion." On June 18, 1953, Rosset would urge, prod, and coax a reluctant Beckett to translate his novels:

> The first order of the day would appear to be the translation [of *Molloy* ... ]. If you would accept my first choice as translator the whole thing would be easily settled. That choice of course being you. That already apparently is a satisfactory condition insofar as the play [*Godot*, which Beckett was then in the midst of translating] is concerned. The agent here tells me that you have agreed to our proposal, and he is drawing up a simple letter contract now which we will mail to you tomorrow. (Gontarski 2001, 25)

Furthermore, Rosset would go on to encourage Beckett to return to writing in his native tongue in the mid-1950s, and Beckett would respond shortly thereafter with a radio play for the BBC, *All That Fall*, and the one-act masterpiece, *Krapp's Last Tape*. On February 5, 1954, Rosset wrote Beckett, "I have been wondering if you would not get almost the freshness of turning to doing something in English which you must have gotten when you first seriously took to writing in French. A withdrawal from a withdrawal—English" (cited in Gontarski 1995, xiv). Thenceforth, Beckett would write in both languages, translating himself into the other. And Rosset was quick to see, perhaps the first, that translation for Beckett was *a part of*, not apart from, the process of creativity. Beckett could see no future to his writing in August of 1954 as he tended his dying brother Frank, and he wrote to Rosset from Ireland on the 21st: "You know, Barney, I think my writing days are over. L'Innommable [*sic*] finished me or expressed my finishedness" (Beckett *Letters* 2011, 497). On September 12, Rosset responded, his own father having recently and unexpectedly died: "Samuel, don't you think that the translation work in itself is still a form of writing for you. If you go on, as you have said you will, with your own translation of the last two books [*Malone meurt* and *L'Innommable*], don't you think it possible that somewhere within them you will find a lead to another deposit" (cited in Gontarski 2010, 28). Beckett did and produced the thirteen short pieces, *Textes pour rien* (*Texts for Nothing*), and another stunning post-*Unnamable* novel, *Comment c'est* (*How It Is*).

Furthermore, in 1963 Rosset's passion for expanding his publishing house into other media culminated in Grove's commissioning a film script from Beckett. The result was the film (Beckett's one and only true venture into that medium and the only one made of a planned series that Grove Press was developing) entitled *Film*. The shooting occurred in New York during the summer of 1964, Beckett himself in attendance. He arrived in New York at what was then Idyllwild Airport (now Kennedy) on July 10, 1964, spending the weekend at Rosset's East Hampton summer home, planning the shooting, playing some tennis, and then returning to Rosset's West Houston Street flat where he resided throughout the filming, departing for Paris on August 6. This would be Beckett's sole excursion to the United States, during which stay he attended a baseball game at Shea Stadium on July 31 (with Richard Seaver and Judith Schmidt) and a showing of the film *The Pawnbroker*, which he disliked (for amusing details, see Seaver 2012, 322–3). Beckett seemed awkward, even uncomfortable during his New York stay, relaxing only at "The Emerald Isle," a Greenwich Village drinking hole. Shortly thereafter, on his sixtieth birthday, Grove Press presented its featured author with a set of thirteen specially bound copies of his books, the first uniform edition of what then were *The Complete Works*. Beckett was emotionally moved by the gesture and wrote on April 16, 1966, as follows: "Gratitude is a poor word for the beautiful set of 13 and the affection it brings me from you all and the way it says how good things always were between us and always will be" (cited in Gontarski 2010, 28; not included in Beckett *Letters* 2016). At the end of his career and only two years before his death, Beckett dedicated the three stories of his late masterpiece, *Stirrings Still*, to Rosset.

Beckett, in turn, would steel Rosset for what would soon become Grove's crusade against censorship. In a letter of June 25, 1953, Beckett suggested not only his own uncompromising position toward his art but set the tone for Rosset's battles against censorship for the next two decades:

> With regard to my work in general, I hope you realize what you are letting yourself in for. I do not mean the heart of the matter, which is unlikely to disturb anybody, but certain obscenities of

form which may not have struck you in French as they will in English, and which frankly (it is better that you should know this before we get going) I am not at all disposed to mitigate. I do not of course realize what is possible in America from this point of view and what is not. Certainly as far as I know such passages, faithfully translated, would not be tolerated in England. (Beckett *Letters* 2011, 385)

Rosset too was unsure what was possible in America. Cautioned by Beckett and on advice of his legal staff, Rosset's initial parry with American authorities was tentative, circumspect. *Molloy* was published exclusively in hard cover at first, its distribution restricted exclusively to New York bookshops, and only to those who had requested it: "Copies of *Molloy* are in all the New York City bookstores that wanted them," he wrote to Beckett on September 24, 1955, "but distribution across the rest of the country has not yet gone out. The post office is now examining the book and I am sure their decision will be very amusing if not pleasing" (Gontarski 2011, XX). In this instance the United States Postal Service raised no objection to the book,[11] and Rosset proceeded with a paperback publication the following year concurrent with the release of *Malone Dies*, which was published exclusively in paperback. (Although actually published in 1956, the paperback *Molloy* retained the 1955 publication date as if it were published simultaneously with the hard cover.)[12] Rosset would not only subsequently persevere with the "obscenities of form" in Beckett, but he would push on to publish and distribute through the mail, in defiance of Postal Service interdictions, two famously banned novels: the unexpurgated *Lady Chatterley's Lover* in 1959, a book even Sylvia Beach of Shakespeare and Company, publisher of James Joyce's *Ulysses*, deemed unsavory in 1928 and Henry Miller's *Tropic of Cancer* in 1961 (although the legal battles over Miller's work persisted until 1964, when the book was finally distributed). These were books that shaped and fueled that social and political upheaval loosely called "the sixties." Battles against censorship became a crusade for Rosset and his Grove Press. In an interview with Italian publisher Giangiacomo Feltrinelli conducted in 1959 for the New York City educational radio station WNET, Rosset articulated what might be considered the ideology of his press: "Mr. Feltrinelli, I would like to interject here that I feel that personally there hasn't been a word written or uttered that shouldn't be published, singly or in multiples. I think that is stating my position" (Gontarski 2001, 8)

From its modest beginning with the publication of *Molloy*, Rosset's battle against censorship became virtually a battle against American legal authority in general. These turbulent years coincided with Richard Seaver's tenure at Grove (1959–71), and his summary of the period is couched in near military terminology:

In 1961, one year after the *Lady Chatterley* litigation ended, we published Henry Miller's *magnum opus*. Ironically, because Lawrence had knocked out both the Post Office and Customs, and won a federal victory, there was no federal case this time. Instead, every local police chief and district attorney felt free to seize and sue, as indeed they did. At one point, Grove was defending some sixty cases around the country, and its paltry reserves[13] were strained to the breaking point as lawyers were hired en masse to defend those attacked. Key staff members, from Barney on down, spent more time in court testifying than they did in the office.

Frankly, I don't remember how we managed to survive the *Tropic of Cancer* litigations, but somehow we did and, bruise and battered but still standing, we went on to test a few more waters: William Burroughs' *Naked Lunch* [...] available in France from Maurice Girodias's Olympia Press but not in the author's native land; Jean Genet, whose dramatic works Grove had been publishing but whose novels, *The Thief's Journal* and *Our Lady of the Flowers,* had generally been deemed too hot to handle even in France and had been published there by a small but audacious publisher, Arbelète. Finally, in 1949 and '51 respectively, the most prestigious French publisher, Gallimard, screwed its courage to the sticking post and brought out both Genet novels. Armed with that house's near-inviolable imprimatur, the Gallic censors, less ardent than the Anglo-Saxon, remained in their corner. But we at Grove had no such illusions about their counterparts here if and when we released those daring works in the States. In the wings close behind Burroughs were two younger Americans, John Rechy and Hubert Selby, Jr., not to mention, again from that country who produce so much of this censorable material, a mysterious woman, Pauline Réage, whose *Story of O* had since the mid-1950s been the talk and rage of Paris; and, finally, the naughty granddaddy of them all:

the infamous, garrulous blasphemer and rebel *extraordinaire,* Donatien-Alphonse-François, a.k.a. the marquis de Sade.[14] [...] Charles Rembar's excellent *The End of Obscenity* details, vividly and accurately, how those battles were fought and, one by one, inch by inch, trench by trench, won over enormous odds. For those of us in those trenches, each day was exciting, exhilarating, rewarding, and exhausting. There were times, too, when it seemed that, to paraphrase Beckett, "We couldn't go on, we must go on."[15] Barney's presumed fortune notwithstanding, the coffers were often dry or close to dry. I remember one day in 1962 Barney, who had disappeared for the morning and most of the afternoon, showed up at four or five o'clock, walked into my office, and announced that he had spent the day trying to get an infusion of capital, without success. So we—the inner circle of Grove that then included not only Fred [Jordan] and myself but Harry Braverman, who went on to become publisher of *Monthly Review Press;* sales manager Nat Sobel [who went on to become a major literary agent]; publicity director Morrie Goldfisher; and an ex–union organizer with little book experience but lots of savvy, Jules Geller—decided that if we were to go down we should do so with guns blazing. Not just our one-a-year bomb but three or four, something to remember us by. In the next two to two and a half years we unleashed upon the world (with *Naked Lunch* now safely behind us) no fewer than half a dozen works which, under normal circumstances, we would have published over a five- or six-year period. In quick succession, and not necessarily in that order, came Frank Harris's monumental *My Life and Loves* (with a final chapter by—pseudonymously— my old *Merlin* colleague and Grove author Alex Trocchi), John Rechy's *City of Night,* Jean Genet's *Our Lady of the Flowers* (the original Olympia Press translation being, to use a kindly term, wooden, I was dispatched to Paris for a month to rework it, line by line, with the translator Bernard Frechtman, a job of delicate diplomacy, since Frechtman "owned" the English language rights and did not take kindly to criticism), followed a year later by his *The Thief's Journal,* Selby's *Last Exit to Brooklyn,* and Pauline Réage's *Story of O.* (Seaver cited in Gontarski 2001, 90–2)

This then would be the house to represent Samuel Beckett in the United States and champion his professional development. And

Beckett was in general sympathy with what might be called the Grove spirit. As early as February 1938 he was approached by Jack Kahane of Obelsik Press, father of Maurice Girodias who would begin to publish Beckett through his Olympia Press, to translate *Les 120 Jours de Sodome*, which Beckett thought, "one of the capital works of the 18th century, which it is for me" (Beckett *Letters* 2009, 604). After considering how such a publication might damage his fledgling literary career ("I don't want to be spiked as a writer" [Beckett, *Letters* 2009, 604]), he reconsidered after Kahane found it necessary to delay publication and Beckett moved on to other projects (see the "Introduction" for further details). But he retained an interest in and a respect for many of the books that Rosset was publishing at Grove. He was delighted to receive Grove edition of the long suppressed Frank Harris work, *My Life and Loves* [edited and with an introduction by John F. Gallagher. (GP-301), 1963], which he acknowledged in his letter of November 24, 1963, and on the 26th he asked Judith Schmidt to airmail a copy to Jack MacGowran in London.

During those years of aggressive publishing and battles against censorship, Beckett did seem to take a back seat to a larger political agenda at Grove, but the politically aggressive press began to unravel in 1970s. Grove faced a dual assault from the emerging women's movement, as employee Robin Morgan led a takeover of the Grove offices, and an unlikely labor union decided to organize the Grove employees. These tandem events managed to accomplish what the forces of American government could not: restrain indeed muzzle Grove Press. Richard Seaver left shortly thereafter, in 1971, as did Judith Schmidt. For the next decade and a half Grove was in a constant state of near collapse and bankruptcy. By March 1985 Rosset would have to sell Grove Press, to oil heiress Ann Getty and British publisher George Weidenfeld for some 2 million dollars, in an effort to revitalize the flagging company. Rosset's thinking was that the new owners would provide "the infusion of capital" that he had sought for over a decade and that such a sale would revitalize the press, but it came at the price of the press itself, or at least Rosset's association with it. Rosset recalls these events thus:

> The unionizing really crippled the company. We were dead broke after that. We had to move back to 11th street—we had a building, [with] the Evergreen Theatre. And from there we moved

into my house, where I lived. And from then on it was a holding operation. For a number of years we were actually making a little bit of money, but we had incurred debts we couldn't pay—it took 12 years to pay them off, month-to-month. We finally did it, but the company was just subsisting for all those years. So when this guy Weidenfeld came along and said, "Oh I've got this woman who's got all the money in the world and she's gonna give it all to me, and I want you. You can do whatever you want. I'll give you all this money to run the company."[16] I was sucked in. And then thrown out. [....] I shouldn't have been surprised. He has a great talent for taking you in and making you feel immune. He told me exactly what he was going to do to everyone and then he did it to me. And that in a nutshell was that. (Rosset 2011)

The terms of the sale in March of 1985 left Rosset as president and CEO, and so he would retain editorial control for some five years, but in April of 1986, on his way to see Beckett in Paris for his author's eightieth birthday celebrations, Rosset was dismissed, and a number of key projects, including the *Evergreen* revival, were scuttled. In his letter to Beckett of June 18, 1986, Rosset summed up his untenable situation: "Time drags rather slowly for me—as my victorious billionaires keep torturing me—for reasons known to them perhaps, but not me." Rosset filed suit over his dismissal, but he finally agreed to a settlement so unfavorable that he had to sign a disclaimer indemnifying his attorney. Rosset's perceptions of his dismissal and his explanation of what he called "personal reasons" for accepting the settlement (that is, beyond his immediate need for the settlement cash) were summarized in an unsent letter he drafted for Ann Getty (but one which nonetheless represents his thinking at the time). Astonishingly, he seemed unaware of any difficulties or tensions with the new owners, and his dismissal apparently took him by surprise: "I do not remember having any disagreement with you, or for that matter any serious one with George [Weidenfeld]." The conflict finally left Rosset "exhausted, traumatized, grief stricken—you name it. But, oddly, there was little anger on my part. Nor has there ever been. And now, my feelings about Grove Press and its personnel are very friendly" (Rosset 2011).

Rosset tried several publishing ventures in the aftermath of Grove Press but he could no longer generate substantial financial backing, and so they remained marginal. Beckett tried to supply him with additional material on occasion, promising at first to translate *Eleutheria* for him (see Chapter 3 for details). Finding the juvenile work impossible to translate, he offered Rosset at first two and then three new but very short texts, which he dedicated to his American publisher and which Rosset (along with John Calder) published as *Stirrings Still*. But such short pieces had little impact on Rosset's ability to start and sustain a new publishing venture. By 1986, then, Barnet Lee Rosset, Jr. was no longer a major force in American publishing, but he still represented Beckett's theatrical interests in the United States. That too came to an end, however, not long after Beckett's death, when Rosset arranged a public reading of the proscribed play, *Eleutheria* (for further details, see Chapter 3). While the reading and subsequent publication of Beckett's first full-length play in the face of the Estate's interdictions was the immediate cause of the rift, Rosset's letters detail a pattern of tensions over rights and royalties between American and French publishers from the earliest days. Aside from the slight volume of stories, *Stirrings Still,* and the American rights to *Eleutheria*, Rosset's professional, and hence economic, connection to Samuel Beckett and his work was fully severed by 1995.

# Notes

1  While influential, particularly in helping develop the Grove Press house magazine, *Evergreen Review*, Donald M. Allen's stay at Grove was short. See "Don Allen: Grove's First Editor," *The Review of Contemporary Fiction* 10.3 (fall 1990): 132–6. He was, however, Grove's first translator of Eugene Ionesco (*Four Plays: The Bald Soprano, The Lesson, Jack or The Submission, The Chairs*, 1958), and he edited two influential anthologies for Grove: *The New American Poetry: 1945–1960*, 1960, and, with Robert Creely, *New American Story*, 1965.

2  One theme of Commins's class that Rosset and Allen learned well was that publishing would have to change dramatically in the postwar era, although Commins himself saw the change as a return to the seriousness of philosophy and the classics (see Dorothy Commins's *What Is an Editor: Saxe Commins at Work* [Chicago: University of Chicago Press, 1978], 100–101).

3  Legendary designer whose *Bookmaking: The Illustrated Guide to Design and Production* (New York: R. R. Bowker, 1965) would become "The unchallenged bible of the publishing industry."

4  Rosset's studies were interrupted at Swarthmore College, U. C. L. A., and the University of Chicago. In New York in 1950 he took advantage of the G. I. Bill to attend the New School, two blocks from his Greenwich Village home. There major literary intellectuals like Wallace Fowlie, Stanley Kunitz, Meyer Schapiro, and Alfred Kazin spurred him on: "Due to their inspiration and the Village atmosphere… I was actually awarded a B. A. in 1952" (Rosset 2011).

5  Rosset would finally convert to the latter.

6  See Beckett's letter of May 5, 1959, for instance: "Internationaux de France on at Roland Garros but haven't been, nearly all the time here in the [Marne] mud [at Ussy]. Saw the France-Wales Rugby match at Colombes, great enjoyment, French a great team, wish I had been in Dublin to see them undeservedly beaten by Ireland" (Beckett *Letters* 2011, 230).

7  See his *"Max Gordon Presents": The Star-Studded Story of His Life on Broadway as Lived and Written by Max Gordon* (New York: Bernard Geiss Associates, 1963) and *Live at the Village Vanguard* (New York: St. Martin's Press, 1980).

8  In a letter of May 26, 1956, Beckett suggested that Grove publish the novel, but the edition never materialized.

9  In 1967, for example, Grove published the university-level *Casebook on "Waiting for Godot,"* ed. Ruby Cohn, and by 1971 the press offered free, 42-page study guides to American high schools, *A Discussion Guide for the Play "Waiting for Godot"* (prepared by Ruth M. Goldstein, Assistant Chairman of English, Abraham Lincoln High School, Brooklyn, New York).

10  Rosset seems already to be hinting at such an appointment in his letter to Beckett of March 23, 1957.

11  It was banned in Ireland, however, as Beckett noted in his letter of February 2, 1956: "I suppose you have heard that all editions of Molloy [*sic*] have been banned in Ireland" (Beckett *Letters* II 2011, 601).

12  Noted in Rosset's letter of March 8, 1956.

13  As Seaver notes, "Barney told me many times in later years that rumors of his fortune, like that of Twain's demise, were greatly exaggerated. Further, to put things in perspective, Grove's total volume of business in 1959 was, if memory serves, $350,000. 'If only we could get to half a million,' Barney said when I took the job in '59, 'we'd make money.' But as the years rolled by, the barrier to profitability seemed always to be raised just beyond our reach, at least till the mid-1960s" (Seaver cited in Gontarski 2001, 90).

14  In addition to his being one of Grove's most aggressive acquisitions
    editors, Seaver was a major translator for the press, the marquis de
    Sade among his most famous translations, particularly *Philosophy in
    the Bedroom and Other Writings* (1965); *The 120 Days of Sodom
    and Other Writings* (1966), both compiled and translated by Austryn
    Wainhouse and Richard Seaver; and *Letters from the Bastille and
    Vincennes*, translated by Austryn Wainhouse and Richard Seaver. In
    his autobiography, moreover, Seaver finally admits what was an open
    secret to many, that he was the translator of the Grove Press edition
    of *The Story of O* (Seaver 2012, 362).

15  The title Seaver chose for his own anthology of Beckett's work was,
    "*I Can't Go On, I'll Go On*": *A Selection from Samuel Beckett's
    Work*, edited and with an introduction by Richard W. Seaver (1977).

16  On Rosset's discharge and the failures of the new owners, see Adam
    Begley, "Ann Getty: Publish and Perish?," *The New York Times
    Magazine*, October 22, 1989, pp. 36–37, 47–51.

# 3

# *Eleutheria*: Samuel Beckett's Suppressed Bohemian Manifesto

*Eleutheria is dithering, dithering and beginning to be spoken of a little. I think it will see the boards in time if only for a few nights. But never those of the Gate [Theatre in Dublin]. SB to Thomas MacGreevy, March 8, 1948*

*Perhaps it is time that someone were simply nothing.* Victor Krap, Eleutheria

In his catalogue of the Samuel Beckett papers at the University of Texas's Humanities Research Center, Carlton Lake outlines the curious publishing history of the work Samuel Beckett was writing just after the Second World War as he turned to writing predominantly in French: "Along with *Watt* and *Mercier et Camier* one of the more long-drawn-out publishing histories in Beckett's career is that leading up to *Nouvelles et textes pour rien*" (i.e., *Stories and Texts for Nothing*) (Lake, 1984, 81). Indeed, this was a period in Beckett's creative life when the time between composition and publication was unusually protracted. *Watt*, for instance, written predominantly in the south of France during the Second World War and completed in 1945, did not see print for some eight years after its completion. It was rejected by more publishers than even Beckett could remember before being published in 1953 by the group Beckett called the "*Merlin* juveniles" (Knowlson, 355) in collaboration with Maurice Girodias and his notorious Olympia Press. On November 18, 1947, Beckett wrote to his English friend and sometime literary agent, George Reavey, about its rejection by Hamish Hamilton: "I knew H. H. was hatching a dead egg, or rather that Watt [*sic*] was under a dead hen. Thanks for all the trouble you have taken" (Beckett *Letters* 2011, 64). On August 6, 1953, Beckett confirmed to his Trinity College friend, A. J. "Con" Leventhal, that "Watt [*sic*] is having a difficult birth but is expected out into the dark of day next week," publication confirmed to his American publisher, Barney Rosset, on September 1, "Watt [*sic*] I believe is now out [jointly from Collection Merlin and Olympia Press] but I have not yet seen it" (Beckett *Letters* 2011, 395, 397).

Beckett's short story "Suite" (later "La Fin" or "The End"), furthermore, was finished in May of 1946 and found publication almost immediately in the July 1946 issue of *Les Temps moderne*, but even that quick publication was not without incident. Beckett had expected the second half of the story to appear in the October issue, but Simone de Beauvoir considered the first part complete in itself and refused to publish the second. Beckett argued that printing half the story was a "mutilation," but Mme. de Beauvoir remained adamant, and it was some nine years before the complete story appeared. As he wrote to Beauvoir "after long hesitations" on September 25, 1946, "Yesterday Madame Clerx told me of your decision on the second half of Suite [*sic*], I regret the misunderstanding which compels you to cut off my story half way. [...] You are immobilizing an existence [his character] at the very moment at which it is about to take its definitive form. There is something nightmarish about that" (Beckett *Letters* 2011, 41–2). Beckett in fact wrote four French stories, *nouvelles*, in 1946, and he expected that they would appear quickly in book form from his first French publisher, Éditions Bordas, which would publish his translation of *Murphy* in 1947 and which had, at least tentatively, accepted "all future work in French & English (including translations), and my affairs are now entirely in their hands" (Beckett *Letters* 2011, 48). In December of 1946 Beckett could write with some confidence to Reavey, "I hope to have a book of short stories ready for the spring (in French). I do not think I shall write very much in English in the future" (Beckett *Letters* 2011, 48). Bordas, however, dropped plans to issue both the four stories, *Quatre Nouvelles*, and *Mercier et Camier* when sales of the French *Murphy* proved disastrous. When Beckett finally found a second French publisher willing to take on the whole of his creative backlog, Les Éditions de Minuit in 1950, he hesitated and finally withheld much of the earliest writing in French, *Mercier et Camier*, one of his four stories, *First Love*, and his first full-length play written in French, *Eleuthéria*. The remaining three *nouvelles* of 1946 were finally published by Les Éditions de Minuit in 1955 and in the United States by Grove Press in 1967, both in combination with the thirteen post-*Unnamable Texts for Nothing*. Both *Mercier et Camier* and *First Love* would eventually be published as Beckett reluctantly yielded to pressure from his publishers hard upon the 1969 award of the Nobel Prize: 1970 in French and 1974 in English.

But these publishing difficulties, rejections, misunderstandings, hiatuses, hesitations, instances of recurrent self-doubt and self-censorship pale before the intractable difficulties surrounding the publication of Beckett's first full-length play, *Eleuthéria*, published only in 1995, nearly half a century after its writing. If the publication history of *Watt, Mercier et Camier*, and *Premiere Amour* is curious, that of *Eleuthéria* is even more so. As was the case with *Mercier et Camier* and his four *Stories*, Beckett was at first quite eager to see *Eleuthéria* published and performed. He saw the play as part of a sequence that reflected a certain continuity to his writing. On July 8, 1948, for example, he wrote to Reavey, "I am now typing, for rejection by the publishers, Malone meurt [*sic, Malone Dies*], the last I hope of the series Murphy, Watt, Mercier & Camier, Molloy, not to mention the 4 Nouvelles & Eleuthéria" (Beckett *Letters* 2011, 80). *Malone Dies* was not, of course, the last of the series. Another play would follow shortly thereafter, *En Attendant Godot* (*Waiting for Godot*), completed in January of 1949, and a third French novel, *L'innommable* (*The Unnamable*), completed a year later in January of 1950 and which, along with *Molloy* and *Malone Dies*, would form a sequence, part of what Beckett would refer to as "the so-called Trilogy."

*Eleuthéria* was begun on January 18, 1947, as a retreat from the problems caused by the revolutionary French prose Beckett was writing at the time. As he apparently told his first biographer, Deirdre Bair, in 1972, "I turned to writing plays to relieve myself

from the awful depression the prose led me into. Life at the time
was too demanding, too terrible, and I thought theatre would be a
diversion" (Bair, 1990, 361). By February 24, he had completed a
draft of the three-act play, and by late March of 1947 he had turned
over a typescript (which he always made himself, mindful perhaps
of the errors and changes introduced into James Joyce's work by
various typists) to Toni Clerkx, sister of Bram and Geer van Velde,
who would, for a time, function as Beckett's literary representative
in France, and had placed "Suite" with Les Temps moderne, and
who was responsible for placing Murphy with Bordas. And, in
fact, Mme. Clerx managed to interest Jean Vilar of the Théâtre
Nationale Populaire in the play, but Vilar insisted on cuts and the
reduction of three acts into a single long act (a structure Beckett
would finally adopt for Fin de Partie in 1957). When Beckett
refused, Vilar dropped his interest. By the fall of 1947 Mme. Clerx
told Beckett that she could no longer represent him and still have
time for her own writing, and so his live-in companion and future
wife, Suzanne Descheveaux-Dumesnil, began to circulate his work
among producers and publishers.

By January of 1949, Beckett had completed a second French
play, En attendant Godot (Waiting for Godot): "I began to write
Godot as a relaxation to get away from the awful prose I was
writing at the time" (Duckworth 1967, 89), this time presumably
Malone meurt (Malone Dies), and that play too was circulated by
Mme. Descheveaux-Dumesnil—without success until she saw a
production of August Strindberg's Ghost Sonata performed at the
Gaité Montparnasse in early spring of 1950. The play, staged by
Roger Blin, an admirer if not a disciple of Antonin Artaud, had
impressed her, and she dropped off the typescripts of both plays at
the box office for him to consider. Blin had heard of Beckett from
the Dada poet Tristan Tzara. He was interested in the plays even
though "he frankly did not understand Waiting for Godot, but he
liked it. He decided that he should probably begin with Eleuthéria
because it was more traditional, and to his mind easier to cope with"
(Bair 1990, 403). But finally economics entered the decision-making
process and, as Blin noted, "Eleuthéria had seventeen characters, a
divided stage, elaborate props and complicated lighting. I was poor.
I didn't have a penny. I couldn't think of anyone who owned a
theater suitable for such a complicated production. I thought I'd be
better off with Godot because there were only four actors and they

were bums. They could wear their own clothes if it came to that, and I wouldn't need anything but a spotlight and a bare branch for a tree" (Bair, 403). With such decisions, then, was theater history shaped.

In October of 1950 Suzanne Descheveaux-Dumesnil, still systematically and assiduously making the rounds of French publishers, delivered the typescripts of three novels, the "so-called trilogy," *Molloy, Malone meurt,* and *L'innommable,* to the desk of Georges Lambrich, an editor at Jérôme Lindon's Éditions de Minuit, a house rapidly gaining a reputation among the Paris avant-garde. By November, Beckett had a French publisher, and the publication of *Molloy* was scheduled for January of 1951 (although it was finally delayed several months) to be followed shortly thereafter by *Malone meurt.* Blin had been making some headway with the production of *Waiting for Godot.* He had interested Jean-Marie Serreau in the play just as Serreau was opening his Théâtre de Babylone, and Blin had gotten a small grant from the French Ministry for Arts and Letters to produce the play. Lindon, too, had seen copies of the two plays and had agreed to publish them both as well as the novels, provided that he was not broke himself by then. The two plays along with the third novel of the trilogy were then announced as forthcoming on the back cover of Beckett's first two French novels, *Molloy* and *Malone meurt.* By June of 1953 Beckett had an American publisher as well, Barney Rosset of the fledgling Grove Press, about which "Sylvia Beach said very nice things" (Gontarski 1990, 81), and a "first version of [the English] *Godot*" was "in the hands of Mr. Harold L. Oram, 8 West 40th Street, New York, who has our authority to treat for the performance rights up till I think November 1st" (Gontarski 1990, 81). The recognition that Beckett had assiduously sought for so long was now within reach, and he pursued it—but not without hesitations. He withdrew from publication *Mercier et Camier, First Love,* and the play that bears a curious relationship to *First Love, Eleuthéria,* which play he then consistently withheld from publication and performance.

Although *Eleuthéria* languished in Beckett's trunk, it was not exactly an unknown work. Beckett preserved typescripts and manuscript notebooks. In fact they were finally sold or donated to major research libraries, namely the Humanities Research Center at the University of Texas, which holds the two manuscript notebooks, Dartmouth College, which holds the original typescript, and Washington University, St. Louis, and the University of Reading (Reading, England), each of which holds a copy of the typescript. In something like an overriding of Beckett's rejection, individual copies circulated freely among Beckett scholars as a sort of *samizdat* underground publication network once Beckett had attracted sufficient reputation among academics in the late 1950s, and a number of important studies of Beckett's theater have included essays on *Eleuthéria*.[1]

By 1986, however, Beckett had relented considerably on his ban against the play's publication. He had allowed almost a third of it to be published in France in the special issue of *Revue D'Esthétique* as part of a tribute volume to honor his eightieth birthday.[2] And several significant pages were published in *Beckett in the Theatre, I: The Author as Practical Playwright and Director: From* Waiting for Godot *to* Krapp's Last Tape (1988), the dialogue between the Glazier and his son, of which Beckett has said, "the source of the dialogue between the boy and Vladimir [in *Waiting for Godot*] is to be found in the unpublished play *Eleuthéria*" (Beckett, 1966, xiv).

In fact in the spring of 1986 Beckett was on the verge once again of releasing the whole *Eleuthéria* to his long-time friend and American publisher Barney Rosset. That spring Parisians were honoring the eightieth birthday of their adopted son, Samuel Beckett. The great museum of modern art in Paris, the Centre Pompidou, sponsored a week-long celebration of Beckett's work with lectures, exhibits, discussions, and performances. The massive special issue of the *Revue D'Esthétique* appeared in the windows of most of the city's bookshops in time for the Pompidou festivities. Beckett himself, slightly embarrassed by the attention, kept his distance, absenting himself, as was his habit, even from performances of his work. He met with friends quietly as they came into town at the café of the Hôtel PLM not far from his Boulevard St. Jacques apartment, but he spent most of the time buried in the "Marne mud" of his Ussy retreat. On his birthday, however, he was back in Paris and was persuaded to attend a small reception at one of his old haunts, La Coupole, which he had avoided for over two decades, preferring the Falstaff around the corner and finally the hygienic anonymity and privacy of the Hôtel PLM.[3] As a group of Beckett's friends (the author included) sipped drinks at the sequestered Bar Américain, Barney Rosset came through the doors in a flurry announcing that he had been summarily discharged from the company he built and ran for over thirty-three years, Grove Press, and so the mood of the evening shifted from celebration to consolation. It seemed impossible that Rosset could be separated from Grove Press; in our minds, of course, they were one. Rosset *was* Grove Press. But he had sold it a year earlier in an effort to recapitalize. The new owners, Ann Getty and Lord Weidenfeld, had pledged to keep Rosset on for five years as editor in chief—or so he thought. One clause of his contract stipulated, however, that Rosset actually served at the pleasure of the new owners, and they were displeased, particularly at Rosset's inability to adapt to the corporate structure of the new owners. We sipped our drinks and shook our heads grumbling that if the decision to publish writers like Beckett rested with boards of directors and sales staff rather than visionary publishers like Rosset, Calder, and Lindon, neophytes all at the time, and was based on marketing surveys, the likes of Beckett would have remained obscure, little-published writers.

Beckett arrived—rather materialized—promptly at eight. No one apparently saw him come in. Suddenly he was just standing there in an outsized gray greatcoat and brown beret. We greeted him and withdrew to a cluster of tables in the corner of the cordoned bar area where Beckett was briefed on what became the Rosset affair. What could be done, he queried? Rosset shrugged his shoulders and muttered, more into the table than to anyone in particular, "Start over, I guess." It was immediately clear from the tenor of the conversation that for Beckett also Rosset was Grove Press. It was Barney Rosset who was Samuel Beckett's American publisher not some corporate entity called Grove Press. Years later John Calder would call Rosset Beckett's "spiritual son," and on that snowy April evening Beckett responded much like a spiritual father. Perhaps he might find something in the trunk to help Rosset begin a new publishing venture yet again.

Rosset and Beckett met several times during the week to discuss details. The obvious choice was for Rosset to publish *Dream of Fair to Women*,[4] the less-than-finished English novel of 1932 that Beckett plundered for two of the stories of what became *More Pricks than Kicks*, which Rosset did publish in 1970. But *Dream* and its subsequent iteration of 1934, *More Pricks than Kicks*, remained sensitive works for Beckett in 1986. *Dream* featured a protagonist who was only a thinly disguised alter ego of the author, and it was a *roman à clef*, the Smeraldina Rima, modeled on Beckett's cousin,

Peggy Sinclair, the Caleken Frica on Ethna McCarthy, the Alba on Mary Manning Howe, and the Syra Cusa on Lucia Joyce, to mention only its female characters, all of whom were transported into the stories of *More Pricks than Kicks*. Some of their models but certainly their descendants were still alive and would surely be embarrassed by its publication. Beckett finally settled on his first full-length play, *Eleuthéria*. He inscribed a copy of the play to Rosset to seal the agreement, and withdrew to Ussy to take on the clearly distasteful task of translating the play into English.

Although he is listed as the translator into English or French on almost all of his work, Beckett never was strictly a translator—of himself or of any other author. Each shift in language produced not a literary or linguistic equivalent but a rewriting and hence essentially a new work. Beckett's translations have always been transformations, a continuation of a creative process interrupted by publication. There simply are no equivalents between Beckett's French and English texts. Theater, moreover, required yet another major transformation, a reconceptualization of the work into stage space. During his twenty-year career as a theatrical director, from 1967 to 1986, Beckett seized these opportunities to review and rethink his plays and so continue the creative process. As a theatrical director of his own work, he revised, at least, and at times wholly rewrote every play he directed. The task of translating *Eleuthéria* then was not the simple academic exercise it at first may have seemed. Looming as well was the possibility, rather the threat of performance once the work was translated and published, and, once released in English, French publication and performance seemed inevitable as well. It came as less than a surprise, then, that shortly after Beckett took on the task, he abandoned it as too complex and too taxing in his eightieth year. It would have meant recreating a play he wrote some four decades earlier. On June 25, 1986, Beckett reluctantly wrote to Rosset: "I had completely forgotten Eleutheria [*sic*]. I have now read it again. With loathing. I cannot translate it. Let alone have it published. Another rash promise. Made with intent to lighten your burden. Now I have added to it. [...] I feel unforgivable. So please forgive me," signed, "Much love from guilt ridden me" (Rosset 2017, 403 [published in facsimile]). Rosset was no more disappointed than Beckett himself, but Beckett offered some consolation: "I'll try to write something worth having for you. If only a few pages" (Rosset 2017, 403). What followed were three short new prose works which he called *Stirrings Still* and which he dedicated to Rosset.

Rosset, however, never abandoned plans to publish *Eleuthéria*. A draconian contract with the new owners of the press forbade his competing directly with Grove, and the publication of *Eleuthéria* would have violated the terms of that agreement. But after Grove Press changed hands yet again, Rosset resumed plans to publish *Eleuthéria* in English. As he notes in his autobiography, "the literary scholar Stan Gontarski started prodding me about this play, which both of us thought of as an important addition to the Beckett *oeuvre* that should see the light of day and eventual theatrical production" (Rosset 2016, 283). What Rosset omits was that the prodding was by way of my sending him my English translation of the play, which I did with my graduate students for research purposes, so that Rosset had a translation that would need some revision, of course, but was essentially ready to publish. On March 2, 1993, Rosset wrote to Beckett's literary executor, the French publisher Jérôme Lindon, to inform him that he was making plans to publish the work that Beckett had offered him in 1986. After some opening niceties, Rosset outlined his disappointment at not being consulted or considered as the publisher for *Dream of Fair to Middling Women*: "I have been puzzled over the last few months; after hearing of the publication plans for *Dream* that I had never been informed about them much less offered a chance to publish the book myself. Only recently was I able to get a copy of the already published book." From there Rosset moved on to his main point; after offering Rosset the play, Beckett could not translate it and so

*Eleuthéria* became temporarily dormant. [ … but] now is the time to publish *Eleuthéria*, and I hope that we can do so in cooperation with each other and avoid the confusion, misunderstandings, in-fighting, and legal battles surrounding the publication of *Dream of Fair to Middling Women*. You may recall that you were prepared to publish *Eleuthéria* in 1953, and even announced it at that time. Sam gave both *Waiting for Godot* and *Eleuthéria* to Roger Blin for production. Blin liked them both [...]. Some time thereafter Beckett withdrew *Eleuthéria*, but at one time he thought (and Blin agreed) that it had equal value with *Godot*. [...] Sam had given *Eleuthéria* to you in 1953 for publication, and in my case he offered it to me in 1986 for publication at that time and never withdrew it. For me at least now is the time to publish Sam's only remaining major unpublished work, *Eleuthéria*. (Rosset 2017, 415–16)[5]

Lindon's initial reply on March 5, 1993, suggested some room for negotiation. While insisting on Samuel Beckett's *interdictum* on *Eleuthéria*, Lindon nevertheless suggested, "I do not believe that much in everlasting perpetuity of steadfast stand-points. It is likely that *Eleuthéria* might be published some day, in some way or other, in French first, then in other languages. When? I cannot possibly tell you for the time being." Rosset replied in a letter faxed on April 19, 1993:

I'm afraid, my dear Jérôme, that you misunderstood the intent of my recent correspondence with you. You seem to be under the misapprehension that I have been asking you for permission to publish the play. May I remind you that I already have permission to do so, that from Sam himself. The purpose of my recent communication was to extend the hand of cooperation to you. [...] I asked you at least to begin making the necessary preliminary arrangements and to establish some sort of time table. That was a courtesy on my part, which I am still willing to extend if a reasonable and mutually agreeable schedule can be established. But do not confuse my gestures of friendship with requests for permission. (Rosset 2017, 417)

Lindon's alternate strategy was to take exception to the translation, which was my translation at first, but, of course, Lindon spoke no English himself. Rosset replied: "In the forty years of our relationship and of my publishing French writers I have never sought your permission for, nor approval of, any translation of French work; and I am not doing so now [....] I have already consulted my attorneys and they have told me that I indeed do have the right to publish Sam's play. If you would like to pursue this line of inquiry further you are welcome to have your attorneys contact them. Their names are appended at the end of this letter" (Rosset 2017, 418). But Rosset was willing to compromise on the issue of translation, commissioning a second from French scholar and translator Albert Bremel and then a third from Michael Brodsky.[6]

On April 22, 1993, Rosset sent a long, remarkably impassioned letter to Beckett's heir and nephew, Edward, which contained an overview of his career and outlined his motives for publication throughout his career. It is in some senses a better autobiography than Rosset's published autobiography (Rosset 2016), and the six-page letter (in print) ends in the spirit of bonhomie and compromise: "Why don't we allow this decision making [to] 'cool off' for a period of time, let us say a month. During that time we can all try to think of some solution which would at least not destroy our ongoing relationship and hopefully might end in a constructive and cooperative undertaking" (Rosset 2017, 419–24). Throughout these deliberations, Rosset continued preparations to publish the play while negotiations proceeded, commissioning a second translation from Albert Bremel and taking on a copublisher, John Oakes and Dan Simon of Four Walls Eight Windows; together they formed a new company Foxrock, Inc. through which they would publish the play. The negotiations between the two strong-willed publishers, however, grew increasingly acrimonious. The conflict was unfortunate in a number of respects, not the least of which was that the two most important figures in Samuel Beckett's publishing life were now at loggerheads with each other, and both were acting out of the firm conviction that they were serving Samuel Beckett's best interests. Lindon as best he could was trying to fulfil Samuel Beckett's final wishes—to the letter. Rosset was acting through the historical imperative that had driven his thirty-three years at Grove Press, that major work by major writers should not be suppressed or limited to an elite that had privileged access to it. Rosset's attitude toward *Eleuthéria* then was no different from his attitude toward *Lady Chatterley's Lover* or the *Tropic of Cancer*, except that Samuel Beckett offered the play to him directly in 1986. Beckett was fiercely loyal to his original publishers. In fact to demonstrate his confidence in Rosset, Beckett made formal in a letter of February 1, 1986, an agreement that they had between them informally: "This is to confirm that I have appointed you my exclusive theatrical agent for North America. This agreement shall remain in effect until such time as either one of us decides to terminate it" (Rosset 2017, 343; letter is *not included* in Beckett *Letters* 2016). That commitment made more explicit what Beckett had explained to Rosset on March 26, 1958, in this case in reference to *Krapp's Last Tape*: "You (B. Rosset) have all and exclusive publication and performance rights

In [sic] UC, Canada, and wherever else you normally exercise them. You are therefore free, without consulting anyone, to publish Krapp [sic] and have it performed in the US, Canada, etc, when, where, how, with whom, by whom, under whom and before whom you please. If this is not clear I'll give up drink" (Rosset 2017, 142, letter *not included* in Beckett *Letters* 2014).

In the aftermath of Beckett's death, however, that rift between Rosset and the Beckett Estate, principally with Beckett's French publisher and confidant, Jérôme Lindon, over, particularly, *Eleutheria* led to the summary termination of the 1986 agreement. The immediate cause of the agreement's termination was that in September of 1994 Rosset announced his intention to bring the play to the attention of a broader public by offering an open reading in New York. Rosset had hoped that a series of favorable reviews from the performance might sway the Estate to sanction publication and performance. Samuel Beckett's nephew, Edward, however, denounced the action to the *New York Times* in broadly sweeping terms suggesting that "all those who might be party to this New York event which deliberately transgresses the will expressed by Samuel Beckett, would of course expose themselves to legal proceedings" (Gussow). Lindon then followed up and wrote to copublishers John Oakes and Dan Simon specifying "all those who might be party to":

> In order to avoid any ambiguity, I made a point of warning Barney Rosset by return post that should he publish *Eleuthéria* then the Beckett estate would prosecute not only the publishers but all those—translators and distributors, among others—who have been accessory to that illicit action.

Those threats were enough to scare off the New York Theater Workshop where the reading was scheduled to be held. Rather than simply withdraw, however, the Theater Workshop demanded a $25,000 bond to indemnify itself in the face of published threats from the Beckett estate. Undeterred by the theater's failure of nerve, Rosset gathered the audience outside the New York Theater Workshop and led the group of thirteen actors and some 100 invited guests through the streets of New York, a procession in search of an author, to his apartment building where space was found for the reading (Rosset 2016, 286; Rosset 2017, 407). Edward Beckett responded on September 30, 1994, "I could no longer let you be the representative in the United States of Samuel Beckett's interests. I will therefore ask you to voluntarily resign that function, failing which I will terminate our agreement under the terms of that agreement" (Rosset 2017, 425). It was in Rosset's nature neither to desist from his public reading nor to resign, as Edward notes in his astonishing "Foreword" to *Dear Mr. Beckett*, a scrapbook of Beckett/Rosset material, in which he acknowledges that Rosset "was a dogged character, not easily deterred once he decided on what he wanted to do" (Rosset 2017, 18). Just over a week after his request for Rosset's voluntary resignation, on November 8, 1994, Edward formally completed the termination: "I have asked Georges Borchardt to be the Estate's agent in the U. S. A. and Canada. I am sorry that I had to take this final step but under the circumstances I felt that I had no alternative" (Rosset 2017, 427). (Rosset has the date of termination at October 13, 1994 [Rosset 2016, 286], but the letter in *Dear Mr. Beckett* is in facsimile.)

At this point of maximum conflict, when it looked as though the only resolution to this drama would be a protracted and costly court battle, the issues were resolved. A third translation was commissioned from the novelist Michael Brodsky and sent to Lindon and in January 1995, Rosset received a capitulation via fax from Lindon as follows:

> I persist in thinking that Sam would not have wanted *Eleutheria* to be published. Yet as I see you are staunchly bent on publishing your translation [now by Michael Brodsky], I bring myself to grant you that publication right for the United States which you have been asking me for two years [...] The one thing I am sure of is that Sam would not have liked us to fight against each other about him in a public lawsuit. My decision—I should say: renouncing—is essentially due to that. (Rosset, 2016, 287, Garbus vi)

Lindon prepared to publish the play in French so that it would appear before its English edition, including a collector's edition of "99 exemplaires numérotés sur Vergé des papeteries de Vizille." The "Avertissment" (*q.v.*) to his edition makes clear, however, that he was publishing the work against his better judgment since Beckett considered it "une piéce ratée." Rosset's position was that such judgments are best left to history. Beckett had often been overly critical of his own work. In the letter to Rosset of February 11, 1954, for example, he noted, "It's hard to go on with everything loathed and repudiated as soon as formulated, and in the act of formulation, and before formulation." In the same letter, Beckett noted that he had to resist Lindon's pressure to publish another *oeuvre inachevée*: "He [Lindon] also wanted to publish *Mercier et Camier*, the first 'novel' in French and of which the less said the better, but I had to refuse" (Beckett *Letters* 2011, 457). And not infrequently Beckett had second thoughts about publication or republication after granting initial consent. On October 20, 1964, Beckett wrote to Rosset, "I have broken down halfway through galley's of More Pricks than Kicks [*sic*]. I simply can't bear it. It was a ghastly mistake on my part to imagine, not having looked at it for a quarter of a century, that this old shit was revivable. I'm terribly sorry, but I simply have to ask you to stop production. I return herewith advance on royalties and ask you to charge to my account with Grove whatever expenses whatever [*sic*] entailed by this beginning of production. I'll be talking to John [Calder] today to the same humiliating effect" (Rosset 2017, 143; Beckett *Letters* 2014, 633). This rejection follows Beckett's initial hesitancy expressed to British publisher, writing to John Calder on April 28, 1964: "Better send me the contract before I start weakening backwards or before I have time to reread the muck" (Beckett *Letters* 2014, 633n1). It has been our good fortune that Jérôme Lindon persisted and finally prevailed, and Minuit published *Mercier et Camier* in 1970, Grove in 1974, and that Rosset and John Calder persisted with Beckett's 1934 collection of stories, *More Pricks than Kicks*, resuscitated and published finally by both houses also in 1970, all these, doubtless, in response to market demands generated by the award of the Nobel Prize in 1969. And with *Eleutheria* Rosset prevailed once again, sort of, since the victory was pyrrhic; he published the play with permission of the Estate, finally, but he was economically devastated, and the punishing termination of his function as Beckett's theatrical agent was never rescinded.

Both American and French publishers had taken considerable risks with Samuel Beckett's work, financial and, potentially, legal, and Beckett was intensely loyal to both, making Jérôme Lindon finally his literary executor and trying to secure Rosset's future by offering him a formal agreement for his continuance as his theatrical representative in North America and by offering him his last major unpublished work for publication. It is to our good fortune, finally, that Beckett's two major publishers came to an agreement about the publication of *Eleuthéria*, but not without a Parthian shaft, a public expression of resistance by Lindon, for whom, "tous les vrais connaisseurs de son travail que j'ai connus considéraient comme une piéce ratée" [roughly, "all the true experts of his work that I have known consider it a failed play"). And major critics like Ruby Cohn, among others, had agreed with Lindon's assessment. Of *Eleuthéria* Cohn has said, "It is not surprising that Beckett refuses to make public this play written in 1947 but rather that he ever considered publishing or staging it." It surprised her, moreover, "that Beckett should have written so relatively conventional a play shortly before creating *Godot*" (Cohn, 245). But how successful *Eleuthéria* is as a play qua play may not be exactly the right or the only question to ask about its significance and so of its publication. Carlton Lake, for one, places the focus on the work's historical significance: "it is a late-blooming transitional work and, even though preceded by other works in French, forms a bridge between Beckett the English language writer and Beckett the French writer" (Lake 1984, 51). And in what is perhaps the most comprehensive historical assessment of the play, Dougald McMillan and Martha Fehsenfeld note:

[*Eleuthéria*] was thus the culmination of [Beckett's] examination of the dramatic tradition of which he was a part. If we do not have for Beckett a direct manifesto like Corneille's *First Discourse on the Uses and Elements of Dramatic Poetry*, Strindberg's prefaces to *Miss Julie* and *A Dream Play*, Zola's preface to *Thérèse Raquin*, or Brecht's *Short Organum for the Theater*, we do have in *Eleuthéria* Beckett's own full statement on dramatic method—a statement which clearly influenced his later plays.

Gogo and Didi did not spring onto the stage full blown from Beckett's brow. Though couched in the humorous language of dramatic parody, *Eleuthéria* contains the serious theoretical underpinnings of a new kind of drama Beckett was to initiate in *Godot*. Many passages in it contain the seeds of Beckett's later work. The holograph bears Beckett's notation, "Prior to Godot." At the time of its composition Beckett clearly regarded *Eleuthéria*

as a serious work to be considered alongside *Godot*. (McMillan
and Fehsenfeld, 29–30)

In addition to such a "full statement on dramatic method" that
contains "the seeds of Beckett's later work," *Eleutheria* might also be
considered as something of a sociological manifesto on the artistic
as opposed to the middle-class life. Shortly after completing *Molloy*,
then, the first of what would become, in English, *Three Novels*,
Beckett developed an explicit even personal statement of cultural
rejection in a character, Victor Krap, who reverses the expected
youthful drive toward success and upward mobility, striving, instead,
for some sort of downward mobility, a move toward a bohemian
life on his way toward total inertia. Like the two parts of *Molloy*,
the set for what became *Eleutheria* is doubled or split between
a bourgeois apartment and a bohemian hovel, and as the play
develops the bourgeois apartment is progressively (or regressively)
swept off the stage. Rosset seems to have responded strongly to the
play's bohemian quality; in anticipation of its summer 1995 book
publication with the newly formed Foxrock, Inc., he published a
considerable excerpt, almost its entirety, in the quarterly magazine
*Grand Street* in its special issue on "Fetishes" (78–111), for which
Rosset commissioned a preface, "Sordid Inertia," from Irish poet
John Montague (76–77). Montague situates Beckett's one and
only three-act play squarely amid his earlier work, "I see a student
when I think of the young Beckett, a disreputable, down-at-the-
heels 'Trinity Scholar,' with a fag at his lip, and a bottle of stout
projecting from his soiled raincoat pocket. This malcontent is the
central character in *Dream of Fair to Middling Women* and *More
Pricks Than Kicks* [...]" (76).

There is no question that Beckett was not happy, finally, with
this play with another version of the "malcontent," "a disreputable,
down-at-the-heels 'Trinity Scholard,'" and he had not yet fully
solved the play's technical problems. Little wonder that he could
not translate or resisted translating it when he tried in 1986. It is
after all a drama in the throes of resisting becoming a drama, as its
principal character is in the throes of resisting becoming a character
by asserting what Montague calls his "sordid inertia." That is,
Beckett wrote a play in which the main character refuses to explain
or is incapable of explaining the motives that drive his behavior,
his principled inaction, motives and action that have traditionally

undergirded the machinery of drama. Victor's desire, his passion is to be inert, to redefine freedom in terms of inertia, to be nothing in short, and Beckett's own unguarded analysis of the play in 1948 is stunning and deeply personal. He wrote to his "old friend," Georges Duthuit, on August 11, in something of a confessional from which *Eleuthéria* is inseparable:

> You know I really have no wish to be set free [Beckett here playing on the title of *Eleuthéria*, Greek for freedom], nor to be helped, by art or anything else. Young people after reading *Eleuthéria* have said to me, but you are sending us away discouraged. [Who are these young people, by the way, and what text did they have access to?] Let them take aspirin [a phrase Beckett will later use to director Alan Schneider as a recommendation to theater critics[7]], or go for long walks before breakfast [as Beckett himself often did]. Nothing will be sufficiently against for me, not even pain, and I don't think I have any special need for it. I say confusedly what comes uppermost, like Browning. [an allusion that Beckett will reprise *Happy Days* in 1961, surprisingly unglossed in the letters, however] Victor (name to be changed incidentally. I need Nick something instead.) is utterly defenceless [*sic*], he *too* can be heard from afar, what he has to say, in order to have the right to be silent, is in the end the old nonsense, he is afraid, he says Mr Inspector sir, he seems to be telling them off, in reality he is licking their boots, talking to them is sucking their arses. (Beckett *Letters* 2011, 97, emphasis added)

With *Eleuthéria*, then, Beckett was learning to risk not only silence and absence on the stage and to reduce or empty theatrical space, first of physical material, then of action, then of character, then of motive, but also to risk direct revelation and explanation if not confession. It would take another play before he would begin to solve this dramatic problem of presenting or evoking "nothing" by, in part, entirely removing the central characters from the scene—Godot—and to make his own voice "heard from afar." *Eleuthéria* is not there yet, but it shows the way, a way, as McMillan suggests. It may be only, say, Krap's first tape, which of course is less developed, less complete than what becomes Krapp's last tape. But *Eleuthéria* is the beginning of "it all." It already anticipates the resistance, absences, and apparitions of the later work. And chronologically nearer, we can see, as well, the novel *Malone Dies* evolving from Victor's futile struggles to explain himself. *Eleuthéria* has its own qualities as well, as Rosset understood and demonstrated in the public reading he organized, and published it is now in the hands of a broader public to decide if and how it fails, if and how it succeeds.

# Notes

1 See, for instance, Ruby Cohn, *Just Play* (Princeton: Princeton University Press, 1980, 2014), 143–62; Guy Croussy, *Beckett* (Paris: Hachette, 1971), 102–3; John Fletcher and John Spurling, *Beckett: A Study of His Plays* (New York: Hill and Wang, 1972), XX; James Knowlson and John Pilling, *Frescoes of the Skull: The Later Prose and Drama of Samuel Beckett* (New York: Grove Press, 1980), 23–38; and most importantly, Dougald McMillan and Martha Fehsenfeld, *Beckett in the Theatre: The Author as Practical Playwright and Director* (New York: Riverrun Press, 1988), 29–45.

2 Numéro hors-série (Paris: Editions Privat, 1986), 111–32. See also Dougald McMillan, "*Eleuthéria*: le Discours de la Méthode, inédit de Samuel Beckett," translated by Edith Fournier, in the same issue, pp. 101–9.

3 Rosset seems to confuse these two Paris locales in his autobiography (Rosset 2016). Rosset's announcement of his dismissal from Grove Press and Beckett's initial proposal of *Eleuthéria* was made at a birthday gathering arranged by Tom Bishop in May of 1986 at La Coupole (Rosset 2016, 281). Stephen Graf misidentifies the locale as well, citing another former haunt of Beckett, La Closerie de Lilas (Graf 74).

4 The novel finally appeared, amid much squabbling among its publishers, from Black Cat Press, Dublin, in 1992, and from Arcade Publishing, in association with Riverrun Press, in 1993, both editions edited by Eoin O'Brien and Edith Fournier. In his letter to the *Times Literary Supplement* on July 16, 1993, however, Eoin O'Brien dissociates himself from the second edition, although he remains listed as its editor: "Both the US (Arcade) and UK (Calder) 1993 editions of this work have been printed without taking into account the necessary corrections I, and my co-editor, Edith Fournier, made to the proofs of the re-set text. It is of deep concern that Samuel Beckett's work be treated in this manner. We can be held accountable," he continues,

"only for the first edition published in 1992 by Black Cat Press in Dublin and can accept no responsibility for the errors in the US and UK flawed editions" (17). See also Tucker (2011).

5 These letters are now published in *Dear Mr. Beckett* (Rosset 2017, 414–24). They were drafted by the current author for Rosset, a practice not uncommon in business generally and with Rosset in particular.

6 Graf notes that the "Bermel's translation, unfortunately, has apparently been lost" (Graf, 89n14), but all three translations are included in and available through the Stanley E. Gontarski Samuel Beckett Collection on deposit in the Library, Trinity College, Dublin. See https://www. irishtimes.com/news/education/tcd-adds-to-samuel-beckett-collection-with-new-works-1.1711136

7 "My work is a matter of fundamental sounds (no joke intended) made as fully as possible, and I accept responsibility for nothing else. If people want to have headaches among the overtones, let them. And provide their own aspirin" (Harmon 1998, 24).

# PART TWO

# A Theatrical Life

# 4

# Textual Aberrations, Ghost Texts, and the British *Godot*: A Saga of Censorship

*questions of art are questions (in the widest sense) of execution; questions of morality are quite another affair [...].*

—HENRY JAMES, "THE ART OF FICTION" (1884)

*There is no such thing as a moral or an immoral book. Books are well written or badly written. That is all.*

—OSCAR WILDE, "PREFACE," *THE PICTURE OF DORIAN GRAY* (1891)

## 1953: "a most unusual play of a surrealist nature"

In an endnote to a letter Samuel Beckett wrote to his French publisher, Jérôme Lindon, on December 1, 1953, the editors of the *Letters of Samuel Beckett* cite Lindon's earlier letter to the effect that "agreement had been reached with [proposed director] Peter Glenville (1913–96) and producer Donald Albery (1914–88) [of Donmar Productions, Limited] regarding an option for the

FIGURE 4.1 Waiting for Godot *playbill for the Lord Chamberlain Approved Criterion Theatre production.*

London production of *Waiting for Godot*." Lindon asked if Beckett concurred that "it would be better to leave the United States rights to Albery and Glenville" (*Letters* 2011, 426n4). Beckett readily agreed, and he confirmed the decision two weeks later to his American publisher, Barney Rosset, "Signed yesterday for London West End production within six months, producer [i.e., director] probably Peter Glenville. [Harold] Oram [holder of the original American option] as you may know is out [that is, Oram's option expired in October]" (*Letters* 2011, 432). The following spring, on March 23, 1954, Albery began to clear the way for a London production by applying for a performance license to Brigadier General Sir Norman Gwatkin of the Lord Chamberlain's office, calling *Godot* "a most unusual play of a surrealist nature" and further noting that "Peter Glenville is to direct it and we hope to get a very good cast to play it. We are thinking in terms of Ralph Richardson for one of the tramps" (LCP Corr July 1954/6597). The travesty of Beckett's subsequent meeting with Richardson as Beckett was passing through London on September 24, 1954, is already well rehearsed. Beckett himself describes it in a letter of October 18, 1954, to Rosset; the meeting seemed at least to dampen Richardson's and finally Glenville's interest:

> [...] had a highly unsatisfactory interview with SIR Ralph Richardson who wanted the low-down on Pozzo, his home address and curriculum vitae, and made the forthcoming of this and similar information the condition of his condescending to illustrate the part of Vladimir. Too tired to give satisfaction I told him that all I knew of Pozzo was in the text, that if I had known more I would have put it in the text, and that this was true also of the other characters. (*Letters* 2011, 507)

While Beckett had some embarrassing interaction with the Censorship of Publications Act of 1929 in his native Ireland over his story collection *More Pricks than Kicks*, writing (but not publishing[1]) a scathing attack on the act in "Censorship in the Saorstat," even citing his own registered case number at the end, 465 (*Disjecta* 84), he seemed to exhibit more than a little naïveté about the workings of the English theater and the restrictions regarding performance in London. At least the narrator of his 1938 London novel, *Murphy*, is well aware of the issues of censorship as he notes, "This phrase [with music as a metaphor for what Murphy calls Celia's 'sausage and mash sex' (37)] is chosen with care, lest the filthy censors should lack an occasion to commit their filthy synecdoche" (76). But in a letter to Irish director Alan Simpson of April 9, 1954, regarding Irish production rights to *Godot*, Beckett noted of the impending London production that "No request for modifications of any text have [*sic*] been made" (*Letters* 2011, 479),[2] this comment a full fortnight after Albery's initial query letter to the Lord Chamberlain. But the die had been cast even as Beckett was writing to Simpson. Sir Vincent Troubridge, assistant examiner in the Lord Chamberlain's office, had already rendered his preliminary judgment by March 28, 1954, that the play had to be sanitized in anticipation of its West End premiere.

Sir Troubridge's "modifications" were officially stamped August 25, 1955, as reconfirmation of his earlier reading dated March 28, 1954. Troubridge's judgments were confirmed by a second, even less flexible examiner, as follows: "With many years on the Council of the old Stage Society [an early name for the English Stage Company], I have had much experience with 'advanced,' 'expressionist,' and [second 'and' struck out] similar imaginative kinds of plays, but I find this one extremely baffling" (LPC Corr July 1954/6597). Recommended cuts [the first judgments bracketed below are presumably Troubridge's] include:

Act I, p. 2.[3] "You might button it up all the same." [Cut Cut]

Act I, p. 3. "(his hand pressed to his pubis)" [Cut Cut]

Act I, pp. 4–5. There is some conversation here between the tramps about the Crucifixion that seems all right to me, but as a precaution another eye should run over it. [Leave Cut (in pencil)]

Act I, pp. 9–10. The lines as marked about a known secondary effect of hanging must come out. [Delete sign Cut]

Act I, p. 27. "Kicking him out on his arse." [Cut Cut]

[Act I—37 "The hard stool" is queried with red pencil on the submitted ts. but no cut is indicated at this point. The line will, however, become an issue with future assessors.]

Act I, p. 40. "Mixed in the nonsense of the first 12 lines [see below, Beckett cites 15 lines to Barney Rosset], I detect a distinct mockery of religion." [Allow Cut (in pencil)]

Act I, p. 40. "Fartov." [Cut Cut] [Part of above speech.]

Act I, p. 52. I don't like Estragon comparing himself to Christ. [Cut Cut] [On this passage Beckett will be unwilling to compromise, and he will eventually prevail.]

Act II, p. 3. "You piss better ... etc." [Cut Cut]
Act II, p. 16. (resumes his foetal posture)
I conceive this to link with I, 3 i.e. with his hand on his pubis, but
I may be wrong. [Cut Cut]
Act II, p. 20. "Gonococcus! Spirochaete!"
(These are the microbes of gonorrhaea and syphilis.) [Cut Cut]
Act II, p. 30. "Who farted?"
(Though used in the plays of Ben Jonson, this word is now out
of favour. [Cut Cut]
Act II, p. 38. "give him a taste of his boot, in ... the privates."
[Cut Cut]
Act II, p. 45. The business of letting down Estragon's trousers,
which may be all right. [Better keep his (i.e., the trousers) up.]
Second comment: "Leave provided he is well covered."
"Otherwise, ["in some bewilderment" added in autograph pen].
RECOMMEND FOR LICENSE [*sic*]
28/3/1954" (LCP Corr July 1954/6597)

Albery subsequently conferred with Beckett. Afterward, on April 26,
1954, he outlined the discussion and offered a list of compromises:
"Memo following a visit with Mr. Samuel Beckett who was very
reluctant to change anything but finally agreed to the following"
(Albery, Donald Box 526.1). Sir N. W. Gwatkin responded on June
21, 1954, agreeing to all changes "except No. 10, [Act II] page
30," for which he asked for further suggestions. After hearing from
Beckett again, Albery responded to Sir Gwatkin on June 28, offering
to replace the earlier, more general change, the suggested "Who did
that?" for "Who farted?" But the Lord Chamberlain still found the
line too suggestive. In a June 15 note to the list of compromises
submitted by Albery, a handwritten addendum dated June 21 is
appended: "The L. C. should stand firm about any business of
breaking wind" (LCP Corr July 1954/6597). Gwatkin replied to
Albery on July 1, as follows: "In reply to your letter of June 28th I
write to inform you that the Lord Chamberlain agrees to the words
'Who belched?' being substituted for 'Who farted?' on [Act II] page
30" (LCP Corr July 1954/6597).

Troubridge's initial recommended cuts would then provoke
protracted and heated negotiations before an official license
for general public performance would be issued. But even as the

DONMAR PRODUCTIONS LIMITED

(Registered Office: Canada House, Norfolk Street, Strand, W.C.2)

Directors:
Donald Albery
Anthony Albery

Secretary:
Dennis Ryland, F.C.A.

New Theatre,
St. Martin's Lane.
London, W.C.2

TEMple Bar 5596, 5650

26th April 1954

"WAITING FOR GODOT"

Memo following visit to Mr. Samuel Beckett who was very
reluctant to change anything but finally agreed to the
following:-

1. The lines to which the Lord Chamber lain objects
   on Act 1 page 2 should be cut.

2. Page 3, "his hand pressed to his pubis" should be
   changed to "his hand pressed to his stomach"

3. Page 9, from "It'd give us an erection" down to
   "Did you not know that?" now to read :-
   Estragon: "What about hanging ourselves?
   Vladimir whispers to Estragon
   Vladimir With all that ensues. Where it falls mandrakes
           grow. That's why they shriek when you tear
           them up. Did you not know that?

4. Page 27, "on his arse" to be changed to
   "on his backside"

5. Page 40, Sir Norman Gwatkin said that he thought it
   might help if the word ""God" was altered. Mr. Beckett
   is willing to agree to the substitution of "deity" for
   "God". Mr. Beckett is prepared to omit "Fartov" substituting
   "Popov".

6. He cannot see any way to change this speech nor does he
   see why it is in any way objectionable.

7. Act II, page 3, "You see, you piss better when I'm not
   there" to be changed to "You see, you eliminate better
   when I'm not there".

8. Page 16 "(he resumes his foetal posture") to be out.

9. Page 20, "Gonococcus": Spirochaete". Mr. Beckett
   suggests substituting "Lord Chamberlain" "Civil Servant".

10. Page 30, "Who farted" to be changed to "Who did that?"

/over

- 2 -

11. Page 38, "and the privates" to be changed to
    "and the guts".

12. Page 54 It is agreed that Estragon will be well
    covered when his trousers fall.

FIGURE 4.2 *Albery, Donald. Memo to Lord Chamberlain, April 26,
1954. Sir Donald Albery Collection. Harry Ransom Humanities Research
Center, University of Texas, Austin. Box 526.1.*

necessary alterations were still in dispute, a version of *Godot* with most of the changes outlined above (but with considerable rewrites to Beckett's text by unknown hands) was performed nearly a month before the Lord Chamberlain's official licensing approval. It opened at The Arts Theatre Club in London on August 3, 1955, some fifteen months after the official submission of the play script, but to a select, invited audience and for a very limited run. In such a private club, plays, skits, and revues could legally be performed without official license, but the venue was small and its commercial possibilities limited.

That fifteen-month negotiation has led to considerable confusion about the chronology of censorship and performances surrounding British productions and publication of *Waiting for Godot*, the confusion abetted by unvetted information dispensed from otherwise reliable sources. The "Chronology 1954" summary in Volume II of the *Letters of Samuel Beckett*, for instance, mistakenly notes of "23 June [1954]": "Objections of the Lord Chamberlain's Office to the text of *Waiting for Godot* resolved" (*Letters* 2011, 440). The Lord Chamberlain's office stamped the submitted script "approved" on August 28, 1955, that is, almost a month *after* the play had opened at The Arts Club, even as Beckett had not yet approved the final cuts that would allow West End performances.

Troubridge's objections persisted, then, well after his preliminary cuts to the text were made in March and reaffirmed in July of 1954. Troubridge wrote to the Lord Chamberlain:

> The play is a modern cry of despair, and Godot, for whom we human tramps are always waiting in expectation, is Death. Pozzo and Lucky are allegorical figures passing before our eyes of how men treat one another, by acts of enslavement that lead to blindness for the enslaver and dumbness for the slave. The best way out is a piece of rope—what Shakespeare called "the charity of a penny cord" ["it sums up thousands," *Cymbeline*, V.4] (LCP Corr July 1954/6597)

Final approval for the West End venue at the Criterion Theatre, however, came only on September 12, 1955, the play's opening night with the substantial cuts to the text, also stamped August 25, 1955. In it, the original fourteen cuts had been reduced to ten:

"This License is issued on the understanding that the following alterations are made:—

1.  Act I, p. 2, omit '(pointing) You might button it all the same'. 'True (he buttons his fly).'
2.  Page 3, for 'his hand pressed to his pubis' substitute 'his hand pressed to his stomach',
3.  Page 9, omit 'It'd give us an erection'.
4.  Page 27, for 'arse' substitute 'backside'.
5.  Page 40, for 'Fartov' substitute 'Popov'
6.  Act II, page 3, for 'you piss better' substitute 'you do it better'. [At one point Beckett suggested first 'eliminate,' then 'piddle.']
7.  Page 16, omit '(he resumes his foetal posture)'
8.  Page 30, for 'who farted?' [sic] substitute 'Who belched?'
9.  Page 38, substitute 'and the guts' for 'and the provates [sic]'.
10. Estragon will be adequately covered when his trousers fall." (LCP Corr July 1954/6597)

The approved cuts stamped August 1955 were almost exactly those Troubridge proposed in March of 1954 and revisited in August, except that the Lord Chamberlain now relented on two of the potential blasphemies. "The Hard Stool" is not mentioned at all (*Godot* F&F [1956] 40). In his letter to Albery of April 14, 1954, Beckett seemed flexible on and so accepted all but two of Troubridge's original suggested changes:

> But two of the passages condemned, those namely numbered 5 and 6 on the [original] list, are vital to the play and can neither be suppressed nor changed. I cannot conceive in what they give offense and I consider their interdiction wholly unreasonable. I'm afraid that this is quite final. Until those two passages are reinstated as they stand, there is no point my submitting amendments to the others. (LCP Corr July 1954/6597; this crucial letter is cited only in part in Beckett *Letters* 2011, 481n3).

Beckett would summarize the issues to Rosset on April 21, 1954, before their resolution:

We were all set for a London West End performance [that is, at the Criterion] until the Lord Chamberlain got going. His incriminations are so preposterous that I'm afraid the whole thing is off. He listed 12 passages for omission! [Sir Troubridge cites 14 above, but Albery's memo cites 12, and the Lord Chamberlain conceded two of those, as above.] The things I had expected and which I was half prepared to amend (reluctantly) but also passages that are vital to the play (first 15 lines of Lucky's tirade and the passage end of Act I from "But you can't go barefoot" to "And they crucified quick") and impossible either to alter or suppress. However Albery (the theatre director) is trying to arrange things in London. I am to see him this week-end and all is not yet definitely lost. It would be a pity as there was talk of Alec Guinness for the role of Estragon [who would join Ralph Richardson's Vladimir]. (Beckett *Letters* 2011, 480; qtd. in Knowlson 1996, 372)

And "arrange things" Albery did. Number 5 in Albery's memo cited above reads as follows: "Page 40 [*sic,* page number of the typescript submitted], Sir Norman Gwatkin said that he thought it would help if the word 'God' were altered. Mr. Beckett is willing to agree to the substitution of 'diety' for 'God'. ['God' was finally retained, however, as was the entire passage (F & F [1956] 43, Samuel French 29).] Mr. Beckett is prepared to omit 'Fartov' substituting 'Popov'" (LCP Corr July 1954/6597). To Beckett's wider objection, number 5, "first 15 lines of Lucky's tirade," and number 6, from "But you can't go barefoot" to "And they crucified quick," he remained adamant ("He cannot see any way to change this speech nor does he see why in any way it is objectionable" (LCP Corr July 1954/6597), and on these the Lord Chamberlain finally acquiesced.

In Mary Bryden's "Preface" to the 2010 edition of *Godot* from Faber and Faber, however, she suggests that these lengthy and potentially blasphemous portions of the play were indeed cut:

It was foreseeable that certain passages of *Godot* would fall afoul of the Lord Chamberlain's blue pencil. These included moments deemed to contain unacceptable religious or sexual content, such as the exchange near the end of Act I where Estragon talks of comparing himself to Christ [...]. *Another casualty* was the opening of Lucky's monologue with its supposedly blasphemous description of a 'personal God quaquaquaqua' [...]. (Bryden 2010, xi, emphasis added)

On those points, of course, the Lord Chamberlain had relented. Bryden is closer to the mark, if still slightly off, when she suggests, "These deletions were restored when the first performance took place in the 'private' space of the arts club [...]" (Bryden 2010, xi).[4] They were, in fact, included for all performances, Arts Club and West End. Bryden's history thus remains a bit confusing since the "'private' space" had nothing to do with the Lord Chamberlain's deliberations. Yet while the Arts Club performances were unaffected by the Lord Chamberlain's review, Hall et al. followed the Lord Chamberlain's first round of cuts and, further, essentially precensored the text with some alterations added either by Albery or by Hall's team. David Bradby continues some of the confusion as he notes, "The cuts demanded by the Lord Chamberlain included references to Christ at the end of Act I from 'But you can't go barefoot' to 'And they crucified quick' and the first fifteen lines of Lucky's 'Think.' Although these deletions were not necessary for the Arts Theatre 'club' production, the offending lines had to be removed when the production transferred to the Criterion, a public theatre" (Bradby 2001, 228n6). Not so. Bradby, who cites Knowlson and not the Lord Chamberlain's archive as his source (Knowlson 1996, 371), is right on the issue of the Arts Club versus the Criterion Theatre productions. But it was unlikely for the cast of *Godot* to have to learn two different sets of lines for the play between the Arts opening on August 3, 1955, and the Criterion opening on September 12, 1955 (the script approved finally only on August 28, 1955). The published 1956 Faber and Faber text calls that move a transfer, so most of the Lord Chamberlain's cuts were accepted for and used in the Arts Theatre production if for no other reason than for technical and professional expediency. That is, the Samuel French Acting edition of 1957 contains the set, text, and blocking for the Arts Theatre production, and it includes the potential blasphemies but not the sexual and excremental references. Bradby is correct, however, in that the legal issue was only with the West End production. But here again, the Lord Chamberlain was more vigilant and attentive to matters of sexuality and scatology than to blasphemy. He finally relented on Beckett's two principal points, those deemed blasphemous; this compromise allowed the play to open at the Criterion as scheduled. He even allowed to stand the mention of those bacteria associated with the sexually transmitted diseases, gonorrhea and syphilis—"Gonococcus! Spirochaete!"— but he drew the line at flatulence. Beckett's witty replacements for "Gonococcus! Spirochaete!" may themselves have outmaneuvered his censors and so put the Lord Chamberlain's office in an untenable position. As offered in Albery's memo of April 26, 1954, Beckett's alternatives were "Lord Chamberlain," "Civil Servant" (Albery, Donald Box 526.1).

Mark and Juliette Taylor-Batty are also more than a little confused about what was censored and for which productions. They suggest, "Beckett was asked to adjust some lewd references ('Fartov' became the anodyne 'Popov,' for example) but he refused to remove the references to erections or the falling of Estragon's trousers, and resisted the deletion of many passages deemed blasphemous (such as Lucky's first fifteen lines) which the censor required before the play might be performed in public" (Taylor-Batty and Taylor-Batty 2008, 59). Beckett did resist most strongly those passages deemed blasphemous, but the references to erections were indeed unacceptable from the first and remained excised for all productions through 1968, and Estragon's falling trousers was never seriously in question as long as he remained completely covered.

An unsigned summary by the Lord Chamberlain's office dated April 29, 1954 (shortly after Beckett wrote to Rosset) outlines the compromises finally accepted:

> In view of Mr. [C. D.] Heriot's report, after attending a Reading[5] [*sic*] of the Play [*sic*] the Lord Chamberlain is now prepared to allow the following to stand:—
>
> (5) "Given the existence as uttered forth" down to "and who can doubt it will fire and firmament" p. 40)
>
> The name "Fartov" to be altered.
>
> (6) from "But you can't go barefoot" down to "and they crucified quick" (p. 52)
>
> (9) "Gonococcus! Spirochaete" (p. 20)
>
> It is understood that the other alterations are agreed upon. (LCP Corr July 1954/6597)

This public reading of the play was evidently central to breaking the deadlock over performance permissions and allowing the play

```
                                                    I-16
POZZO      Be careful! He's wicked.

                    (VLADIMIR and ESTRAGON turn towards Pozzo)
           With strangers.

ESTRAGON   (Undertone) Is that him?

VLADIMIR   Who?

ESTRAGON   (Trying to remember the name) Er...

VLADIMIR   Godot?

ESTRAGON   Yes.

POZZO      I present myself; Pozzo.

VLADIMIR   (To Estragon) Not at all!

ESTRAGON   He said Godot.

VLADIMIR   Not at all!

ESTRAGON   (Timidly, to Pozzo) You're not Mr. Godot, Sir?

POZZO      (Terrifying voice) I am Pozzo! (silence) Does
           that name mean nothing to you? (silence) I say
           does that name mean nothing to you?

                    (VLADIMIR and ESTRAGON look at each other
                    questioningly)

ESTRAGON   (Pretending to search) Bozzo...Bozzo...

VLADIMIR   (Ditto) Pozzo...

POZZO      PPPOZZZO!

ESTRAGON   Ah! Pozzo...let me see...Pozzo...

VLADIMIR   Is it Pozzo or Bozzo?

ESTRAGON   Pozzo...no...I'm afraid I...no...I don't seem to...

                    (POZZO advances threatingly)

VLADIMIR   (Conciliating) I once knew a family called Gozzo.
           The mother embroidered doilies.

ESTRAGON   (Hastily) We're not from these parts, Sir.

POZZO      (Halting) You are human beings nevertheless. (he
           puts on his spectacles) As far as one can see.
           (he takes off his spectacles) Of the same species
```

FIGURE 4.3 *Typescript page of reproduced* Waiting for Godot *submitted for approval to Lord Chamberlain. Sir Donald Albery Collection. Harry Ransom Humanities Research Center, University of Texas, Austin. Box 526.1.*

to open in the West End. But public objections would continue well after official approval and the play's opening at the Criterion Theatre. Lady Howitt's complaint, that the play's displays of "lavatory necessities is offensive and against all sense of British decency" (LCP Corr July 1954/6597), prompted the Lord Chamberlain's office to send a representative to the Criterion Theatre to view a performance and so revisit the issues, the emphasis now on excretions. The report of November 30, 1955, reads as follows[6]:

> Lady Hewitt's [*sic*] case is not proved. There are lavatory references, of course, but where the whole text is more or less offensive and in doubtful taste, no useful purpose could be served by pruning—and the Lord Chamberlain might endanger the dignity of his office if he rescinded his license at this point in the play's run. Having passed, this carbon copy of "Ulysses," he has, it seems to me, satisfied the demands of those who claim it to be Literature with a capital L. Let him leave it at that (with a non-committal answer to Lady Hewitt [*sic*]) and allow public opinion quietly to disperse this ugly little jet of marsh-gas. (LCP Corr July 1954/6597)[7]

# 1964: "I am directing 'Waiting for Godot' and am working closely with Mr. Beckett, who is here for rehearsals"

The issues of textual modifications to Beckett's first performed play are further muddled by curators at the venerable University of Texas Harry Ransom Center (or their vice-curators, often appointed interns, students essentially, as such matters unfold these days) who proclaimed the English theatrical censors dissolved by 1964. According to its 2006 web-published exhibition catalogue called *Fathoms from Anywhere: A Samuel Beckett Centenary Exhibition*, the section devoted to performances of *Waiting for Godot* proclaims, "It wasn't until December of 1964—after the office of the Lord Chamberlain had finally gone out of business [hardly an academic turn of phrase]—that the unexpurgated version of *Godot* was performed, with official British sanction, at the Royal Court Theatre in London, under Beckett's supervision" ("Waiting"). The claim is not only wrong (as is other material in the online catalogue), but the errors remain uncorrected to this day. Admittedly, the historical error was gleaned (without appropriate citation) from an unexamined and under-researched error in Deirdre Bair's 1990 biography: "The first unexpurgated version of *Godot* in England [...] opened at the Royal Court on 30 December 1964" (Bair 1990, 613).

In fact, the Lord Chamberlain's office has not "gone out of business" at all. It still functions to this day as the senior official of the Royal Household. His public, theatrical censorship function begun with the (Theatre) Licensing Act of 1737 was dissolved not in 1964, as the Ransom website proclaims, but by the Theatre Act of 1968. (The British production of *Hair*, originally denied its license in that year, opened hard upon the act's passage.) Even "under Beckett's supervision," the 1964 Royal Court revival adhered to the 1954/5 cuts as follows, acknowledged in a letter dated December 23, 1964: "we will, of course, comply with the Lord Chamberlain's requirements in respect of the changes in the script" [for an opening of December 30 at the Royal Court] (LCP Corr 1964/4604).

The bulk of the Lord Chamberlain's performance restrictions would hold sway then for well over a decade, even as Faber and Faber finally relented and published an un-Bowdlerized text of the play, contemplated first in 1962 but not effected until 1965. The impending—if tardy—publication of it prodded a revival of the play by the Royal Court Theatre in 1964. While it was a much-altered text of *Godot* that opened at The Arts Club on August 3, 1955, as the Lord Chamberlain's office was still reviewing the text for its West End opening, the *Godot* performed by the Royal Court, even "under Beckett's supervision," was still this censored text of 1954/5. The Royal Court, however, submitted for approval a version of *Godot* that Faber and Faber was apparently about to publish as its revised and uncensored text. But that uncut text was not the version performed at the Royal Court in 1964.

In fact the reestablishment of the censored text by the Lord Chamberlain may have prompted Faber and Faber to delay yet again the publication of the uncensored text it had prepared to issue in 1962. An unusually restrained Beckett made his plea to Charles Monteith of Fabers for an unexpurgated edition of the play in a letter of November 15, 1963:

[...] on the subject of GODOT [*sic*] there is something I should like to ask you. The version published by you is the playing version authorized by the Lord Chamberlain and differs considerably from the unexpurgated version published by Grove. I appreciate the necessity of their being available in England a text securing theatre management from trouble with censorship. At the same time one is depressed by the mutilations involved and which so weakens the meaning in certain places as to make it scarcely intelligible. I have been wondering recently if it would not be possible, now that there seems to be a more liberal view of what can be said on the stage than when GODOT [*sic*] was first purified to bring your version closer to the original. [...] The whole question was brought forcibly to my mind by the first volume just published of Suhrkamp's trilingual edition of my plays in which he has used quite unnecessarily your text instead of the integral one. [...] (Beckett *Letters* 2014, 580)

Faber and Faber apparently had the unexpurgated text set in type by the time of Beckett's letter, but it did not formally publish it until 1965 nor did it release in 1962 or 1963 an "integral" text to Suhrkamp for its trilingual edition, the publisher a tad late in screwing its publishing "courage to the sticking-place," as Lady Macbeth might have it (*Macbeth* I:7). The text submitted to the Lord Chamberlain by The English Stage Company for performance at The Royal Court was a retyped or proof version, some of it curiously, perhaps comically, precensored, so quite certainly Beckett never saw this almost "integral" version. Page I–16 of the typescript submitted to the Lord Chamberlain in 1964 reads, as it had in 1954 (LCP 1954/23), for instance, as follows: "(*Conciliating*) I once knew a family called Gozzo. The mother embroidered doilies" (LCP Corr 1964/51). A decade after the Lord Chamberlain's original censorship of *Waiting for Godot*, the guardians of public decency and morality in Britain had still not warmed to the 1964 revival of the play as written (i.e., warts and all) by the English Stage Company at the Royal Court Theatre, even as the venerable house of Faber and Faber already had plans to publish, if hesitantly, the fully uncensored text.

As it turns out, then, this curious substitution of "doilies" or "d'oylies" (see Figure 4.3) for "warts" or "clap" was part of the original typescript submitted in 1954 (LCP 1954/23). It was, even more curiously, if not inexplicably, published commercially in 1957 by Samuel French, Ltd. as French's Acting Edition No. 510, apparently another "authorized" edition of the play, which follows the Criterion cuts of August 25, 1955, and so those of the 1956 Faber and Faber text. This edition includes, "The mother embroidered d'oylies" (*Godot* [Samuel French] 12), something of a ludicrous rendering of the censored line used in the 1955 West End Criterion production, "The mother had warts—," and as published in the original 1956 Faber and Faber edition (*Godot* [F&F 1956] 22). Beckett's original, of course, had her suffering from gonorrhea, "The mother had the clap" (*Godot* [F&F 1965] 22). The revision from "clap" to "warts" figured not at all in the Lord Chamberlain's deliberations in 1954/5, so that the change must have been made somewhere in house before the play was originally submitted to the Lord Chamberlain's office.

The reproduced typescript or early proof text (stapled with magenta semi-soft cover) submitted by The Royal Court Theatre on December 1, 1964 (so stamped), follows not the Faber and Faber editions of 1956 (mcmlvi) and 1959 (mcmlix), but the version printed or typeset in 1962 (mcmlxii) as already the unexpurgated text, at least in a proof stage (LCP 1964/51). It includes the usual Faber and Faber copyright and performance details that appear in the printed text, and already includes the note that the "textual deletions" of 1954/5/6 "have been restored in the text printed here." The character designations throughout, too, are those found in the F&F editions, all capitals in the left margin followed by a colon. This version of the text, hand numbered 22 on the title page, is not paginated consecutively, however, as the printed F&F texts are, but are paginated as follows: I–2 (page I–1 having no designation) through I–59, thence II–2 (page II–1 having no designation) through II–52. It is, then, despite its 1962 copyright date, essentially the F&F text as it will finally appear in 1965 into which the Lord Chamberlain's 1954/5 objections were reinscribed by one of its readers.

The Lord Chamberlain's markups, then, return to the deletions of the 1954/5 production. The offensive passages are noted in blue pencil as follows, with "The Hard Stool" and "Ballocksed" now added as new objections:

The business with Vladimir's fly (I–2);
Pubis (I–4);
Gestures ... like those of a pugilist and erection (I–10);

Erection (I–11);
Arse (I–30);
The hard stool (I–40);
Fartov (I–44);
Piss (II–3);
Ballocksed (II–31);
Who farted (II–34) (LCP 1964/51)

This text also included Beckett's original line, "I once knew a family called Gozzo. The mother had the clap." The passage remained unmarked in this text and so presumably it slipped through (I–18), perhaps because it was never at issue in 1954/5 where the mother was precensored as one who "embroidered doilies" (LCP 1954/23). The original strategy of self-censorship had now apparently proved successful since no attention was given to this line in 1964. The Lord Chamberlain's men were thus not reading as attentively as one might expect; they seem to have been focused only on restoring the original cuts.

Anthony Page,[8] a successor to Beckett-defender George Devine as artistic director of the Royal Court and director of this *Godot* revival, appealed to the Lord Chamberlain on December 17, 1964, to lift the ban, noting, "I am directing 'Waiting for Godot' and am working closely with Mr. Beckett, who is here for rehearsals" (LCP Corr 1964/4604). Page made a special plea as follows: "It is very important to show that the spirit of Vladimir suffers from a disability of the bladder, (so that there is no ambiguity about the reason why he leaves the stage). This is the only passage which explains it clearly, [hand written asterisk here] and as we had been rehearsing it, he turns his back to the audience for 'buttons his fly'" (LCP Corr 1964/4604). A handwritten note to the asterisk reads, "No if this is clear there is no need to emphasise it with the fly-buttoning gesture" (LCP Corr 1964/4604). In reference to "An erection," Page asks that "When the play was done before, there was no cut after the word 'erection', i.e., 'With all that follows' to 'Did you know that?' was allowed. I am not quite clear whether this passage is allowed or not" (LCP Corr 1964/4604). An asterisk marks this passage as well to which the following comment applies: "this does look as if it was permitted in the original. The reference (if erection is cut) is very obscure. Only readers of Joyce will understand—or friends of the hangman"

(LCP Corr 1964/4604). These are apparently the comments of Charles Heriot, for a note of December 21 [1964, affirmative confirmation added on December 22] contains the following: "I agree with Charles Heriot's recommendations. May I please check that you will disallow the fly-buttoning (Act I–2) and 'Who farted' (Act II–34)?" (LCP Corr 1964/4604).

In his report to the Lord Chamberlain dated December 4 for performances scheduled to begin on December 30, 1964 (and stamped December 24), an exasperated C. D. Heriot continued his assault on the play:

> More nonsense has been talked and written about this inflated piece of simple symbolism [Roger Blin had described it as Expressionism] than any other play of its kind during the past decade. Reading it again after several years (and after having seen it is [*sic, recte* "in"] performance) I am inclined to think that the excellence of the actors in the original performance dazzled the critics into accepting dross for gold. Maeterlinck, for all his dead *art nouveau* presentation, did this sort of thing much better, and avoided indecency while conveying his "message."
>
> All the cuts made in the original have been restored [that is, they remain in effect] and at least one new one [has been added]. This I have listed together with two warnings based on the complaint received from Lady Howitt (File no. 440/55) [see above, these principally against miming or simulating urination, or as she put it in her letter of complaint, overt display of "lavatory necessities is offensive and against all sense of British decency"]. (LCP Corr 1964/4604)

As late as 1964, then, the Lord Chamberlain not only reinstated the cuts of 1954/5 but added cuts of "The Hard Stool," contemplated but not enforced in 1954/5 (I–37), "arse" (I–27) (for which "backside" was substituted and printed, F&F [1956] 31), and "ballocksed," of which Heriot noted, "This is new [and it was]. It was 'banjaxed' in the original," that is, in the 1954 typescript (II–27) and oddly "banjoed" in the 1957 Samuel French edition (57). Heriot further noted, "At no point during the action of the play must there be any miming of urination or excretion on stage (Lady Howitt complained of this without indicating when it occurred" (LCP Corr 1964/4604).

The ever vigilant Lord Chamberlain's team, principally Sir Troubridge and C. D. Heriot, seem to be calling, on behalf of the Lord Chamberlain (or rather Lady Howitt), for something of what Henry James called a "shy" literature or, more generally, an art "addressed in a large degree to 'young people,' and that this in itself constitutes a presumption that it will be shy" (n.p.). James's focus is primarily on the novel or "the Modern English" novel, but he takes on the general and prevailing Victorian ethos as justification that British fiction, and so all art, finally, ought to have a "conscious moral purpose," a proposition that puzzles James as he notes, "questions of art are questions (in the widest sense) of execution; questions of morality are quite another affair [...]" (n.p.). This is apparently not the case for the Lord Chamberlain's office in post-Victorian, post–Second World War Britain, however. Rather than a mark of strength, individual and national, James found in English fiction "moral timidity of the usual English novelist; with his (or with her) aversion to face the difficulties with which, on every side, the treatment of reality bristles" (n.p.).

## Ghost text to "definitive text"

Between those Faber and Faber copyright dates, the 1956 of the original edition (and subsequent reprints in 1957 and 1959) and the 1962 restoration of Beckett's full text (but not generally available until 1965), a Samuel French Acting Edition appeared in 1957, a much-altered Hall/Snow set now foregrounded and detailed. In fact, the entire text is here much altered. Rather than Beckett's simple, now-iconic "A country road. A tree. Evening," we find the first and third parts of Beckett's description in place, then Hall's (or Hall's team's) expansive rendering: "*A rostrum in the form of a bank or piece of high ground runs back stage [...], with a slope or ramp R leading down to stage level*" (*Godot* [Samuel French] 1). This then is a stage mounted on a stage. "*The bank LC is shaped in the form of a low mound to serve as a seat. On the rostrum C is a leafless tree. There is a tree stump C and an empty tar barrel lies on its side LC*" (*Godot* [Samuel French] 1). This Samuel French edition also contains a full photograph of this Snow set (by Houston Rogers) at the beginning of the play and a detailed sketch of it with a list of props at the end (71). The Samuel French edition opens thus: "*When the Curtain rises, Estragon is seated on the mound, trying to remove one of his boots*" (1). Faber and Faber has Beckett's original, simpler version: "*Estragon, sitting on a low mound, is trying to take off his boot*" (F&F [1956] 9).

In fact, the Samuel French version is filled with what Beckett might call "explicitation." Take Vladimir's initial entrance, for example. In the text published by Faber and Faber (and Grove Press, we might add), we have "*Enter Vladimir*" (F&F [1956] 9, Grove 7). In the Samuel French edition we find a visual emphasis of Vladimir's urination difficulties, "*Vladimir enters up R. with short, stiff strides, his legs wide apart*" (1), a visual image of the lines the Lord Chamberlain had censored. Someone in the British production crew—Hall, Snow, or an eager member of his staff—decided to improve Beckett's prose and to make him a more complete playwright by adding stage and blocking details. As a result, portions of this readily available and much used text are not Beckett's; the performance edition of *Godot* seems to have been improved by professional theater folk. The Samuel French edition then details how added props are to be used, and these directorial notes are printed as part of the text. In Lucky's speech, for example, for some the centerpiece of Act I, the Samuel French text contains blocking details, again, as if they were part of Beckett's text. At first Beckett's description, "*During Lucky's tirade* [...]," is simply cut (F&F [1956] 42; Grove 28); in its place we have the following interventions: "(Vladimir *takes off his hat*)"; "(Pozzo *sits on the barrel*)"; "(Estragon *sits on the stool*)" (Samuel French 29), etc. Evident throughout, then, are not only the alterations imposed by the Lord Chamberlain but alterations or "theatrical improvements" imposed by someone in the Peter Hall company.

One year after the 1964 re-censored, Royal Court production, Faber and Faber finally issued its much-delayed, unexpurgated *Godot*, what it called the "definitive" text. Its publication caused something of a flutter of productions. An Oxford University group submitted the now-published, revised Faber and Faber text, the copyright page for which now reads:

*First published in mcmlvi*
*Reprinted mcmlvi, mcmlvii* [which reprint already anticipates F & F's publication of *All that Fall*], *and mcmlxi* [no mention

here of the 1959 (*mcmlix*) reprint noted in the Royal Court text above.]
*This revised and unexpurgated edition first published mcmlxv* [again, no mention here of the 1962 (*mcmlxii*) reprint noted in the Royal Court text above.]

The Lord Chamberlain's stamp on the endpaper reads October 22, 1964, and the notice of "A New Edition" is printed on the inside flap of the dustcover, which also carries the announcement: "The author has made a number of important revisions to the text of *Waiting for Godot* since it was first published and this new edition, complete and unexpurgated, has been authorized by Mr Beckett as definitive" (LCP 1964/51). The dustcover bears the Lord Chamberlain's form with the identifying number 304, the requesting theater, the Playhouse, Oxford, and is dated October 26, 1965. Permission to perform this newly printed, unexpurgated script in Oxford again was denied, the 1954/5 cuts reimposed, thus:

Date of production, 25 October 1965
Report dated 22 October 1965

This is a performance [at the Oxford Playhouse by the Hertford College Dramatic Society] from the definitive printed edition of the play [i.e., the F&F 1965 edition]. The cuts are the same as for the production by the English Stage Company in 1964 [but that text was a reproduced version or copy of the Faber edition of 1962 that was never published, and hence it remains something of a ghost text].

[Cut] p. 10. Omit the business and speeches about the fly buttons.

[Stipulate] p. 11. Estragon presses his hand to his stomach, *not* his private parts.

[Cut] p. 16. Estragon omits all gestures of encouragement while Vladimir is relieving himself off-stage.

[Cut both] p. 17. Omit "It'd give us an erection" and "and erection!" [*sic*].

[Cut] p. 40. Omit The Hard Stool.[9]

[Alter] p. 43. Omit "Fartov" (Mr. Page used Poppoff [*sic*.])

[Alter] p. 59. Omit "You see, you piss better when I'm not there." (Mr. Page used "You do it better ... ")

[Alter] p. 79. Omit "ballocksed" (Mr. Page used "banjaxed")

[Alter] p. 81. Omit "Who farted?"

[Warn] Also: At no point during the action of the play must there be any miming of urination or excretion on stage.

Otherwise

Recommended for license

[Signed] C. D. Heriot (LCP Corr 1965/304).

In something of a rush, Ian Collyer, writing for the Hertford students, acceded as follows: "I am pleased to say that our director has agreed to all your disallowances and wishes to make no substitutions; and therefore I hope a license for the performance will be issued" (LCP Corr 1965/304). Some two years later, November 7, 1967, Alan Player-Mason wrote the Lord Chamberlain on behalf of the St. Luke's College Dramatic Society (at Oxford) to ask again about the F&F publication of *Godot*, noting that "On page 81 Estragon says 'Who farted?' The directors and myself were concerned as to whether during a public presentation, this might offend the laws of censorship. [...] the disallowances will be observed" (LCP Corr 1965/304). As they were.

## "the start of modern drama"

*Waiting for Godot*'s first British director, Peter Hall, as he assessed this period some forty-two years later while reprising the play in 1997 (opening June 27 and playing through December, with Ben Kingsley and Alan Howard as the principals), saw his 1955 production as a watershed moment of British theater. Hall calls it the "reinvention of British theatre" and "the start of modern drama":

> It is often thought that 1956 and the first night of John Osborne's *Look Back in Anger* was the re-invention of British theatre. Suddenly all young writers saw that they could write for the theatre, and write about now. Out went the slim volumes of verse and the imitations of *Lucky Jim*, and the Royal Court revolution was under way. All this was wonderful, but nonetheless faintly

parochial, which *Godot* wasn't. *Look Back in Anger* now looks a very dated play; it uses the theatre in a very conventional way. [...] By contrast, *Waiting for Godot* hasn't dated at all. It remains a poetic masterpiece transcending all barriers and all nationalities. It is the start of modern drama. (Hall, 1997)

One would not be far off the mark if one saw Hall's assessment as bordering on the grandiose and self-serving, but he is on the mark about the conventionality of *Look Back in Anger*, especially in retrospect. Hall's 1955 Beckett production of *Waiting for Godot* would lead to a call from Tennessee Williams, who had already run afoul of the Lord Chamberlain in 1949 with *A Streetcar Named Desire*, a production directed by Laurence Olivier,[10] which itself might have anticipated the John Osborne "kitchen sink" theatrical revolution. But Hall at least continued and developed that revolution:

One morning the phone rang and a gentle voice from the South announced improbably that it belonged to Tennessee Williams. He had seen *Godot* [in Miami and New York, and had invested in the New York production] and wished to meet me. He gave me the rights to direct his plays in London. (Hall, 1997)

Hall went on to stage a production of *Camino Real*, which opened at the Phoenix Theatre on April 8, 1957, and offered an unexpurgated production of *Cat on a Hot Tin Roof*, but not without doing battle with the Lord Chamberlain once again. With *Cat on a Hot Tin Roof*, Hall would evade the Lord Chamberlain by using the same initial strategy he had with *Godot*. He produced it at a theater "club," first at The Arts Club in November of 1955 and then at the Watergate Theatre Club in January 1958, although the commercial West End production would again be subject to cuts so severe that no commercial license was issued.[11] Hall's *Godot*, then, did at least accelerate profound, postwar European and American influences on the insular British stage that were already in place. Beckett would remain a central part of that cross-channel force, doing battle once again with the Lord Chamberlain over his next play, *Endgame*,[12] in 1957 as the Lord Chamberlain's office seemed determined to ensure that theater, at least, remain shy, genteel, and un-modern, its ethos part of—if not mired in—an earlier age.

# Notes

1   The 1935 essay was commissioned by and written for *The Bookman*,
    which ceased publication before the essay appeared. It was collected
    finally in *Disjecta*, 84–8, reprinted in Carlson (1990), 142–6 (published
    for "Article 19: International Centre on Censorship," a watchdog
    organization named for Article 19 of the 1948 Universal Declaration
    of Human Rights) and discussed in Ó Drisceoil 2011, 294.

2   Writing to John Barber of Curtis Brown on April 29, 1961, Beckett,
    surprised by the production, would try to stop Alan Simpson's
    revival of *Godot* at Stratford East, London, a production billed as
    "uproariously funny": I "do not authorize it. Please tell Mr. Simpson
    to stop his production" (*Letters* 2011, 413n5). Beckett finally
    relented, but with a damning stipulation: no transfer to the West
    End. In 2009, a revival of *Godot* at least in the "uproariously funny"
    tradition that Beckett detested and starring English acting nobility, Sir
    Ian McKellen and Sir Partick Stewart, was wildly successful both in
    London and on world tour that included New York.

3   Given subsequent anomalies and interventions, the first text
    submitted to the Lord Chamberlain, although retyped, is quite close
    to what Faber and Faber would publish as the first edition, excepting
    the excisions from the Faber and Faber text of the alterations finally
    agreed. The page numbering in the Lord Chamberlain reports
    refers to this duplicated script, numbered 6597 on a form glued
    to the cover, "Lord Chamberlain's Office," noting, handwritten,
    "Criterion Theatre," and dated "1.7.54." These stapled pages with
    external, black, vertical, reinforcing-binding are numbered I–2 (page
    I–1 having no designation) through I–54, thence II–2 (again no
    designation for II–1) through II–46. Each of the offending lines is
    marked in the text with a vertical red line in the right margin. At one
    point, some sort of pasted marker was affixed to the top of the pages
    with uncertain material, but those have since been removed, perhaps
    when the red lines were substituted to specify the precise offending
    passages. A red, handwritten number 12 appears in the upper-right-
    hand corner of the bluish-green, semi-soft cover. This text already
    includes the precensored line, "I once knew a family named Gozzo.
    The mother embroidered doilies" (I–16). The censored F&F edition
    of 1956 has "I once knew a family called Gozzo. The mother had
    warts—" (22). Page I–30 also bears an additional late note, numbered
    (1) followed by "All four wear bowlers." This is in the middle of page
    I–30 but refers to the line "Pozzo takes off his hat" on page I–29. The
    note appears at the foot of page 33 in the Faber 1956 edition and is

perhaps in response to the Ian Emmerson drawing on the cover of the Criterion playbill in which one of the tramps wears a stovepipe hat (see above). In Beckett's letter to Charles Monteith of November 15, 1963, he wrote to explaining the note in the text on Bowler hats (and used the occasion to urge Faber and Faber to publish the unexpurgated version of *Waiting for Godot*—see above): "I alone am responsible for the bowlers and the note concerning them" (Beckett *Letters* 2014, 580).

4  We might note that among the blunders associated with this 2010 reprint in the first complete works of Beckett published in the UK, Faber and Faber has the American edition of *Waiting for Godot* listed on the formal copyright page as appearing only in 1974: "First published in the United States in 1974." The American edition appeared from Grove Press in 1954, two years before the 1956 Faber edition, as noted by Bryden in her "Preface" (xi). For a more comprehensive account of Faber and Faber's publishing miscues, see Gontarski, "A Centenary of Missed Opportunities."

5  Details of this reading are available in Knowlson (371), but his conclusion is incorrect: "All to no avail; cuts would have to be made, they were informed, or no license for public performance could be given" (371). The next sentence is ambiguous, "But for production in a public theater cuts still had to be made" (371). This is true, but not the blasphemies, on which the LC had relented. Knowlson's note on the censorship issue refers to a script from Paul Daneman in which the line "'Hmm. It would give us an erection' was added in pencil for the private club production" (Knowlson 1996, 698n134).

6  Much of this material from the Lord Chamberlain's files is now digitalized and available through the British Library; see also: https://amp.theguardian.com/books/2017/sep/11/early-responses-to-waiting-for-godot-showcased-online-samuel-beckett

7  A touring company was established shortly after the Criterion production, produced by Michael Wide and Richard Scott Ltd., directed by Richard Scott. Called in the *Playbill*, "priceless, inimitable [...] the most discussed play in London following its success at the Criterion Theatre" (see listing in World Cat: http://www.worldcat. org/title/michael-wide-and-richard-scott-ltd-present-samuel-becketts-priceless-inimitable-waiting-for-godot-playbill-the-most-discussed-play-in-london-following-its-success-at-the-criterion-theatre/ oclc/50726293), the production played at least at The Birmingham Repertory Theatre (July 9, 1956), The Opera House, Manchester (August 6, 1956), Leeds Grand (August 30, 1956), and The Royal Lyceum Theatre in Edinburgh (1957). The touring production

featured Harold Lang, Michael Hichman, Edward Caddick, and Michael Peak. For more details and a fuller list of tour stops, see McMullan et al. 2014, 11–33; for more details on the "varying interrelated cast" (15) of the touring productions, see McMullan et al. 2014, 30n5.

8  Curiously, in his book-length study, David Bradby omits any serious mention of this production even as Beckett himself was a major consultant on and so a major contributor to it, if not finally its de facto codirector. Likewise, Mark and Juliette Taylor-Batty mention neither Anthony Page nor his Royal Court production, the first production in English with which Beckett was seriously involved.

9  The line remains intact in the 1957 Samuel French Acting Edition, p. 27.

10  For production and hence censorship details, see "On Stage." (Gontarski 2006).

11  First query from The Arts Theatre was in October 29, 1955, by Manager Anne Jenkins, called by Peter Woodthorpe "Donald Albery's Factotum" (Knowlson and Knowlson 2006, 122). The L.C. report by Charles D. Heriot is dated November 2, 1955, and begins thus:

> Once again Mr. Williams vomits up the recurring theme of his not-too-subconscious. This is the fourth play (and there are sure to be others) where we are confronted by the gentlewoman debased, sunk in her private dreams as a remedy for her sexual frustration, and over all the author's horror, disgust and rage against the sexual act. (file LPC CORR 1964/4496)
>     See also, Hope-Wallace, Philip, "*Cat on a Hot Tin Roof* Eludes Censor."

12  See Gontarski (2016b), "'I think this does call for a firm stand.'"

# 5

# "nothingness/in words enclose?": *Waiting for Godot*

Godot *is "the thing [...] in its simplicity, the waiting,
the not knowing why, or where, or when,
or for what."*

*I went to Godot last night for the first time in a long
time. Well played, but how I dislike that play now. Full
house every night, it's a disease. SB to Pamela Michell,
August 18, 1955.*

Almost secreted amid the "Addenda" to Samuel Beckett's second
published novel, *Watt* (Beckett 1959, 247–254)—discards, notes,
scraps and other "precious and illuminating material" that "Only
fatigue and disgust prevent its [the 'Addenda''s] incorporation" into
the body of the text—one finds one of Beckett's most emblematic,
poignant, and accessible poems, one sufficiently trenchant to be
reprinted in various collections of his poetry, particularly in the
splendid variorum compilation, *The Collected Poems of Samuel
Beckett* (Beckett 2012, 109):

who may tell the tale
of the old man?
weigh absence in a scale?
mete want in a span?

the sum assess
of the world's woes?
nothingness
in words enclose?

This untitled, eight-line interrogatory offers a fundamental
challenge to anyone tempted to verbalize his or her insights about
not only *Watt* but the work of Samuel Beckett in general. The most
profound response to the nothingness enclosed in words, that is, the
entire Beckett canon, may finally be silence (a strategy that might
find more sympathy among oriental rather than occidental readers).
And so the most direct approach to *Waiting for Godot* might
simply be silence; the perfect lecture would then be one where the
lecturer stands silently before his auditors for—say—an hour. That
audience might then grow conscious of not only its own heartbeat
and breathing but of the physicality of the act of *waiting*—for
something to happen, for something to break the silence, to relieve
the boredom, the emptiness of the present moment. After a while its
members might begin to look for ways to fill time, to amuse itself.
Individuals might begin to read, talk, doodle, play little games,
but basically the spectators would wait. Audiences generally enter
theaters, lecture halls, classrooms, or bookstores with expectations,
preconceptions about the rituals and even the contents of plays,
lectures, books; that is, we've all internalized cultural codes and
conventions which shape our expectations, and an hour's silence,
rather an hour's worth of random ambient sounds, since even John
Cage's pioneering composition, *4' 33,"* during which a musician
sits before a piano for *precisely* that length of time playing *nothing*,
is not full of silence (and the phrase "full of silence" strikes at the
heart of the paradox). The audience coughs, its members shift
about in their seats, some may get up and walk out, even noisily,
an hour's worth of non-action, non-lecture or anti-lecture, or non-
music certainly disrupts those expectations. Or one might begin
the lecture, then leave the room for a bit, to go to the toilet, say,
as Vladimir does; that too would upset expectations and certainly
cause some tittering. Perhaps the most profound lectures on or
performances of *Waiting for Godot* are those that never take place.
The most significant production of *Waiting for Godot* may not have
been Herbert Blau's 1957 version with the San Francisco Actor's
Workshop which played in San Quentin Prison to an audience of

650 condemned convicts (see also Esslin), or even Samuel Beckett's own mounting of the play performed at the Schiller Theater in Berlin on March 8, 1975, but the production Jan Jonson staged in Stockholm in April of 1986 with "five inmates of the country's top maximum security jail. [...] Four out of five, all drug offenders, absconded through an open dressing room window just before the first night at the City Theatre in Göteborg" (Rosset 2017, 450). For all we know that audience may still be waiting.[1] In something of an echo of the San Francisco Actor's Workshop production, Jonson then restaged a prison performance of *Waiting for Godot* in San Quentin in 1987, but, having learned his lesson, perhaps, kept his prison actors confined within the prison walls (Rosset 217, 450). In his subsequent meeting with Beckett, Jonson responded to Beckett's question, "Why have you done all this," with the following: "I love the silence in your work. I even love the silence in your face ..." (Rosset 2017, 451).

Having already stained the silence myself, to borrow one of Beckett's oft-cited metaphors, I have shown myself without the courage to remain silent. Offered the opportunity to direct the play, moreover, I would no doubt bow to convention and dutifully raise the curtain at the appointed hour and hope that the actors actually appeared. With an absence of occurrence, or rather an occurrence of absence, however, we might have replicated something of the early audience experience of *Waiting for Godot*, a play in which, as Irish critic Vivian Mercier so wittily observed, "nothing happens, twice" ("The Uneventful Event," *The Irish Times*, February 18, 1956, cited in Cronin). We come to theaters to watch *something* happen, prepared for action, so to speak, acts, at any rate. It's what actors do: they "act" or "play." Watching nothing happen, no less twice–can be profoundly unsettling. The trick is in how we read Mercier's aphorism. What *happens* is nothing. Certainly no one leaving City Theater in Göteborg that April evening in 1986 felt that *nothing* had happened, but rather that nothing had *happened*. That is, that audience experienced not an *absence* of happening, but the *happening* of absence, the intense dramatization of nothing, a theme announced in the play's opening line: "Nothing to be done" (Beckett 1954, 7). That is, not only is there no solution to the problems at hand, of tight boots, say, and by extension the plight of humanity in the universe (i.e., in the words of mad Lucky that "in spite of strides in alimentation and defecation [man] wastes and pines" [Beckett 1954, 29]), but what needs to be done during an hour's silence, or the days of our lives, is nothing, the nothingness that is daily life, the nothingness of filling time while we wait, the nothingness which keeps the nothingness within at bay.

When asked by Colin Duckworth about the sources of *Godot*, Beckett suggested that "If you want to find the origins of *En attendant Godot*, look at *Murphy*" (Beckett 1966, xiv). He might have suggested *Watt* as well. The full implications of Beckett's suggestion have yet to be explored by critics who find more immediate links to *Godot* in Beckett's first extended piece of French prose fiction, *Mercier et Camier* (1946). Certainly, one link between *Godot* and *Murphy* is its direct allusion to the Greek philosopher Democritus the Abderite, the laughing philosopher, who proclaimed in his version of atomic theory that air is not mere emptiness. The phrase he used which had become so appealing to Beckett is that "Nothing is more real than nothing." Only after Murphy's chess game with the potential apnoeist, Mr. Endon, can he find some temporary solace in the nothingness:

> Murphy began to see nothing, that colorlessness which is such a rare postnatal treat, being the absence (to abuse a nice distinction) not of *percipere* [to perceive] but of *percipi* [being perceived]. His other senses also found themselves at peace, an unexpected pleasure. Not the numb peace of their own suspension, but the positive peace that comes when the somethings give way, or perhaps simply add up, to the Nothing, than which, in the guffaw of the Abderite, naught is more real. (246)

Murphy's solace in his nothingness is short lived. Even he recoils from an emptiness, from the microcosm he so assiduously sought, drawn back to the music, Music, MUSIC of the macrocosm and Celia. Chance, however, intervenes, and Murphy is atomized into superfine chaos. Didi and Gogo, sobriquets for Vladimir and Estragon, on the other hand, find not even temporary solace but terror in the possibilities of nothing. As Estragon suggests, "Nothing happens, nobody comes, nobody goes, it's awful!" Phrases like "Nothing happens" are, of course, double edged. What the tramps feel is the happening of nothing, nothing as physical entity, and their one hope against it is Godot, ironically the primary, informing absence of the play. In the novel *Watt* the terror is expressed in a phrase which might itself gloss *Godot*: "Nothing had happened, a thing that was nothing had happened, with the utmost formal directness" (73).

Refusing to accept the very indeterminacy and contingency of their plight, and by extension that of all of human existence, Vladimir and Estragon find the ambiguity of nothing to be done, nothing these two tramps, who resemble the tragic comedians of American silent film like Laurel and Hardy, Buster Keaton, and the character whom the French call Charlot, Charlie Chaplin, can do about tight boots, or hair lice, prostrate problems, about their day-to-day lives, about their place in the universe, about an empty universe, about their having been born into it.

Vladimir (Didi) picks up the cosmic implications of Estragon's (Gogo's) complaint, "Nothing to be done," of being unable to remove his boot: "I'm beginning to come around to that opinion. All my life I've tried to put it from me, saying, Vladimir, be reasonable, you haven't yet tried everything. And I resume the struggle" (7).

The play is now over sixty-five years old, having had its premiere at the Théâtre de Babylone in Paris in January of 1953, and it seems almost tamed by its official designation as a modern classic (whatever that oxymoron might mean) and by its inclusion on the lists of set texts in international universities and even secondary schools. Those early audiences, however, were at least divided. Some found it boring, irritating, and incomprehensible. But the play had its early defenders too. The perceptive French dramatist and critic Jean Anouilh compared the premiere of *Godot* to the opening of Pirandello's *Six Characters in Search of an Author* three decades earlier in 1923, and he described this new work as "a music hall sketch of Pascal's *Pensées* as played by the Fratellini clowns" (cited in Graver 2004, 92). In France and England the play received respectful reviews, if rather small audiences. The American premiere, however, was pure farce. It opened at the Coconut Grove Playhouse in Miami Beach, Florida, and it was billed as "the laugh hit of two continents" (cited in Soloski). Audiences of vacationing sun worshippers looking for easy diversion were, to say the least, not amused: "Audiences left in droves, demanding refunds" (Soloski). But America was also the scene of an amazingly apposite early performance. The San Francisco Actor's Workshop took Herbert Blau's production into San Quentin Prison, a maximum-security prison, in November of 1957. While the rest of the world puzzled over the meaning of

Godot—God? Happiness? Eternal Life? Christian salvation? Any sort of salvation? The future (which by definition is never *present*)— the inmates of San Quentin Prison, who in a painfully Beckettian phrase, were "condemned to life," or "got life," understood the play on an immediate, primary, visceral level. For them *Waiting for Godot* was straight realism. Those convicts might not comprehend critical theory, Surrealist or Dada manifestoes, Existential philosophy, or phenomenological aesthetics, but they knew well the waiting game, waiting for change in their condition, waiting for the mail, for appeals, for pardons. Waiting and having nothing happen, and so having to fill the time. As the inmate reviewer for the *San Quentin News* of November 28, 1957, wrote, "It asked nothing in point. It forced no dramatized moral on the viewer, it held out no specific hope. [...] We're still waiting for Godot, and shall continue to wait. When the scenery gets too drab and the action too slow, we'll call each other names and swear to part forever but then there's no place to go" (Esslin 1987, 26). "That's how it is on this bitch of an earth," says Pozzo (Beckett 1954, 25b).

In the aftermath of *Godot*, theater conventions have never been the same. It was one of those culture-altering artworks that changes the way we see the world around us. It was so unexpected a play, and yet it now seems so inevitable, so necessary. It captured something which perhaps had never been staged before, even as there was nothing new about it. Its elements have been imbedded in our Judeo-Christian, Western culture for thousands of years, if not always realized in art. As Vladimir says early on, "Hope deferred maketh the something sick, who said that?" (Beckett 1954, 8). The allusion is to the wisdom literature of the Old Testament traditionally attributed to Solomon, Proverbs XIII, 12: "Hope deferred maketh the heart sick; but when desire cometh, it is a tree of life." The tree stands before us on stage, leafless and so apparently lifeless in the first act, but with "four or five leaves" in the second. The tree of life looks suspiciously at first like the tree of death, especially as Vladimir and Estragon plan to commit suicide by hanging themselves from its boughs. The tree, however, does sprout leaves in the second act, perhaps even overnight. It thus suggests at least a minimum degree of vitality in a place or a space otherwise arid. Where trees sprout leaves, that is, when life still changes, when time passes, hope remains. To Vladimir's "Time has stopped," Pozzo replies almost brutally, "Don't you believe it, Sir, don't you believe it .... Whatever you like, but not that" (Beckett 1954, 24b). In his 1981 prose work, *Company*, Beckett returned to the quotation from Proverbs with a bit more optimism, "Better hope deferred than none," qualified almost immediately with, "Up to a point" (26). But as Beckett suggested in the opening of his study of the French novelist Marcel Proust, time is "a double headed monster of damnation and salvation." The passing of time may fuel hope, but in its passing humanity deteriorates, physically "wastes and pines."

But if we focus on one head at a time, we can find in Lamentations III, 26, "It is good that man should both hope and quietly wait for the salvation of the Lord." In Romans VIII, 24–5, however, we learn that the process of waiting, in order to have meaning, *must* be elusive, irresolute, nothing; salvation and hope remain, must remain out of reach like water from the parched lips of Tantalus: "We are saved by hope: but hope that is seen is not hope; for what a man seeth, why doth he yet hope for? But if we hope for that we see not, then do we with patience wait for it." "We are saved by hope," says the author or authors of Romans; in *Molloy*, Moran calls it "hellish hope." Beckett's two tramps waiting on stage may have initiated a fundamentally new sort of drama, but its concerns, its themes, are at least as old as the Western Judeo-Christian tradition.

Psalm 40 begins, "I waited patiently for the Lord; he inclined to me and heard my cry. He drew me up from the desolate pit, out of the miry bog and set my feet upon a rock, making my steps secure." In fulfilment of that prophecy in the New Testament, the rock was Simon Peter, the foundation of the Christian church, the first in line of the apostolic succession. Beckett parodies this imagery in Lucky's speech where the labors of two rocks, Steinweg (stone road in German) and Peterman (i.e., Rockman), are "lost." The rock upon which the hope of the world was to be built has become a waste land, as in the third section of Lucky's speech where the theme "earth abode of stones" is repeated four times and alluded to at least twice more. But the theme of waiting is not only biblical. It has as well entered our popular culture. An advertising campaign for a popular brand of chewing gum dispensed through machines in the Paris Métro was visible at every Metro stop. It said simply, "En attendant ...." One could easily picture a traveling Beckett confronted by the elliptical slogan, stop after stop after stop, and wondering, "while waiting for what?"

One reading of *Waiting for Godot* sees the play as an autobiographical account of Beckett's and his future wife Susanne's flight from Paris to the Vaucluse, during which journey they slept by day in haystacks and walked all night, tired, hungry, and without food. The autobiographical reading is plausible since *Godot* contains at least one allusion to the Roussillon exile, a man called Bonnelley, from whom Beckett occasionally got food, but the play is fundamentally about emptiness and stasis, not an arduous journey. Some of the dialogue and the strains of hiding from the Nazis may have been borrowed from the escape to unoccupied France, but the core of the play, the stasis, the uncertainty, the emptiness, the difficulty of filling time, indeed the waiting, must have come from another source. A more plausible possibility is the one suggested by Beckett's close friend and English publisher, John Calder, who offers an alternate autobiographical interpretation. Despite his fluent French, Beckett would be easily identified as an alien during his exile because of his Irish accent, and even if Beckett had little to fear from the local representatives of the Pètain government, Hitler violated his agreement with the Vichy government in order to help protect his southern flank from an expected allied invasion and ordered the seizure of unoccupied France on November 10, 1942. From then until the Americans entered Roussillon on August 24, 1944, Beckett was in considerable danger despite his Irish passport, Ireland having remained neutral during the Second World War. The threat of German patrols passing through the region would send Beckett and perhaps Susanne, or more likely another alien like Henri Hayden, a Polish jew, who would be in danger even from local collaborators sympathetic to Hitler's Jewish policies, to hide in the forest and wait, sometimes for days, for word to return. Hiding in the woods and fields, confused about potential rendezvous sites, perhaps even forgetting code words whispered during a lunch break or across café tables, they never knew when they heard someone approach whether it would be a Nazi patrol, French collaborators, or friendly villagers. But finally what is of most concern is less the character of the author than the characters in the drama.

What finally are we to make of our waiters? Are they simply foolish, maintaining hope in the face of overwhelming evidence to the contrary, the thrust of the work, finally, satiric? Or, quite the contrary, are the waiters the very epitome of Christianity, the imagery of which permeates the play, maintaining at least as much faith as Job, maintaining hope in the face of overwhelming evidence to the contrary? To each of those questions Beckett might simply answer, "perhaps," the most important word in his plays, he told one interviewer. And the questions are further complicated by other developing themes. Even if salvation were available its dispensation seems arbitrary, depending more on chance, opportunities of the moment, than on anything like lifetime commitment. Vladimir refers to the Gospel according to Saint Luke XXIII, 39–43, when he suggests that "one of the thieves" crucified with Christ "was saved. It's a reasonable percentage" (Beckett 1954, 8b) he concludes, that is, 50/50. In *Murphy*, Neary cites the tale of the saved thief as solace, "and do not despair. ... Remember also one thief was saved" (213). Yet the more reflection Vladimir gives the matter the more he realizes that the odds are considerably slimmer than 50/50. Only one of the four Gospels mentions the saved thief even though all four of the Apostles were there, or thereabouts. Now it's 50 percent of 25 percent, one of the four. And even when salvation appears possible, its dispensation seems arbitrary. Was one thief saved or not? One Gospel says yes, one says no. Were any thieves at all crucified along with Christ? Two Gospels say yes, two suggest perhaps not. This salvation business seems very much a crapshoot, as chancy as one of Estragon's feet being in pain, the other functioning well, pain free. Of this dilemma Beckett has said, only half jokingly, that one of Estragon's feet is saved, one is damned. And if one thief was saved, why? Was salvation dependent on a chance remark issued forth in the midst of torture, which is, after all, what crucifixion was, a means of slow self-strangulation.

The pattern of reward and punishment seems arbitrary throughout the play. Estragon spends the night in a ditch where he is beaten evidently regularly for unspecified offenses. Further, near the end of the first act Vladimir asks what appears to be Godot's messenger about his master. "He doesn't beat you?" "He beats my brother, Sir," the boy replies (Beckett 1954, 33b). In Beckett's inversion of the biblical story, it is the minder of the goats who is spared, the minder of the sheep who is punished. In the traditional version in the "Gospel According to St. Matthew" XXV, 32–3, the shepherd is saved, the goatherd punished. Beckett's reversal again throws into high relief the arbitrary nature of the whole system of rewards and punishment, salvation and damnation. Even if Godot arrived, his actions would be unpredictable. "And if we dropped him?" Estragon asks. "He'd punish us," Vladimir replies. A few lines later, to Estragon's, "And if he comes?" Vladimir replies, "We'll be saved." But saved from what? When Vladimir suggests that they might repent, Estragon is confused, "Repent what? [...] Our being born?" (Beckett 1954, 8b). But, of course, it is too late for that.

That sort of deep existential pessimism, if not nihilism, is not, however, peculiar to modern man's alienation and angst. The comment is simply a restatement of the traditional Christian view of this world as a place of suffering, a vale of tears, a *via dolorosa*. But it is also the dark side of Hellenic culture, an element of what Nietzsche would call its Dionysian quality. In *The Birth of Tragedy from the Spirit of Music*, Nietzsche quotes the exchange between Midas and Silenus, companion to Dionysus. When Silenus finally fell into Midas's hands, Midas forced him to reveal what was "best and most desirable of all things for man." Silenus answered, "oh wretched ephemeral race, children of chance and misery, why do ye compel me to tell you what it were most expedient for you not to hear? What is best of all is beyond your reach forever: not to be born, not to be, to be *nothing*. But the second best for you is quickly to die" (Nietzche 1995, 8). Such a view is not only a theme in *Godot*, it is Beckett's view of tragedy.

But *Waiting for Godot* is not only somber tragedy. Beckett calls this work a tragi-comedy. Its sources are the tradition of harlequin in tears, *Il Pagliacci*, Charlie Chaplin's sad clowns. Such is the view proposed by Schopenhauer described in decidedly theatrical terms. "Viewed overall and in a general manner and extracting only the most significant features, the life of every individual," Schopenhauer notes, offering us something of a definition of what Beckett will call "tragi-comedy"

> is in fact always a tragedy; but worked through in detail, it has the character of a comedy. The urges and the nuisances of the day, the restless taunts of the minute, the hopes and fears of the week, the accidents of every hour, all of which are brought about by chance playing practical jokes—these are true comic scenes. But the unfulfilled desires, the thwarted striving, the hopes that have been mercilessly crushed by fate, the fatal errors of the whole of life, with increased suffering and then death at the end, this always makes for tragedy. So as if fate wanted to add mockery to the misery of our existence, our lives have to contain all the

grief of tragedy, but we can not even assert out dignity as tragic players [evident most directly in Hamm's opening remarks, for instance]; instead in the expanse of life's details we cannot escape the roles of foolish comic characters. (Schopenhauer 2010, 348)

Yet, in the face of such insufficient justification for or redemption of humanity's suffering, amid suggestions of the arbitrary, capricious salvation, Vladimir, at any rate, steadfastly retains hope, his hope for and faith in a rational world. To Estragon's insistence that he "wasn't doing anything" and yet he was beaten, Vladimir play's the role of "Job's comforter," "But it's the way of doing it that counts, the way of doing it" (Beckett 1954, 38b). Vladimir insists that Estragon's beatings are caused by some offensive behavior. For him, the world is causal and so rational.

The odds against salvation are further increased through the uncertainties of identity. What exactly would Godot look like if he did arrive? Would he (she?) be recognizable? Would he recognize Didi and Gogo? He would certainly not simply identify himself to every stranger he met along the road like a parody of a contemporary politician. Might it not be possible for him to arrive and depart without their and our knowing it. After all, few recognized the face of salvation when it appeared some two thousand years ago. And Beckett himself entertained the possibility in an early draft of the play that Pozzo might himself be Godot. But even in the published text some hints to Godot's identity can be teased out of the shroud of uncertainty which envelopes the play. When Pozzo first appears, for instance, his name sounds enough like Godot for Estragon to say, "He said Godot." And Didi and Gogo are quite capable of mishearing names. Even Vladimir is unsure if the name of the visitor is "Pozzo or Bozzo?" (Beckett 1954, 15b). And it is Pozzo who admits, "I am perhaps not particularly human" (Beckett 1954, 19b) (again, *perhaps*). Does he mean only that he is a slave master, or something more divine? And once Pozzo and Lucky leave, Vladimir notes, as if he knew them, "How they've changed!" and insists to Estragon, "Yes, you do know them. ... We know them, I tell you. You forget everything. ... Unless they're not the same." Estragon is curious as to why Pozzo and Lucky did not recognize them. "That means nothing," Vladimir replies, "I too pretended not to recognize them. And then nobody ever recognizes us" (Beckett 1954, 32). Shortly thereafter, in an apparent development of Vladimir's insight, a boy appears, and Vladimir answers to the name of Mr. Albert. Is he indeed Vladimir Albert or Albert Vladimir? Did the boy mistake him for someone else? Does Vladimir know himself who he is? Perhaps he is finally more representative than individual. He may be Man(kind) and so can answer to any name. To calls for help from Pozzo in the second act Vladimir intones "Vehemently," "To all mankind they were addressed, those cries for help still ringing in our ears! But at this place, at this moment of time, all mankind is us, whether we like it or not." Further, to Pozzo's "What is your name," Estragon answers, "Adam" (Beckett 1954, 25).

The vessel of personality here seems fractured as being seeps, oozes beyond traditional containment. When after their second encounter with Pozzo and Lucky, in Act II, Estragon asks, "Are you sure it wasn't him?" [i.e., Godot], Vladimir answers, "Not at all! (*Less sure.*) Not at all! (*Still less sure.*) Not at all" (Beckett 1954, 58). And we are not always certain that Vladimir and Estragon themselves are independent entities. Each act ends with "Yes, let's go," followed by the stage direction, "*They do not move*" (Beckett 1954, 35b, 60b). Vladimir and Estragon are tied to each other as securely as they are tied to Godot, as tightly as Lucky to Pozzo. Admittedly, they move about the stage more or less freely, but they enjoy only the freedom of two arms attached to a single trunk. The phrase that Beckett used to talk about *Mercier and Camier* applies here too, "a pseudo couple." Vladimir and Estragon might thus be seen as two aspects of a single entity, the mental and the physical, for instance, a dichotomy in keeping with Beckett's early interest in and critique of Cartesian dualism. Personality is as problematic in the play as is the identity of Godot.

Our discussion has moved from the problematics of salvation to the problematics of identity and personality, and yet they are sides of the same epistemological coin. They both entail the search for core realities, the absence of which destroys so many of Beckett's characters, like Watt and Moran, who cannot face the fact that reality may be, like the core of the onion or the center of a whirlpool, an absence. In fact, the line separating dream from what we commonly call reality (if indeed there is a distinction) is not always clear. Vladimir suggests the problem near the play's end:

Was I sleeping while the others suffered? Am I sleeping now? Tomorrow, when I wake, or think I do what shall I say of today?

That with Estragon my friend, at this place, until the fall of night,
I waited for Godot? That Pozzo passed with his carrier, and that
he spoke to us? Probably. But in all that what truth will there be?
(Beckett 1954, 58)

The comment is remarkable for questioning the veracity of what
we have just witnessed on stage. In fact the whole landscape has a
dreamlike quality to it. The Moon rises "in a moment"; trees sprout
leaves overnight. Pozzo and Lucky go blind and dumb respectively,
overnight! To Vladimir's insistence that they were in the same spot
yesterday, Estragon replies, "I tell you we weren't here yesterday.
Another of your nightmares" (Beckett 1954, 42b). If nightmare,
however, it seems to recur nightly. In Act I, Estragon falls asleep
and dreams. When Vladimir wakes him, Estragon wants to relate
his dream, but Vladimir insists, "Don't tell me!" Estragon's reply
as he "gestures toward universe," is, "This one [i. e. this dream] is
not enough for you?" (Beckett 1954, 11). To Vladimir's, "Do you
remember [the tree]," Estragon replies, "You dreamt it" (Beckett
1954, 39).
   But this dream world of *Godot* is no simple hierarchical
dichotomy between dream and reality. Neither of those terms is
privileged. Nor is the dream single, but we have dreams within
dreams suggesting an infinite regression and progression, as the two
acts of the play are but two days of a greater series. Asked why two
acts for *Godot*, Beckett replied that one would be too few, three too
many. Vladimir looking again at the sleeping, dreaming Estragon
can say, "At me too someone is looking, of me too someone is
saying, He is sleeping, he knows nothing, let him sleep on" (Beckett
1954, 58b). Instead of a simple dream/reality dichotomy we have
a multiplicity of interpenetrating dreams, all of which displace our
epistemological grounding.
   Moreover, the nightmare motif also helps explain the fluidity
of time, which at times appears almost to have stopped, but at
other times races forward so that Pozzo, having lost his watch, can
scream, "Have you not done tormenting me with your accursed
time! It's abominable! When! When! One day, is that not enough
for you, one day I went blind, one day we'll go deaf, one day we
were born, one day we shall die, the same day, the same second,
is that not enough for you. They give birth astride of a grave, the
light gleams an instant, then it is night once more" (Beckett 1954,

57b). Shortly thereafter, Vladimir resounds the theme: "Astride of a grave and a difficult birth. Down in the hole, lingeringly, the grave digger puts on the forceps" (Beckett 1954, 58). In *Godot*, time seems much more subjective than objective, much more personal and psychological than chronological.

And still they wait; they remain faithful. For Kierkegarrd, reason could only take us so far, to the edge of the precipice. What was necessary then was a great leap, of faith. That leap toward belief is unsupported by any empirical evidence. It is a reason-transcending leap, and one must choose to leap or not. It is, as the title of one of Kierkegaard's books suggests, *Either/Or*. That leap by definition is irrational, absurd.[2] Likewise, the empirical evidence of the play suggests that waiting is absurd, irrational. The tramps don't really know what Godot looks like. They are to meet him by "the tree," but is the plant conspicuously before them mid-stage a tree at all and not rather a shrub or a bush. Vladimir asks, "What are you insinuating? That we've come to the wrong place?" "He should be here," Estragon replies, and Vladimir is forced to admit, "He didn't say for sure he'd come" (Beckett 1954, 10). The tramps have apparently been waiting for days, that is, the two nearly identical acts, the fact that nothing happens twice, suggests that they are caught in a cyclical existence, and yet no Godot, or, perhaps, no Godot yet. There seems no rational reason for their continued waiting, and yet they wait, for this is what faith means: to hold a belief when empirical evidence is insufficient to substantiate it. Doubting Thomas seems to have had no faith. If evidence were available, there would be no need for faith. We would have knowledge. Vladimir and Estragon have made the great leap of faith into absurdity, into unreason, not that they have many alternatives, and that leap is spine chilling. Amid all the epistemological uncertainties of the play, the one certainty seems to be their faithfulness: "*What are we doing here*," Vladimir intones, a bit too poetically, "*that* is the question. And we are blessed in this, that we happen to know the answer. Yes, in this immense confusion one thing alone is clear. We are waiting for Godot to come." And then he immediately halves his certainty, "Or for night to fall. ... We have kept out appointment and that's an end to that. We are not saints, but we have kept our appointment. How many people can boast as much?" The apparent seriousness of Vladimir's assertions is immediately undercut with Estragon's "Billions" (Beckett 1954, 51b). That is, they are not so very exceptional. Is this faith, this persistence of belief in the face of overwhelming evidence to the contrary, heroic or foolish? Do our tramps embody a Christian ideal or an existential foolhardiness? Are the two tramps to be admired or derided? The play offers no more answer to such questions than does life itself. But the play does contain strong elements of satire. Vladimir's speech on their faithful waiting is delivered while Lucky and Pozzo are crying for help. The longish speech begins with the advice, "Let us not waste our time in idle discourse!" (Beckett 1954, 51). And yet he does. Cries of help, of humanity in distress, punctuate Vladimir's pronouncements: "All I know is that the hours are long, under these conditions, and constrain us to beguile them with proceedings which how shall I say which may at first sight seem reasonable, until they become habit" (Beckett 1954, 51b). What we have here is another example of the inability of the intellectual to act, a fault that may in part also account for Lucky's imprisonment. What finally entices Vladimir to action is not reason nor any concern for humanity, but the promise of payment. Vladimir's deliberations in the face of immediate appeals from a suffering humanity finally reinforce again the problematics of salvation and satirize the impotence of the intellectual. The other ineffectual thinker in the play, the other obviously impotent character, is Lucky, a strange name for a slave, and yet, apt. Within the epistemological uncertainties of the universe where an apparently personal God "loves us dearly with some exceptions," where, as Beckett himself describes the first part of Lucky's speech (Beckett 1954, 28b–29b), it is about "the indifference of heaven, about divine apathy." The second part is, he tells us, about "man shrinking ... man who is dwindling." The third is "earth abode of stones." If Vladimir and Estragon are "blessed" in their knowledge that they are waiting for Godot, Lucky too is "blessed," blessed as perhaps only one could be blessed in an absurd world, he is "blessed" or "lucky" that amid an uncertain, indifferent universe where God functions "from the heights of divine apathia," where human reason has made no progress in solving the fundamental questions of human existence like who are we and what are we doing here?; that is, incidentally, why we euphemistically call the themes of the Greek drama "universal"; we simply have not been able to solve those fundamental human problems. Within universal flux and social chaos, Lucky is lucky to know that he has a place, a definite function: to carry the bags and obey the orders of Pozzo, even if the bags are only filled with sand. And he is "lucky" that Pozzo will have him at all. "The truth is," says Pozzo, "you can't drive such creatures away. The best thing would be to kill them" (Beckett 1954, 21b).

Despite the play's questioning of the nature and purpose of human existence, it is fundamentally not an existential play, or rather, it is existential, miniscule not majuscule. One of the tenets of Existentialism, at least as it is defined by Jean-Paul Sartre in his essay "Existentialism is a Humanism," is freedom. Man enters the world without essence and is free to define himself. But Beckett's play is about imprisonment and impotence, not about the power of self to create itself. *Waiting for Godot* is about being tied, sometimes visibly with a rope as Lucky to Pozzo, but also Pozzo to Lucky, sometimes invisibly but just as firmly, by cosmic and/or cultural forces as Didi to Gogo, as both to Godot. Moreover, the theme of restriction, of restraint is sounded as well in the minor key. Estragon who is formally tied to Vladimir but less so to Godot rejects the restrictions of having his shoes laced. "No, no, no," he shouts, "no laces, no laces!" (Beckett 1954, 44). And the theme of Lucky's dance is the net. "He thinks he's entangled in a net" (Beckett 1954, 27), says Pozzo. Vladimir and Estragon are the victims of expectations, victims of hope, but hope in others not in themselves. And so they are tied. And yet, perhaps they choose to be helpless, choose to make the existential leap of faith, choose freely their own lack of choice and freedom. Are these characters existentially free or determined, biologically, culturally, or theologically? Again the play has no firmer answer than does life itself.

One way out for our trapped characters might be death. "What about hanging ourselves?" asks Estragon, and he is excited to hear that hanging might give them an erection. Freud makes a similar point in the *Interpretation of Dreams* analyzing the "May-beetle dream" where he notes that a female patient has told her husband "'Go hang Yourself.' It turned out that a few hours earlier she had read somewhere or other that when a man is hanged, he gets a powerful erection" (Freud 1965, 326). But what was finally a life-affirming dream in Freud's analysis becomes another inevitable disappointment in Beckett. Even if that were the case, the result would also be sadness, a post ejaculatory depression. Of Estragon's excitation about the possibilities of erection, Vladimir says, "With all that follows. Where it falls mandrakes grow. That's why they shriek when you pull them up." Vladimir's associations with sexuality hardly suggest joy or the affirmation of life.

There are practical as well as ethical problems with suicide, moreover. The bough of the flimsy tree would never support them. The rope would surely break. They could not even jump, "Hand in hand from the top of the Eiffel Tower" (Beckett 1954, 7b), for now, looking like bums, they would not even be allowed up the edifice: "We were respectable in those days. Now it's too late" (Beckett 1954, 7b). Moreover, suicide, as Schopenhauer reminds us, is a useless act since it has no effect on the plight of humanity:

> Suicide is related to the negation of the will in the same way that the individual thing is related to the Idea. The person who commits suicide negates only the individual not the species. We have already found that for the will to life, life is always a certainty, and suffering is essential to life, so it follows that suicide, the willful destruction of one single appearance that leaves the thing in itself untouched […] is a futile and foolish act. (Schopenhauer 2010, 426)

General editor of the Cambridge Schopenhauer, Christopher Janaway, glosses the issue thus: "The person who commits suicide because he has suffered greatly and sees no fulfilment in the world for his striving, is deluded: he still regards fulfilment of his individual strivings as something in principle attainable and valuable. Greatly superior to this is continuing to exist with an attitude of resignation in the face of all suffering" (Cf. Sisyphus) (Schopenhauer 2010, xxxviii–xxxix). While Schopenhauer critiques an individual's behavior and action, his emphasis remains finally on the "transcendental." As Janaway continues,

> In a letter to one of his most philosophically astute correspondents, Johann August Becker, Schopenhauer explains that the value moral actions have for the one who performs them is a 'transcendental' one; such actions lead him on 'the sole path of salvation, i.e. deliverance from this world of being born, suffering and dying.' The person who is so morally good that the distinction between him- or herself and others begins to fall away, feels all the suffering throughout the world as if it were his

or her own. This leads to resignation, tranquillizing of the will, or its recoil away from life. (Schopenhauer 2010, xxxix)

And Vladimir at least is concerned with the ethics of how the two represent the species: "Let us represent worthily for once the foul brood to which a cruel fate has consigned us" (Beckett 1954, 51).

Any number of ethical, theological, and philosophical themes thus wind through and interconnect or overlap in *Waiting for Godot*: the problematics surrounding salvation, the ethics of human behavior, issues of epistemology, time, and being itself, but the play engages politics as well. Beckett is rarely thought of as a political writer, and rightly so in the most overt, agitprop way. He is not political the way, say, Jean-Paul Sartre or Bertolt Brecht is, but a power struggle is going on in *Waiting for Godot*. Making people wait is itself an exercise in power. When the telephone company puts us on hold when we call, when doctors or professors are half hour late for an appointment, they are exercising their power. The waiter is powerless, the menial. The assumption within this power paradigm is that the waiter's time is valueless. The words themselves, *waiters, attendants*, what used to be *ladies in waiting*, are ideological.

Finally, what are we to make of this Samuel Beckett. Is he merely the poet of doom and depression, of human worthlessness, of pure pessimism, pure darkness? Is Beckett a poet without alternatives? He is perhaps finally no more pessimistic than the late Beethoven or the brooding Brahms whose pessimism is expressed within the harmonious formal structures of music. Hope in Beckett, some cause for optimism, and these are words that admittedly one does not often use in regard to Beckett's work, resides not within the systems man has traditionally used to order his life, religion, law, any political system, or even language itself, but in the formal, essential, transcending artwork. Despite the epistemological uncertainties and pessimism of *Godot*, we have the play itself, this elegant tribute to tomorrow, a sublime transcendence of its own themes. Played against the epistemological and existential uncertainties in the text is the text itself, a formal balanced exposition of absence and chaos in the face of which humanity continues. If the play is a nothing, it is a beautifully shaped nothing, in nearly symmetrical halves. Beckett's view of art may be close to that expressed by Nietzsche in *The Birth of Tragedy out of the Spirit of Music*: "when the will is most imperiled, art approaches, as a redeeming and healing enchantress; she alone may transform these horrible reflections on the terror and absurdity of existence into representations with which man may live. These are the representations of the *sublime* as the artistic conquest of the awful, and of the *comic* as the artistic release from the nausea of the absurd" (Nietzsche 1995, 23).

# Notes

1   "Audience Wait and Wait for Prison Godots," *The Times* (April 31, 1986).

2   For an exceptional reading of Kierkegaard, see Boris Groys, Chapter 1, "Soren Kierkegaard," *An Introduction to Antiphilosophy*, 2–32.

# 6

# An End to Endings: Samuel Beckett's End Game(s)

*If happiness or if, in some sense or other, a reaching*
*out for new happiness is what holds the living onto*
*life and pushes them forward into life, then perhaps*
*no philosopher has more justification than the cynic.*
*(Friedrich Nietzsche, "On the Use and Abuse of*
*History for Life" [1873])*

No, there are no accidents in Endgame, it is all built on
analogies and repetitions. (Beckett in Berlin)

*Endless ending breath. "Ceiling," For Avigdor 1981.*

Those of us who spend much of our professional lives exploring
the profound depths of Samuel Beckett's work need on occasion
to remind ourselves of its direct simplicity, often signaled by the
unexpected bluntness of Beckett's titles. *Waiting for Godot* is, after
all, a play about waiting, which may be the most common social
activity of our lives. It is an image of life paused, "on hold," as it
were, where indeed we spend most of our lives. The French title of
the play, *En attendant Godot*, accents the burden of waiting in its
title more directly than does the English. The title might well have
been rendered into English as **While** *Waiting for Godot* (as it is

in Japanese, say), but Beckett omitted the adverb from his English translation. The titular emphasis on time, "while," may have resonated more with those members of the French audience who may remember a popular brand of chewing gum sold through Métro vending machines for many years with the slogan, "En attendant ...," "While waiting ...." The two-word teaser focuses attention on the inaction of waiting—in this case for a train at least—and hints at some remedy to the implied boredom of nothing happening. But if one were on "A country road" and not in a Métro station, as the text tells us Vladimir and Estragon are, one might well wait forever for that train, with no chewing gum to break the boredom and help time pass. What then to do while waiting on that road, and, of course, therein lies much of Beckett's innovation, turning the most ordinary of human activities into the extraordinary, turning life's simplest action on its head—inaction as the action of our lives. And so the waiting for Godot is not *prelude* to some major event or action; it is that event or action itself.

The characters of *Endgame* are, quite simply, still waiting, if only for an end to waiting, as Hamm shouts "Let it end then ... with a bang (Beckett 1958, 77)." If end does indeed come in this play, it does so not with a bang but a whimper, to borrow the climactic phrase from T. S. Eliot's poem, "The Hollow Men." Like its predecessor, the preoccupation of *Endgame* is bluntly announced in its title, which Beckett thought to hyphenate as *End-Game* until just before the American text went to press. The original Faber and Faber text retains the hyphen. The play begins with Clov's announcing that end as almost a direct pronouncement to the audience (for, after all, whom else might Clov be addressing, since the rest of this happy family sleeps): "Finished, it's finished, nearly finished, it must be nearly finished" (Beckett 1958, 1), he tells us. It is a recitation from the play's opening words of what Hamm will summarize near its end, as if beginnings and endings have not so much been reversed as redoubled, the play ending where it began, with its ending. One complication in this *Endgame*, then, is not that the play has no ending, but that it has too many, or that it has only endings. Hamm may say, "It's the end, Clov, we've come to the end. I don't need you any more" (Beckett 1958, 79), but he might say this at almost any point in the play. Moreover, he also tells us that "The end is in the beginning," and knowing that, somehow, "you go on" (Beckett 1958, 69). That sense of doubled endings may call to mind one of

Beckett's favorite jokes: everything has an end—except, goes the punch line, the sausage. It has two, and one at either end, we might add so which might be the beginning, which the end is indeterminate. It takes us some while into the play to realize such doubleness, the doubling of endings; that is, Clov opens the play not only with its first ending, but with a plagiary as well, making his announcement in words not his own. At the very beginning of the play, the *Beginning to End*, as Beckett entitled a series of recorded readings by one of his favorite actors, Jack MacGowran, Clov is already an echo of innumerable other games, of countless previous performances, of speech he has heard with uncountable frequency—and we hear it *as if* for the first time. Like most actors, Clov, an actor playing an actor, is mouthing the words of another. If Hamm were awake, he would certainly realize that his carefully crafted diction has been appropriated, if the words were Hamm's to begin with, and that Clov may be rehearsing his future, on stage, before us, like an understudy anticipating his turn to sit on the throne and make such grandiose pronouncements—"preluding" Beckett called such performance in anticipation of performance in *The Unnamable*. The implication from the play's first words is thus of a possible succession, a turn from the steady decline of life catapulting toward its end, to a return to the end that is a beginning, some form of regeneration, if only in the recycling of words and images, as in all theatrical performance. Like all actors, Clov has almost no language of his own, is always already an echo.

From his opening announcement of an end, Clov might then offer some exposition, some detail of what exactly is finished: the morning ritual, the day itself (which has apparently just begun, if days begin or end at all in this world without end, with the unveiling, though Hamm wants to be recovered, to go back to sleep, that is, to end the day, almost immediately once he's awake). But exposition suggests a middle, something that comes between a beginning and an end. With only end or ends, there is no place for a middle. What comes in the middle are perhaps more ends.

More apocalyptically, Clov announces (or repeats Hamm's vision of) an end to their physical existence, to all physical existence, to time itself. That would be the "bang" Hamm so desires since it would be a retrospective look at the whole of a life and so give it some meaning. And Clov might offer an explanation of daily life in the shelter, the "day after day" alluded to in the play, if he indeed had a

r voice of his own. But he does not, and such revelation is
written. Clov can, of course, only recite what is already
written, or at least given. The biblical injunction in John I:1 that "In
the beginning was the word" might be restated, with only a slight
shift of emphasis, as "In the beginning was the word, there already."
Instead of exposition then, Clov repeats additional stolen language,
Hamm's metaphor of the grains and the heap, a philosophical
paradox: "Grain upon grain, one by one, and one day, suddenly,
there's a heap, a little heap, the impossible heap" (Beckett 1958, 1).
The allusion is admittedly arcane; nonetheless, it provides much of
the underpinning to this play. The mantra that Clov has absorbed
and now reiterates is the paradox of the one and the many or the
part and the whole, that is, that the part is already the whole, or
that the whole has nothing to add to the smallest part, the single
grain already the heap, the single instant of experience already the
whole of a life. As Hamm puts it, "Moments for nothing, now as
always, time was never and time is over, reconing closed and story
ended," at which point Hamm beins his story anew (Beckett 1958,
83). Clov's repetition or echo at the opening of the play of what
is essentially Hamm's metaphor (that is, Hamm's or the Eleatic
philosopher Zeno's or whomever Zeno is echoing) renders the issue
of time in terms of wholeness, as a heap of grain, a life: at what
point does one individual grain added to other individual grains
add up to a whole, a discrete singularity that we might call a heap?
At whatever point we agree on heapness, its definition relies on
the one, single grain, the last grain added. Subsequent grains add
nothing to that notion of heapness, except perhaps to extend it, to
enlarge it, to repeat it, but not to alter its wholeness, its heapness. In
the literary echo of the paradox, we are left to ponder the paradox
of literary fragments: at what point do separate fragments, without
clear end, perhaps, added to other fragments, also without end, add
up to what we might call a work of art, a play, perhaps, or in Hamm's
case a life chronicle, that is, at what point is Hamm's story finished,
ended? At what point does it, like his life, achieve a wholeness, a
totality, its heapness. Hamm himself states the paradox in terms
of ontology—at what point do separate moments of existence,
piling toward a heap, add up to a life, "And all life long you wait
for that to mount up to a life" (Beckett 1958, 70), he muses. That
conception of not just the metonymy or synecdoche, the part, some
part, representing the whole but, more radically, the part as coeval

with the whole, informs much of Beckett's art of the fragment, an art of incompletion, an art for which endings are superfluous since they already exist in the instant of beginning. Hamm's repetition of the paradox at the end of the play, then, underscores the fact that Clov's opening is already Hamm speaking, as if already from the dead, is already the whole of the play, beginning and end. Later Clov snaps at Hamm's objection to his language with, "I use the words you taught me. If they don't mean anything any more, teach me others. Or let me be silent" (Beckett 1958, 44). Here Clov is again an echo, this time of Caliban's malediction to Prospero in *The Tempest*: "You taught me language; and my profit on't/ Is, I know how to curse: The red plague rid you/For learning me your language!" (I.ii.365–7). Being always already an echo, Clov apparently is without substance, has no being of his own because he has neither memory nor language, except those written for him by Hamm; that is, Clov has what memory Hamm has supplied for him in his forgetting. Clov's history and so his memory are simply Hamm's afterthoughts expressed at least partially in his narratives. If they happen to agree on memory at all, it is, as Malone tells us in *Malone Dies*, an "agreement [that] only comes a little later, with the forgetting" (Beckett 1956, 217).

With the final themes, or the themes of finality, already established at the opening (one hesitates to say beginning), with the dumb show, the twin, almost symmetrical opening monologues, and the sequence of five unveilings, the play moves into its dramatic conflict, the tempo of which Beckett, as director of his own play, described to his actors thus: "There must be maximum aggression between them from the first exchange of words onward. Their war is the nucleus of the play" (McMillan and Fehsenfeld 1998, 205). One trope Beckett used to express that war is a hammer (Hamm) driving three nails: Clov (from the French *clou*), Nagg (from the German *Nagel*), and Nell (from the English *nail*). Asked directly by his German cast if *Endgame* is a play for a hammer and three nails, the circumspect Beckett would only respond, "If you like." Mother Pegg, whose light has died, as Hamm's is dying, might constitute yet a fourth beaten nail. Furthermore, in the resonance of Beckett's imagery, hammers and nails almost always suggest Christ's passion. Throughout the play, then, all the banging—including Hamm's tapping on the wall, Nagg's tapping on Nell's bin lid, Clov's tramping his booted feet— echo the theme of human suffering but ultimately of the incarnate

Christ's crucifixion, a death that itself was not a death, an ending that entailed a new beginning, at least for believers. Another time Beckett explained the Hamm-Clov relationship in terms of fire and embers or ashes, one character agitating the other, and from that stirring of embers flames flare afresh. Clov's goal throughout these conflicts is withdrawal, retreat: to his visions, to his kitchen at least, but on this day (which appears to be different from the others because the grains of millet may have reached a critical mass, the impossible heapness, or the accumulating moments of human existence may have added up to a life, which is evident only at its ending, in retrospect, only at its finale, after the curtain falls) Clov's larger goal is, finally, escape, from Hamm to his kitchen at least but ultimately to the without. But Hamm stirs the embers, "outside of here it's death" (Beckett 1958, 9), he tells his servant. Hamm's goal is then to detain, and thereby to retain his lackey in his place (in both senses of that term), and so, like the characters in *Waiting for Godot*, Hamm and Clov are "ti-ed" to this spot, and to each other, to Hamm's memories and, faced with the prospect of filling time, they abuse each other. As Beckett told the original Clov, Jean Martin, "You must realize that Hamm and Clov are Didi and Gogo at a later date, at the end of their lives [...]" (McMillan and Fehsenfeld 1998, 163).

Hamm has another means of passing the time *en attendant*, his narrative. "It's time for my story" (Beckett 1958, 48), he announces. In Beckett's direction it was clear that Hamm's chronicle too is already a repetition, the recovery or creation of memory, and so a set piece for performance with four distinct voices: "First Hamm carries on a monologue," Beckett told his German cast, "second, he speaks to the beggar he is imagining lying at his feet, third, he lends the latter his own voice, and he uses the fourth to recite the epic, linking text of his own story. Each voice corresponds to a distinct attitude" (McMillan and Fehsenfeld 1998, 205). This lending of his own voice is apparently his gift to Clov as well, and "His own story" is Hamm's struggle not to forget the memory to which all can agree. That is, Hamm struggles to create a world that is predictable, with him at or as center. The atmospheric reports sprinkled amid his monologue are to be spoken, according to Beckett, as though they were "filler" while Hamm is inventing or remembering the next episode of his story (as in history), thinking about how to continue it. The meteorological statistics give the story its shape, suggest a formal, circular structure to the tale, 0–50–100, then back to 0, another end already in the beginning. The return to zero may foretell the play's potential end, and so perhaps the end of existence, of humanity, but at the same time, the return to zero suggests a loop, the possibility of a new cycle, zero the beginning not the end of the number system, not an absence but the starting point of all numbers, the cipher pregnant with infinite numeration. Dramatically, the theme is developed with Clov's sighting, or his feigning sight of, a small boy, who potentially can enter the shelter to replace Clov, who may replace Hamm, who may replace Nagg: something, in short, is taking its course. The sighting of the boy seems to be Clov's appropriation of what was, heretofore, Hamm's story, to move himself into the story, to become its center, perhaps. Clov has made earlier attempts to write or co-write the story (and so history) by telling Hamm more of the boy in Hamm's story, "He would have climbed the trees" (Beckett 1958, 61). But with the sighting of the boy, he seems to have taken charge of the narrative, and so of memory. He (Clov) now lends the latter (Hamm) *his* own voice, which may have been Hamm's to begin with. In the cycle that we call theater such a change may also suggest a cast replacement in performance, and it is a change for which Clov has been preparing, that is, rehearsing, from his opening monologue.

The performative nature of Hamm's chronicle is also evident in his need for an audience to witness his performance and so to validate his story (and thereby his existence as well), and it brings to the fore the theatrical metaphor for the entire play, the "game" or "games" in *End-game*, which is, after all, play about a play. Hamm is always in need of an "other," an audience. Alone if not lonely, abandoned by his parents, say, Hamm needed another, something like a Clov-like factotum. Even as a child, then, the apparently solitary and lonely Hamm needed a witness to his "babble, babble, words," and so had to turn "himself into children, two, three, so as to be together, and whisper together, in the dark" (Beckett 1958, 126). Hamm thus creates an audience for himself. Beckett would return to this image of doubleness or multiplicity in *That Time* (1976) where the protagonist of narrative A describes hiding as a child, "making up talk breaking up two or more talking to himself being together that way" (Beckett 1984, 230). The repetitions (the French term for rehearsals, after all) of dialogue and action suggest that the characters are caught in a play, in a Möbius strip of narrative, in a chamber where the only sounds are echoes, a prevalent Beckett theme from his first collection of poetry, *Echo's Bones and Other Percipitates* (Europa Press, 1935). Clov threatens departure with the phrase: "What's there to keep me here?" Hamm answers, "The dialogue," then cues Clov to the next set exchange for which each has a part already written: "I've got on with my story" (Beckett 1958, 58). Clov is needed more as a witness, a subject, an audience than as a domestic. Nagg and Nell, Hamm's "accursed progenitors" evidently, no longer function in life (hence their relegation to dustbins) *except* that on occasion they too are needed to witness Hamm's performances and so to certify to his existence—or to witness his dying. And Nagg's music hall story of the tailor, complete with multiple voices, needs Nell's audition and so parallels Hamm's need for an audience.

On this extraordinary day, in a world where nothing is left to change, where nothing can change—in essence—where everything seems to have run out, especially pain-killer (a palliative mentioned seventeen times in the play), something *has* changed, as Clov observed from, or even before, the raising of the curtain: Nell dies and a flea appears, one life simply—symmetrically—replacing another. The lowly flea then terrifies Hamm as he shouts: "But humanity might start from there all over again" (Beckett 1958, 33). As terrified of ending as he is that a purported rat in the kitchen might feed on his flesh even before his death, Hamm has a corresponding fear, that of not ending, that is, of a cyclical, recurrent, monadic, repetitious existence. Critics have long noted the anti-creation themes in *Endgame*; Hamm, an echo of Ham, the cursed son of Noah and progenitor of Cush, Mizraim, Phut, and Canaan, fears that the whole cycle of humanity (and so suffering) might start anew from the flea, and so all this suffering—his own and humanity's—may have come to naught but a repetition, his suffering too a repetition and a rehearsal. Hamm would thus be a one of the many, and not the center of the universe, the One. And the setting, the shelter, takes on the qualities of a refuge, Noah's ark, from which, according to Christian mythology at least, humanity was restarted, repeated, as if the antediluvian period were mere prelude or rehearsal.

Although Hamm fears an actual end, the greater fear is that what *appears* to be an end may signal only a new beginning. In the earlier, discarded two-act version of the play, a Clov-like B reads directly an excerpt requested by the Hamm-like A, from Genesis 8:21–2 and

11:14–19, the story of Noah, and Beckett apparently reread those passages during the play's composition. Dissatisfied with the passage, A asks for another, and B reads from the generations. The emphasis on procreation excites A sexually, and he calls for one Sophie with whom he too might beget. But when a barely disguised B appears as Sophie, eager for coitus, A demurs for fear of procreation. Although Beckett cut such overt material, it remains as a trace or afterimage in the flea scene, while Hamm's desire for sexual gratification remains implicit: "If I could sleep, I might make love" (Beckett 1958, 18). The threat of cyclical existence is also suggested by the play's chess imagery since one outcome in the endgame is stalemate as well as checkmate. And in the theater, of course, action resumes in almost exact repetition the following night. The final irony of the *play* (in both senses of that term) is that while Hamm has been resisting the end, he is finally coming to terms with finality, ready to say "yes" to the nothingness, by the end of the play as he commences his own re-veiling with the stauncher. The gesture is belied, betrayed, by Clov's silent, unresponsive presence, his continued witness to Hamm's ending, a persistence that impedes Hamm's ending, his disappearance, and suggests at least one more turn of the wheel may remain. If Hamm comes finally to accept his end, which may validate if not exalt his suffering, he may be deceived yet again. Clov may have outplayed him in this "end game," or Hamm may have outwitted himself with his insistence on witnesses. But even as part and not the whole, each of Hamm's moments is already a life, subsequent moments merely repetitions in a series; the whole show will (must) resume again at each moment, complete in itself. Such a series cannot end despite Hamm's apparent resolve. Clov's presence thus thwarts Hamm's (and the play's) ending. It is Clov's best joke, one that itself must be validated by an audience.

Or is the joke on Clov? Early critics have observed that the set of *Endgame* suggests the inside of a human skull, the action thus a monodrama. What appear to be discrete characters may merely be aspects of a single consciousness: Hamm as reason, Clov his senses, and Nagg and Nell memories and dreams. As such, Clov could never simply walk away, as Hamm well knows, no matter how often he threatens to do so. The retreat from the external world into the sequestered shelter echoes the solipsistic retreat (perhaps of an artist) into the recesses of the self or mind, only to find that it proves no retreat at all since consciousness, perception, and memory are themselves unreliable and conflicted rather than unitary and serene. If the mind offers asylum, it does so in the dual sense of Beckett's favorite paradox since the word suggests both haven and incarceration.

But we began this analysis with a discussion of the direct simplicity of this play and have wandered instead into its deepening complexities. It is, however, the complexity of the simple examined more closely than it has been heretofore. Moreover, despite the emphasis on the self-reflexive, the play's turning back on itself like an uroboros, the play devouring itself in the playing, many of Beckett's comments as a director have tended to return us to the play's more quotidian, naturalistic features. What is surprising is that this paragon of avant-garde theater asked his actors in Berlin for a realistic presentation: "the play is to be acted as though there were a fourth wall where the footlights are," he told them. While, on occasion, Beckett would say, "Here it oughtn't to be played logically," more often he would provide direct logical motivation. For the line "Have you bled," he told Clov, "you see something in his face, that's why you're asking." Examining the parasite in his trousers provides Clov with the occasion for asking Hamm, "What about that pee?" Hamm's "Since it's calling you" should be choked out to trigger Clov's response about his voice, "Is your throat sore?" And Clov's opening speech is motivated by some barely perceptible change that he appears to perceive while inspecting the room. In his notebook, Beckett wrote, "C perplexed. All seemingly in order, yet a change" (Beckett 1992c, 197)

When Beckett was directing *Endgame* with the San Quentin Drama Workshop in 1980, I watched the rehearsals for two weeks. It was not unusual for visitors to be invited to sit in for a day or so, and one of those visitors was the American author Larry Shainberg, who had just published a book called *Brain Surgeon: An Intimate Look at His World* (1979). He sent it to Beckett, and Beckett responded on July 15, 1979:

I received & read yr. book before yr. letter reached me. It impressed me strongly. I read it too fast and shall read it again. Mere decay is a palty affair beside the calamities you describe. It is all I can speak of. And the ever acuter awareness of it. And the preposterous conviction, formed long ago, that here in the end is the last & by far best chance for the writer. Gaping into the synaptic chasm. Forgive such poor private response to yr book & letter. I am a poor hand at this form of communication. (Beckett *Letters* 2016, 506)

Beckett subsequently invited him to sit in on rehearsals of *Endgame* in London. During the break Beckett asked me to join him and Shainberg for lunch, which consisted of a glass of Guinness on a bench along the Thames River outside the Riverside Studios. It was clear that Beckett was fascinated with the intricate details of Shainberg's book and had read it carefully as he asked Shainberg numerous questions about the techniques and repercussions of brain surgery. Most of the discussion focused on the implications of cerebral hemorrhages and the recently developed surgical technique of using a clip to seal the burst blood vessel. The surgical results were amazingly free of all side effects, except that each of the patients reported a continued sensation that something was dripping inside their head. Shainberg was amazed that Beckett had intuited such a condition of aneurism surgery well before the current surgical technique was developed. For Shainberg, thus, much of *Endgame* was at least framed by neurological impairment and its resulting paralysis. For many of us then the play is at once simple and complex, realistic and self-referential, literal and symbolic, and that duality, that interplay of opposites, is evident in the best stagings as Clov remains present in his absence, that presence symbolized by the open door. Something of a Japanese mood pervades the closing moments of the drama, this in keeping with the spirit of Hamm's final monologue, where he transforms Baudelaire's poetic voice into, if not strict Haiku, certainly a poem in the spirit of Haiku: "You cried for night, it falls. Now cry in darkness" (Beckett 1958, 83).

Where finally this theatrical exploration of endings begins or ends, then, one cannot exactly say. If we return tomorrow to this same place, at the same time, we may witness the game re-played. And will the outcome be different tomorrow, or the day after, or the day after that? Will Clov have gone by tomorrow, or will he have replaced Hamm in the chair at the next showing? These are the questions the play, suspended in its irresolution, paused at its conclusion, leaves us with. Will tomorrow be different? Well, we will just have to come back to see. Moreover, that is where the play began. What one might say is that *Godot* may indeed arrive at some point, perhaps on a third (or subsequent) day.

# 7

# Samuel Beckett's Art of Self-collaboration

*I should prefer the text not appear in any form before production and not in book form until I have seen some rehearsals [...] I can't be definitive without actual work done in the theater. S.B. to Barney Rosset, May 18, 1961*

*I have asked Faber, since correcting proofs, to hold up production of the book. I realize I can't establish text of* Play, *especially stage directions, till I have worked on rehearsals. S.B. to Richard Seaver, November 29, 1963*

Godot *in my opinion is insufficiently "visualized" during writing. The other plays I saw more clearly, as the stage directions show. S.B. to Christian Ludvigsen, December 8, 1966.*

Samuel Beckett's transformation from playwright to theatrical artist, his acceptance of what he will call "the real thing," is one of the seminal developments of late Modernist theater and yet one slighted in the critical and historical discourse. A lack of theatrical documentation may account for some of the neglect as scholars and critics traditionally privilege print over performance, i.e., the apparent stability or consistency of the printed text over its performative realization or completion. The absence of Beckett's direct work on stage from the historical equation, however, distorts the arc of his aesthetic evolution, his development as an artist committed to the performance of his theater as its full realization. Beckett was to embrace theater not just as a medium where a preconceived work was given its accurate expression, but as *the* means through which theater is created and texts completed. As Beckett evolved from being an observer then advisor on productions of his plays to taking full charge of their staging, an apprenticeship of some fifteen years, practical theater offered him unique opportunities for self-collaborations. Theater became a heuristic through which he rewrote himself, that is, reinvented himself as an artist, and in the process revisioned late Modernist theater. Beckett was unusually explicit about such issues writing to Christian Ludvigsen on December 8, 1966:

> The mental stage on which one moves when writing and the mental auditorium from which one watches it are very inadequate substitutes for the real thing. And yet without them it is impossible to write for the theater. My experience is that the mental vision and the consequent stage directions are valid on the whole but have often to be *corrected*, and even *altered*, in function not only of the real theatre space, but also of the performers. Thus in our last production of *Endgame*, with the Irish actors [Patrick Magee and Jack MacGowran] I found it necessary to simplify very considerably the opening mime (windows, ladder, etc.) (Beckett *Letters* 2016, 54, emphasis added).

In retrospect it may seem self-evident to assert that the Samuel Beckett who authored *Waiting for Godot* in 1948 and the Samuel Beckett who staged it at the Schiller Theater, Berlin, in 1978 were not one and the same person, no less one and the same artist. Beckett provided his own theoretical paradigm for such process as early as his 1931 treatise on Marcel Proust: "We are not merely more weary because of yesterday, we are other, no longer what we were before the calamity of yesterday" (Beckett 1957c, 3). The Samuel Beckett who came to *Waiting for Godot* as its director thirty years after having written it was that "other," and the conjunction of the two, the writing self of 1948 and the directing "other" of 1978 (or the reverse, the directing self of 1978 and the writing "other" of 1948), is one of the critical and defining moments of late Modernism. Such conjunction occurred some sixteen times on the stage and another six times in the television studio; during each of those interventions, Beckett seized opportunities to play both self and other: that is, to refine if not to re-define his creative vision, to continue to discover latent possibilities in his texts, and to reaffirm a fundamentally Modernist aesthetics by expunging anything he deemed extraneous, and so to demonstrate afresh his commitment to, if not his preoccupation with, like a sculptor, the aesthetic, imagistic shape of his work. Beckett's own theatrical notebooks for what was a pivotal play in this protracted, developing sensibility, *Spiel* (*Play*), alone contain some twenty-five separate, complex, and full outlines of the play as Beckett combed his text for visual and aural parallels, reverberations, echoes in preparation for his own revisioning.[1] Beckett's direct work in the theater, particularly between 1967 and 1985 when he directed most of his major work, led publisher John Calder to declare, "I have no doubt that posterity will consider him, not just a great playwright and novelist, but a theatrical director in the class of Piscator, Brecht and Felsenstein."[2] Beckett, in short, develops into not only his own best director but a major theoretician of the theater in the process of staging and rewriting his plays.

Even before he became his own best reader, Beckett was less observer than active participant in staging his plays, at least in France. From the first, he was concerned with setting what he would call "a standard of fidelity" for his work. That is, primacy, if not hegemony, was initially given at first to the playwriting self. On January 9, 1953, four days after the opening in Paris of *En attendant Godot* (*Waiting for Godot*), the ever-vigilant Beckett wrote his French director, Roger Blin, to admonish him for deviations:

There is one thing that bothers me: Estragon's trousers. Naturally I asked [future wife] Suzanne if they fell down properly. She tells me that he holds on to them half-way down. They must not do—it's utterly inappropriate. It wouldn't occur to him at that moment—he doesn't realize that they have fallen down. As for any laughs that might greet their falling right down, to the great detriment of that touching final tableau, there's absolutely no objection to them. They'd be of the same order as the earlier ones. The spirit of the play, in so far that it has one, is that nothing is more grotesque than the tragic, and that must be put across right to the end, and particularly at the end. I have lots of other reasons for not wanting this business not to be underplayed but I'll spare you them. But please do as I ask and restore it as it is in the text, and as we always planned in rehearsals; and let the trousers fall right down, round his ankles. It must seem silly to you but to me it is vital. (Beckett *Letters* 2011, 350–1)[3]

Despite the difficulties afforded by distance Beckett tried to maintain similar vigilance over American productions. On February 2, 1956, he wrote to his American publisher, Barney Rosset, who had begun, almost by default at first, acting as his American theatrical agent, in order to forestall what Beckett called "unauthorized deviations" in the forthcoming Broadway production of *Godot* with new director and cast, and a producer conscious of the play's dismal failure in its Miami premiere:

I am naturally disturbed [...] at the menace hinted at in one of your letters, of unauthorized deviations from the script. This we cannot have at any price and I am asking [London producer Donald] Albery to write [American producer Michael] Myerberg to that effect. I am not intransigent, as the [bowdlerized] Criterion production [in London] shows, about minor changes, if I feel they are necessary [see Chapter 4 for full details], but I refuse to be improved by a professional rewriter [in this case American playwright Thornton Wilder had been proposed, and Wilder, as play doctor, had drafted a re-translation of *Godot* and had thus revisioned it]. (Beckett *Letters* 2011, 600–1)[4]

Aside from his general naiveté at this stage of his career about the workings of commercial theater into which he had plunged headlong, Beckett seems not to have realized that he had already been "improved by a professional rewriter" by February 1956, and, in fact, that such "improvements" were and are routinely made for "theatrical," that is, commercial reasons, and especially for neophyte playwrights. It was the bowdlerized version of *Godot* to which Beckett alluded above that Faber and Faber would publish in 1956, even as the dossier of Lord Chamberlain's office was restricted to public performance and so had little control over publication per se. The Ministry of Information generally restricted political information, and so the censorship of the British publication seems to have been matter of self-censorship, and the publication of *Godot* would not be the venerable publisher's final instance of such.[5]

After completing *Krapp's Last Tape*, which, as he said, he "nearly entitled [...] 'Ah Well,'" Beckett wrote to his American publisher on April 1, 1958, to set some guidelines for its premiere, telling Rosset, "I'd hate it to be made a balls of at the outset and that's why I question it's [*sic*] being let out to small groups beyond our controp [for control] before we get it done more or less right and set a standard of fidelity at least" (Beckett *Letters* 2014, 123).[6] The issue was personally sensitive for Beckett because he was responding to a request from Mary Manning, whose Boston troupe, the Poets' Theatre of Cambridge, MA, Rosset had preliminarily authorized, but Beckett at this point deemed the group not seasoned enough for so technical and specialized a play: "Mary Manning is intelligent and knows the theater, but I'm afraid her actors won't have the weight and authority that are needed. The Magnetophonics too are difficult and will want a great deal of precision" (Beckett *Letters* 2014, 123). He was, moreover, already looking to London and the Royal Court for that level of technical proficiency he anticipated. Nine days later Beckett wrote to Rosset that he was off to London to oversee directly the Royal Court Theater's production, "where I hope to get the mechanics of it right" (Beckett *Letters* 2014, 127). It was this "standard of fidelity" and the degree of direct oversight entailed in getting "the mechanics of it right" that in good part finally lured, rather drove, Beckett to the semi-public posture of staging his own plays, and, even more important, which allowed him to move to a new phase of his creative development, that which critics usually refer to as the "late plays."

But the move to staging himself was made reluctantly, hesitantly, accomplished, as it were, in as well as on stages, as Beckett learned what theater itself had to offer him as an artist. He quickly saw that his direct involvement in productions offered opportunities beyond authorial validation and textual fidelity. By the late 1950s, the physical theater became a testing ground for him, an arena for creative discovery, even self-discovery. *Krapp's Last Tape* seems to have been the watershed, as he realized that the creation of a dramatic text was not a process that could be divorced from performance, and that mounting a production brought to light recesses previously hidden, even from the author himself. In his April 1 letter to Rosset, Beckett expressed the clarity of his preproduction vision of *Krapp*: "I see the whole thing so clearly (appart [*sic*] from the changes of Krapp's white face as he listens[7]) and realize now that this does not mean I have stated it clearly, though God knows I tried" (Beckett *Letters* 2014, 123). Writing to Rosset six months later, on November 20, 1958, *after* the Royal Court *Krapp*, Beckett seems to have got more than "the mechanics of it right" in this production with Patrick Magee, directed by Donald McWhinnie. In fact in late 1958 Beckett began sounding very much like a director himself:

I arrived in London a week before the opening and 5 days before the 1st dress rehearsal, My intention was to concern myself only with Krapp [*sic*], but on arrival I found Endgame [*sic*] in such a state that I had to take it on too. Impossible to do much in so short a time. But Krapp [*sic*] made up for everything. Unerringly directed by McWhinnie[,] Magee gave a very fine performance, for me by far the most satisfactory experience in the theater up to date. I wish to goodness that Alan [Schneider] could have seen it. *I can't see it being done any other way. During rehearsal we found various pieces of business not indicated in the script and which now seem to me indispensable.* If you ever publish the work in book form I should like to incorporate them in the text. A possible solution in the meantime would be for me to see Alan again (hardly feasible) or to write to him at length on the subject and prepare for him a set of more explicit stage directions. Blin and Martin saw it in London and were bowled over by Magee. [See also SB's letter to Schneider November 21, 1958.] (Beckett *Letters* 2014, 176, emphasis added)

The following day Beckett reprised his enthusiasm to Mary Manning: "Powerful week in London rehearsing Krapp [*sic*]. Terrific performance by Magee, pitilessly directed by McWhinnie. Best experience in the theatre ever. Endgame [*sic*] not good though MacGowran could have been" (Beckett *Letters* 2014, 179). At fifty-two years of age, having had two major plays staged in two languages and having completed his first radio play,

Samuel Beckett seems to have discovered theater. The discovery was monumental. It would transform thenceforth the way he wrote new plays, and finally force him to rethink, revision and so rewrite his earlier work as well. By the early 1960s, then, working directly in the theater became an indispensable part of his creative process, and he wanted those direct theatrical discoveries incorporated in his published texts, before initial publication, at first; then as he began directing work already published, he assiduously revised those texts in terms of his production insights, completing them, as it were, on stage. Writing to Grove Press about *Happy Days* on May 18, 1961, Beckett said, for instance, "I should prefer the text not to appear in any form before production and not in book form until I have seen some rehearsals in London. I can't be definitive without actual work done in the theater" (this crucial letter is not included in Beckett *Letters* 2014).[8] On November 24, 1963, he wrote to Rosset about his wife's disappointment with the German production of *Spiel (Play)*[9]:

> Suzanne went to Berlin for the opening of *Play*. She did not like the performance, but the director, Deryk Mendel, is very pleased. Well received.
> I realize I can't establish definitive text of *Play* without a certain number of rehearsals. These should begin with [French director Jean-Marie] Serreau next month. Alan's [Schneider's] text will certainly need correction. Not the lines but the stage directions. London rehearsals begin on March 9th [1964]. (letter not included in Beckett *Letters* 2014)

In fact, after having read an initial set of proofs for *Play* from his British publisher, Faber and Faber, Beckett panicked and so delayed publication so that he could continue to hone the text in rehearsals. He wrote to Charles Monteith of Faber and Faber first on November 15, 1963, "I received yesterday proofs of PLAY [*sic*]. I'm afraid I shall have to make some rather important changes in the stage directions of PLAY [*sic*]. If they seem to you excessive please charge them to my account" (Beckett *Letters* 2014, 580–1). On November 23, 1963, Beckett was even more insistent: "I suddenly see this evening, with panic, that no final text of *Play* is possible till I have had a certain number of rehearsals. These will begin here, I hope, next month [they were delayed as indicated above], and your publication should not be delayed [that is, publication should follow soon after production]. *But please regard my corrected proofs as not final"* (emphasis added) (letter not included in Beckett *Letters* 2014). Beckett confirmed this decision to Grove Press editor Richard Seaver six days later, on November 29, 1963: "I have asked Faber, since correcting proofs, to hold up production of the book. I realize I can't establish text of *Play*, especially stage directions, till I have worked on rehearsals. I have written to Alan [Schneider] about the problems involved" (letter not included in Beckett *Letters* 2014). Seaver confirmed in his reply of December 4, 1963, "We won't do anything on the book until we hear from you." Shortly thereafter, however, Grove resumed its pressure to publish *Play* and proposed to couple it with a work by Harold Pinter. In his rejection of that project Beckett returned to his theme of the indispensability of production to his theatrical work:

> Quite frankly I am not in favour of this idea, particularly as your text of *Play* is not final and cannot be till I have had some rehearsals, i.e., not before the end of next month. It is all right for the purposes of Alan's [Schneider's] production, because I have left it open for him and he knows the problems. But not as a published work.[10] (letter not included in Beckett *Letters* 2014)

This insistence on completing a text of his play only after "some rehearsals" or "a certain number of rehearsals" would become, then, a central part of Beckett's method of composition from *Krapp's Last Tape* onward. Well over a decade later Beckett sounded the same theme about the text of *Not I* in a letter to Barney Rosset of August 7, 1972: "With regard to publication, I prefer to hold it back for the sake of whatever light N. Y. & London rehearsals may shed. I have not yet sent the text to Faber." While the letter previously cited is not included in Beckett *Letters* 2014, a letter of August 9 to Anne Atik and Avigdor Arika does note, "Good reaction by the Royal Court on receiving *Not I*. They want to put it on in the main theatre with *Krapp*, that is the same pairing as the East Side Playhouse. [...] Have revised the text one last (?) time before sending it to New York and London" (Beckett *Letters* 2016, 304). Without working on stage directly himself, then, Beckett seemed less than sure if his late work, in this case the metonymical *Not I*, was even drama, shaken perhaps by the difficulties Alan Schneider encountered staging the world premiere (that is, setting its "standard of fidelity") with actress Jessica Tandy at New York's Lincoln Center.[11] Beckett wrote to Rosset on November 3, 1972, "Had a couple of letters from Alan. They seem to have been having a rough time. Hope smoother now. Hope to work on *Not I* in London next month and find out then if it's theater or not" (letter not included in Beckett *Letters* 2016).

As we trace the archeology of Beckett's theater works from the late 1950s onward, it becomes clear that publication was an interruption in the ongoing, often protracted process of creation, which occurred on the stage as often as on the page. On the other hand, Beckett the author, with a long history of rejection from publishers, was unable to resist publication pressures or even to control its pace. After publication, however, he continued as a director to collaborate with the author of the texts, that is, himself or, more psychoanalytically, his "other" to continue the creative process. Moreover, such self-collaboration would not be merely a "one off." Beckett very quickly found that staging a play, even directing it himself, did not necessarily produce a final text. The principle of waiting for direct work in the theater before publishing, then, did not always insure what he variously called "corrected," "accurate," "final," or "definitive" texts in part because the process of staging as an act of textual revision, as an act of creation, seems to have become for Beckett open-ended, continuous, the "definitive text," *de facto*, mercurial, elusive, multiple, a perpetually deferred entity. On the other hand, commercial pressures from producers in various countries were incessant after the success of *Waiting for Godot*, as were pressures from publishers. The letters from this period testify to the growing professional pressures on Beckett as an international artist (if not as an international commodity), pressures that would only intensify with the so-called "catastrophe" of the Nobel Prize in 1969. Much of this international attention forced a shift from an artisanal approach, literature as a cottage industry, say, to what seemed to be its mass production. The practical results were an inevitable diminution of quality control which took the form of a proliferation of published and produced texts. Several versions of the same text often circulated among producers, directors, and even publishers; that is, as he continued to direct, he continued to revise, and so Beckett's own creative practice, his evolving creative methodology, contributed to a proliferation of textual variants in the written record. The text of *Play* is a case in point. As Beckett continued to revise the text through British and French productions, which were occurring simultaneously in 1964, various versions of the play circulated in typescript.[12] Working through British agent Rosica Colin, Beckett sent Charles Monteith "a revised text" of *Play* in July 1963. On November 23, 1963, Beckett sent his "panic" letter to Monteith and requested a second set of "virgin" proofs, a request he reaffirmed on December 5: "I need a fortnight's work on *Play* in a theatre. The French production will go into rehearsals this month I hope. As soon as I have exact dates I'll let you know when to expect final proof. Could you let me have another proof (virgin)" (letter not included in Beckett *Letters* 2016). In an internal Faber and Faber memo of December 9, 1963, then, Monteith announced the delay in publishing *Play* to the staff of Faber:

> I think that *Play* will almost certainly have to be postponed until much later in the spring. Beckett wont pass his proofs for press until *Play* has been rehearsed and he decides what changes are necessary for an actual production. The latest news I have about this is that rehearsals will start in France some time this month; and he says he will need a fortnight's work on it in theatre.

Because of the scheduling delays Beckett finally acquiesced to his British publishers' pressures to publish. He wrote to Montieth on "January 9, 1963" [*recte* 1964], "I shall ... re-correct your proofs of *Play*. Rehearsals here [i.e., in Paris] are delayed and I don't want to hold you up any longer, especially as Grove Press seem set on publishing this play in the near future" (letter not included in Beckett *Letters* 2016). Beckett then sent Monteith the second set of corrected proofs on January 17, 1964, before rehearsals began in either country, and Faber and Faber published the work on March 27, 1964, in order to have a text available for the play's London opening. But between Beckett's correcting the second set of proofs on January 17 and the play's opening on April 7, 1964, Beckett revised the text yet again. Working uneasily in Paris with French director, Jean-Marie Serreau, on staging the French text, *Comédie*, before the London rehearsals had begun, it became clear to Beckett that additional revisions were not only desirable but necessary, and he wrote to British director George Devine on March 9, 1964, less than one month before the scheduled opening and while the Faber text was in final production, to warn him of necessary revisions, this just as the published version of the play was about to appear in Britain:

> The last rehearsals with Serreau have led us to a view of the *da capo* which I think you should know about. According to the text it is rigorously identical with the first statement. We now think it would be dramatically more effective to have it express a slight weakening, both of question and of response, by means of less and perhaps slower light and correspondingly less volume and speed of voice. (Beckett *Letters* 2014, 594)[13]

Before those rehearsals, however, Beckett believed that he had got things right in the second set of galleys he revised for Faber, and writing to Grove Press on August 17, 1964, that is, after British and French productions (in which, as he wrote to Monteith on the same day, "I was happy with production and actors and think we got pretty close to it") regarding a Swedish translation, Beckett at first confirmed the Faber text: "As to your MS text, it is less likely to be accurate than the Faber published text for which I corrected proofs" [i.e., at least twice] (letter not included in Beckett *Letters* 2014). But the same letter suggested the need for further revisions, another version which would reflect more of the theater work (as well as an uncharacteristically cavalier attitude about his text in Swedish translation): "[Grove editor Fred] Jordan suggested publishing in *Evergreen Review* the text *in extenso* [i.e., at full length] (as played in London and Paris), i.e., giving changed order of speeches in the repeat and indicating vocal levels. This is quite a job to prepare and I suggest we reserve this presentation for Grove and let translations follow the existing text, simply correcting 'Repeat play exactly' to 'Repeat play'" (letter not included in Beckett *Letters* 2014). When Barney Rosset's personal assistant, Judith Schmidt, compared the Faber text of *Play* to the Grove Press typescript, she wrote to Beckett on August 26, "I can see that there are a good many changes." Jordan then wrote to Beckett on the same day, "We are using the Faber and Faber text in the next issue of *Evergreen Review*, but I believe you asked to have one word changed [i.e., the deletion of 'exactly,' as above]. Could you indicate what the change is, giving me page and line number, assuming we both work from the same edition." If we wonder at the complexities of the

textual (and so performance) history of Beckett's work, here is
a case in point: two editors of the same firm writing their major
author on the same day each proposing to publish a different
version of the same work. Beckett solved some of this confusion,
but only some of it, on August 28, by fully revising his work again,
"Herewith corrections to Faber text of *Play*" (letter not included
in Beckett *Letters* 2014) which text then became the basis of the
*Evergreen Review* (hereafter *ER*) version. The *ER* text of 1964
then was the text of *Play in extenso*, the one for which Beckett made
his final revisions, but it is a text generally ignored by Beckett's
English language publishers and producers. The revisions were
never fully incorporated into any Faber text, and inexplicably it
was not its own text *in extenso*, which Grove Press published in
book form in 1968.[14]

The American book publication was taken some four years
later not from Grove's own fully "corrected" *ER* text but from the
penultimately revised Faber edition. The *ER* text, for instance, was
the first to include Beckett's major postproduction revision, the
note on "Repeat" (the *Cascando* edition of 1968, four years after
Beckett made the revision, does not include this note at all but it
does delete the word "exactly" from the phrase in the *first* Faber
edition, "Repeat play exactly"). The *ER* edition, moreover, is the
first printing in which the opening instructions on lighting were
emended by deleting "not quite" from the original Faber version,
"The response to light is not quite immediate." The Grove book
edition, subsequently, retained "not quite" even after it was cut from
its own *ER* text. But the *ER* text has its own corruption; the sentence
subsequent to the revision was illogically retained, as it is today in
both Faber and Grove standard editions (but not in the collected
editions, *Collected Shorter Plays* [Grove Press and Faber and Faber,
1984] and *Complete Dramatic Works* [Faber and Faber only, 1986,
revised and corrected paperback edition 1990] [hereafter *CSP* and
*CDW* respectively] in which the problem was essentially remedied):
"At every solicitation a pause of about one second before utterance
is achieved, except where a longer delay is indicated." Logically, the
response to the light must be either "immediate" or delayed, not
both, and so the retention of the phrase "of about one second" in
the *ER* version seems clearly to have been a major oversight.[15]

Such a revision may at first seem minor, little more than a
technical adjustment, instructions to the lighting designer. But in

the delicate balance of verbal and visual images which constitutes
Beckettian theater, such changes are fundamental, thematically
potent, especially since light can function as a character in Beckett's
theater. This is the case with *Play* in particular. If a delay exists
between light's command and the response, then a certain amount
of deliberation is possible among the subjects. The situation of
the urn-encrusted characters is thus humanized some. In Beckett's
revision, the final vestiges of humanity (and humanism) are drained
from an inquisitorial process, which Beckett ironically calls *Play*.

The textual history of the dramaticule (Beckett's coinage),
*Come and Go*, is here illustrative as well since it combines the
three dominant problems affecting Beckett's dramatic texts: a
proliferation of versions on initial publication, adjustments made in
translation, and revisions Beckett made for production, in this case
well after the work's initial publication. An uncertain publication
history plagued the initial publication of *Come and Go* in 1978
even though Beckett read proofs for the first edition. The opening
four lines of the parallel English and German text Beckett reviewed
as he prepared to direct *Kommen und Gehen* (*Come and Go*) in
1978 were as follows:

VI: Ru.
RU: Yes.
VI: Flo.
FLO: Yes.

These lines were not, however, included in the first edition published
by Calder and Boyars in 1967. When Beckett read proofs for
Calder's edition he suggested in a letter of December 7, 1966, that
something was amiss: "Here are the *Texts for Nothing*. I return
to Paris tomorrow and shall send you the other proofs corrected,
including *Come and Go*, which at first glance doesn't look right"
(Beckett *Letters* 2016, 53). Whatever didn't "look right" to
Beckett, his review of the proofs did not result in the inclusion
of the opening four lines in the Calder edition. The opening lines
did appear, however, in the first American edition, *"Cascando"*
*and Other Short Dramatic Pieces*, published by Grove Press the
following year, and in all translations, particularly the French and
German. More important they were also part of the final English
text which Beckett reviewed carefully and revised for the Schiller

Theater production in 1978 (which, although Beckett prepared to direct, it was finally directed by Walter Asmus). Subsequent English texts by Faber and Faber were then based on the Calder and Boyars text of 1967 and not the Grove Press text of 1968 that included the four fugitive lines. Since both the *CDW* and *CSP* were projects initiated by Faber and Faber and photo-offset by Grove Press, the British publisher reprinted the incomplete Calder and Boyars edition. Those fugitive lines, then, appear in no major English text other than the first American edition until Faber and Faber accepted the omission in its first uniform edition of Beckett's work in 2009: *Krapp's Last Tape and Other Shorter Plays* (73, see also xii).[16]

In addition the French and German texts include revisions introduced by Beckett after the publication of the English and American editions. FLO invokes the names of the two other characters before her final "I can feel the rings." This final incantation then echoes the opening recitation of names, but it appears in no English language text. Finally, Beckett made a significant textual revision for his 1978 production which changed the speaker for two speeches: RU's first speech was given to FLO, and FLO's "Dreaming of ... love" was given to VI. Although Beckett finally did not direct *Kommen und Gehen* (*Come and Go*), he reviewed both English and German texts in anticipation of production and so clearly established the English version of the text. Had he directed the production himself, he may have made further discoveries and so made additional revisions, but he did not. To date then no English language text includes Beckett's final revisions. These additional closing lines, then, a reinvocation of the added opening lines, are not included in the 2009 text published in *Krapp's Last Tape and Other Shorter Plays* (74), even as the argument for their inclusion is made in the volume's "Preface" (xiii).

With *Footfalls* Beckett also revised the published English text at various times for various stages. He directed three productions of the play in three languages: with Billie Whitelaw at the Royal Court Theater in London in 1976; shortly thereafter with Hildegard Schmahl, on the bill with *Damals* (*That Time*) also in 1976; and finally with Delphine Seyrig at the Théâtre d'Orsay in 1978. Beckett revised the English script in detail, changing, for example, the number of May's pacing steps from seven to nine. Most, but not all, of those revisions were incorporated into subsequent revised English texts,

*Ends and Odds*[17] at first, and then in both the *CDW* and *CSP* both published by Faber and Faber (but Grove Press has never published the *CDW*). But Beckett also made significant lighting changes that he never incorporated directly into any English text, changes that were central to and consistent in all three of his productions. For each of his stagings, for instance, he introduced a "Dim spot on face during halts at R [right] and L [left]" so that May's face would be visible during her monologues. In addition, he introduced a vertical ray of light which seemed to be coming through a door barely ajar, this to counterpoint the horizontal beam on the floor along which May paces. These lighting changes were not only part of all three of Beckett's productions, they were incorporated into the French translation and certainly should be part of any English text or production. Without these final revisions, the only accurate text of *Footfalls*, that closest to Beckett's final conception of the work, is the French text, *Pas*.

The textual problems outlined here were the result, then, of Beckett's continued work in the theater and his desire to have his published texts reflect his most recent theatrical insights, discoveries that could only have been made in rehearsals. It was Beckett's at least tacit acknowledgment that theater is its performance, and the theater space, as Peter Brook has insisted for years, is an arena for the theatrical equivalent of archeological research and creative discovery. At first such revisions as those with *Play* were restricted to works not yet in print. But much of Beckett's most intense and concentrated theatrical work with his texts occurred well after their original publication when as a director he turned to them afresh. Staging himself even well after initial publication would mean revising himself and would allow him to move forward by returning to the past, implement, refine, revision, and extend his creative vision to work published before he came to be his own best interpreter. In retrospect such self-collaboration seemed inevitable since Beckett's theatrical vision was often at odds with those of even his most sympathetic directors. "He had ideas about [*Fin de partie*]," recalled Roger Blin, his first French director, "that made it a little difficult to act. At first, he looked on his play as a kind of musical score. When a word occurred or was repeated, when Hamm called Clov, Clov should always come in the same way every time, like a musical phrase coming from the same instrument with the same volume" (Bishop 1986 [2014], 233).[18] Ten years after writing *Fin de partie* [*Endgame*] Beckett would score the play to his satisfaction in his own Berlin production. "The play is full of echoes," he told his German cast, "they all answer each other," and he revised his texts accordingly. His final revisions to the texts of *Play, Come and Go,* and *Footfalls* reflect just such musical preoccupations.

During his nineteen-year directing career, from 1967 to 1986, Beckett staged (or videotaped) over twenty productions of his plays in three languages: English, French, and German. Each time he came to reread a script to prepare its staging, he usually found it wordy, encumbered, and incompletely conceived for the stage, and so he set about "correcting" it, the word he used most often for the process of theater, the continued development and refinement of his work that directing afforded. Such a commitment protracted the creative process. For Beckett composition, that is, the act of creation, did not end with publication, and certainly not with initial production, even those on which he had worked closely, but was continuous, subject to constant refinement if not on occasion redefinition. As I concluded in my edition of Beckett's *Theatrical Notebooks,* "... from the 1967 [today I would say from the 1958 *Krapp,* as this essay details] *Endspiel* [*Endgame*], Beckett used directorial opportunities to continue the creative process, cutting, revising, tightening his original script. Once Beckett took full control, directing was not a process separate from the generation of a text but its continuation if not its culmination. Writing, translating and directing were of a piece, part of a continuous creative process" (Beckett 1992c, xiii).

\* \* \*

It was this direct work in the theater, this extension of the creative process, Beckett's re-intervention into his own established canon, into texts that were not only already in print but often well established in critical discourse, that has forced to the fore unique questions not only about Beckett's individual texts but about the relationship of theatrical performance to its published record and so about the nature, the quality, the validity of the theatrical experience itself. The sheer complexity of Beckett's creative vision, however, has forced some analysts into critical denial. For Beckett's theater, performance would become his principal text. The results of that direct theatrical process, that fastidious attention to the aesthetic details of the artwork, a salient characteristic of late

Modernism, need to enter our critical and performative equations if we are not to underestimate and so distort Samuel Beckett's creative vision and his own theoretical contributions to Modernist theater as playwright and director.

That's the theory. The practice, that is, the actual accommodation of performance into a written record, is not always easily achievable. As he began increasingly to work directly on stage, to trust his direct work in theater, Beckett did not, unfortunately, always record those insights or revise his texts accordingly. For some productions Beckett simply never got around to making the full and complete revisions to his English text, that is, never committed his revisions to paper, revisions which were clearly part of his developing conception of the play, but let the production stand as the final text. The most obvious and stunning example is the ballet (or mime) called *Quad* in English. Beckett's final version of the work, the production for German television, broadcast on October 8, 1981, is called *Quadrat I & II*, a title that suggests at least two acts, if not two plays. Near the end of the taping, Beckett created what amounted to an unplanned second act for the play. When he saw the color production of *Quad* rebroadcast on a black-and-white monitor, he decided instantly to create *Quad II*. Beckett's printed text (in any language) was, however, never fully revised to acknowledge this remarkable revision of the work's fundamental structure. No printed version of the play bears the title of the production, and so no accurate version, one that includes Beckett's revisions, exists in print. Beckett's own videotaped German production, then, remains the only "final" text for *Quad*.

Finally, for his own television version of his stage play, *Was Wo* (*What Where*), Beckett again revised the German text extensively, but he never fully revised the stage directions of the original. This omission was due in part to Beckett's continued work on the central visual image of the play through rehearsals up to the final taping. He wrote to Reinhart Muller Freienfels of Süddeutscher Rundfunk on January 1, 1984 outlining what was fundamentally his theory of theater:

As performers I would again suggest mimes. All four to be made as alike as possible by means of costume and make up however excessive. Attitudes and movement strictly identical. Speech mechanical and colourless. Marionettes. No 'interpretation.' A balletistic approach. Bodily control the most important requirement as in Quad and Nacht u. Traume [*sic*][.] In a work discipline and selflessness hardly to be expected of 'seasoned actors and in[d]eed too much—or too little—to ask of them.' (Beckett *Letters* 2016, 632–3)

By this stage of his directing career, Beckett had developed enough confidence to trust the collaborations that theater entails, indeed that it necessitates, that he was creating his theater work almost wholly in rehearsals, directly on the stage (or in this case, in the studio), although he kept a theatrical notebook for the production as well. As his long-time cameraman and technical assistant, Jim Lewis, recalled:

> If you want to compare this production [of *Was Wo*] with the others for television, there's one major difference. And that is his concept was not set. He changed and changed and changed. [...] I've never experienced that with him before. You know how concrete he is, how precise he is. Other times we could usually follow through on that with minor, minor changes; but this time there were several basic changes and he still wasn't sure. (Fehsenfeld 1986, 236)

Lewis's observation suggests the single most significant element in Beckett's evolution from playwright to complete theater artist, from writer to director: his commitment to the idea of performance. In practical and literary terms such a commitment meant that nothing like a "final script" for his theatrical work could be established before he worked with it and reworked it directly on stage. What he insisted to his American publisher about *Play* he reiterated at the same time to his principal American director, Alan Schneider, in response to Schneider's queries. Beckett expressed what had become obvious and axiomatic to him: "I realize that no final script is possible until I work on rehearsals."[19] With *Play* Beckett's emphasis on performance had been necessitated by his revision of the work between its English publication and its French and English performances, and it was such demanding technical difficulties as *Play* presented which finally prompted Beckett to take full charge of directing his work.[20] With *What Where*, however, Beckett went on to revise French and English stage versions of his play after he had adapted and taped the German television production, but again without revising the opening stage directions. A clear diagram and a paragraph describing the revised stage set, however, were part of his theatrical notebook for *Was Wo* (*What Where*), and so those passages could be adopted for a revised text by simply substituting Beckett's exact words for the original.[21]

One can, however, easily overstate Beckett's attraction to theater, even romanticize it. While the process of working on stage was fruitful and grew finally indispensable to his theatrical thinking, it did not always proceed smoothly. At times Beckett seemed exasperated by the whole process of theatrical collaboration, even as his letters were filled with theater gossip. With the unexpected success of *Godot*, demands for new work, for advice on productions and translations of his work, from all over the world, became almost suffocating. Much in his expanded semi-public role as director did not sit comfortably with him, in particular the practical demands of differing theaters, the constraints of deadlines, and the inevitable intercourse with an intrusive broader public. Reporters with cameras managed to insinuate themselves into rehearsals all too often, and Beckett periodically announced his abandonment of theater. On March 23, 1975, for instance, he wrote to his friend, publisher and some-time literary agent, George Reavey: "rehearsing French *Not I* with M. Renaud, with yet another *Krapp* to eke it out, opening April 8. Then farewell to theater" (letter not included in Beckett *Letters* 2016). On April 14 he reaffirmed his retirement: "*Pas Moi* off to a goodish start. Vast relief at thought of no more theater" (letter not included in Beckett *Letters* 2016) (Lake 1984, 155). But a year later, in April of 1976, he was in London directing Billie Whitelaw in *Footfalls* at the Royal Court Theater, to which he returned three years later to stage what was perhaps his English language directorial masterwork, Billie Whitelaw's *tour-de-force* performance of *Happy Days*, which premiered in June of 1979. In 1977, two years after his supposed retirement, Beckett only began his long directorial relationship with the San Quentin Drama Workshop, directing its founder Rick Cluchey in *Krapp's Last Tape* at the Akademie der Künst in Berlin in 1977, and *Endgame* with the company in May of 1980 at the Riverside Studios in London. In July of 1983 Beckett announced the end of his directorial career yet again: "Omitted to mention in my last, in reply to your evocation of the Riverside rehearsals [for the San Quentin *Endgame*], that I have done with directing, or it with me. Never again" (letter not included in Beckett *Letters* 2016).[22] But as he wrote to his American publisher and theatrical agent in 1959, "the call of the theater is strong," and it remained so through most of the 1980s. He wrote to Rick Cluchey on July 2, 1983, about a staging of *Godot* for a theater festival in Adelaide, Australia,

> I am past directing my plays, so do not expect from me in Paris the irretrievable means I possessed in Berlin & London, but only my imperfect memory of those productions.
>
> Beckett directs (directed) B is correct for Endgame & Krapp [sic], but can hardly apply to your Godot [*sic*] which I have not seen.
>
> In other words, dear Rick, whatever I still have to offer is yours, as always, with a heart point five. But please understand that it no longer amounts to much. (Beckett *Letters* 2016, 616–17)

But Beckett also agreed "to review your work in Paris next February, prior to the Adelaide Festival" (Beckett *Letters* 2016, 617n1), which he actually did in London as he wrote to Anne Atik and Avigdor Arikha on January 24, 1984, "I have to go to London February 19th for 10 days, to 'vet' San Quentin Godot [*sic*]. Alas" (Beckett *Letters* 2016, 634). In February of 1984, then, Beckett was back in London at least supervising Walter Asmus's recreation of Beckett's own 1978 Berlin staging of *Godot*, now with the San Quentin Drama Workshop. In the course of what was intended as simple supervision or vetting of the 1978 staging, Beckett again revised, refined, corrected his earlier staging significantly.[23] By early 1984, moreover, he had also already accepted an offer to adapt and direct his stage play *What Where* for German television. As he noted in the Atik/Arikha letter above, "Seeing Jim Lewis this evening re What Where [*sic*] for Stutgart TV, production in May" (Beckett *Letters* 2016, 634). The work was finally delayed until June of 1985, however, after which he would re-revise the play for the stage. His revisioning of *What Where* from stage to TV studio to stage again and to TV again would mark Beckett's final work in and for the theater.

But as useful as working directly in the defined space of theater turned out to be, it did not always resolve all creative and textual questions. Having worked closely with Anthony Page on the Royal Court Theater production of *Not I* in January of 1975, for instance, and having directed it himself at the Théâtre d'Orsay later that year in April 1975, then again in April of 1978, Beckett remained uncertain, hesitant, ambivalent about several fundamental details of the play, even how many characters it should contain, for example. The best advice he could offer a pair of young American directors in 1986 was "simply to omit the Auditor. He is very difficult to stage (light position) and may well be of more harm than good. For me the play needs him but I can do without him. *I have never seen him function effectively*" (Beckett *Letters* 2016, 680, emphasis added). Beckett's assessment of Auditor's ineffectiveness presumably includes the 1973 Royal Court production with Billie Whitelaw that he supervised and that was eventually taped for broadcast by the BBC. For the videotape Auditor was, of course, dropped in favor of a tight close-up of actress Billie Whitelaw's bespittled lips. And for his own 1978 French production (his second) with Madeleine Renaud, he omitted Auditor entirely.

To call even those texts which include all of Beckett's theatrical revisions "definitive," however, as Beckett occasionally did (if offhandedly), is not only to evoke the discourse of another era but to shift the emphasis away from the process of textual evolution which they represent. The revised texts are "final" only in the sense that Samuel Beckett's physical life is now final, that is, over. Clearly those who worked with him in the theater understood that had he directed any of his plays again, he would have generated more refinements, additional corrections, another revised text. The revised texts do, however, come closer to being finished than those originally published in the sense that Maurice Blanchot used the term in his 1955 work, *L'Espace littéraire*: "A work is finished, not when it is completed, but when he who labors at it from within can just as well finish it from without" (Blanchot 1982, 54). If Beckett's revised and corrected plays are "finished" it is because Beckett has approached them from "without," as an-other, as a reader and *metteur-en-scène*. Like any good reader, Beckett saw more in his texts at each reading, and directing offered him the opportunity of intense rereading.

What the revised and corrected texts represent, finally, is Beckett's physical work in the theater, a period of self-collaboration, a revisioning that all but dominated the final two decades of his life. They emphasize that his direct work with actors and technicians, while not always tranquil, was always productive and of no less importance, of no less value than the work he did in the seclusion of his study to produce and translate the first versions of his play scripts. Beckett's theatrical texts, however, were created not in his study but in the theater, and as such they stand as testimony to Beckett's creative vitality into the eighth decade of his life and to his faith in the living theater as a vital, creative force in the waning days of the twentieth century.

# Notes

1   These notebooks are on deposit at the University of Reading's Samuel Beckett Archive and were published in facsimile and transcription in *The Theatrical Notebooks of Samuel Beckett, Volume IV: The Shorter Plays,* ed. and with an Introduction and Notes by S. E. Gontarski.

2   John Calder, "Editorial and Theater Diary," *Gambit: International Theater Review* VII. 28 (1976): 3.

3   The translation here seems a bit clumsy but it is the official translation in the Beckett *Letters.* Frankly, I prefer my earlier translation:

> One thing which annoys me is Estragon's trousers. I naturally asked [future wife] Suzanne if they fell completely. She told me that they were held up half way. They must not, absolutely must not. [...] The spirit of the play, to the extent that it has any, is that nothing is more grotesque than the tragic, and that must be expressed until the end, and especially at the end. I have a stack of other reasons for not wanting to ruin this effect but I will spare you them. Just be good enough to restore the scene as written and performed in rehearsals, and let the pants fall completely to his ankles. That must seem stupid to you but for me it is paramount (Beckett 1992c, xiv).

4   Unless otherwise stipulated, letters throughout are in the respective publishers' archives, Grove Press, Faber and Faber, and John Calder [Publishers] Ltd., and are used with permission of the publishers and Samuel Beckett. The Rosset/Beckett material in particular is held at the "Stanley E. Gontarski Grove Press Research Materials" in Special Collections and Archives, Strozier Library, Florida State University. http://fsuarchon.fcla.edu/?p=collections/findingaid&id=4024&q=&rootcontentid=158770

5   See also my "Bowdlerizing Beckett: The BBC *Embers,*" *Journal of Beckett Studies* 9.1 (fall 1999): 127–32.

6   It would, of course, be Alan Schneider who would set the "standard of fidelity" for the American *Krapp's Last Tape.*

7   This problem was finally solved when Beckett directed his own production and eliminated Krapp's white face and red nose. See Beckett 1995b.

8   Editorially speaking, it is important to note that the preponderance of citations in this study to letters germane to Beckett's creative process but absent from the four-volume *Letters of Samuel Beckett* series suggests a deficiency or an insufficiency of that collection for research purposes. Omitted letters are thus not easily available, but included letters are available in other compilations, like those to Alan Schneider, for example, and so are duplicated in the Cambridge collection. If space was the issue for such omission, one might legitimately question the editorial decision to repeat material so easily to hand elsewhere.

9   This would be Deryk Mendel's world premiere production, *Spiel* at the Ulmer Theater, Ulm-Donau, June 14, 1963.

10  Beckett had apparently given up on Schneider's production of *Play*. His instructions to Alan Schneider were that "*Play* was to be played through twice without interruption and at a very fast pace, each time taking no longer than nine minutes," that is, eighteen minutes overall. The producers, Richard Barr, Clinton Wilder, and, of all people, Edward Albee, threatened to drop the play from the program if Schneider followed Beckett's instructions. Schneider, unlike Devine, capitulated, and wrote to Beckett for permission to slow the pace and eliminate the *da capo*: "For the first and last time in my long relationship with Sam, I did something I despised myself for doing. I wrote to him, asking if we could try having his text spoken only once, more slowly. Instead of telling me to blast off, Sam offered us his reluctant permission." See Alan Schneider, *Entrances: An American Director's Journey* (Viking Press, 1986), 342. The exchange to which Schneider alludes may have been verbal since it does not appear in *"No Author Better Served": The Correspondence of Samuel Beckett and Alan Schneider*, Harmon 1998.

11  When actress Jessica Tandy complained that the play's suggested running time of twenty-three minutes rendered the work unintelligible to audiences, Beckett telegraphed back his now famous (but oft misinterpreted) injunction, "I'm not unduly concerned with intelligibility. I hope the piece may work on the nerves of the audience, not its intellect." For a discussion of Tandy's performance see Enoch Brater, "The 'I' in Beckett's *Not I*," *Twentieth Century Literature* XX (July 1974): 200.

12 For details on the production of *Play* see "De-theatricalizing Theater: The Post-*Play* Plays," *The Theatrical Notebooks of Samuel Beckett, Volume IV: The Shorter Plays*, 1999, pp. XV–XXIX.

13 The letter is also published in facsimile in *New Theatre Magazine: Samuel Beckett Issue* XI.3 (1971): 16–17.

14 *"Cascando" and Other Short Dramatic Pieces* (Grove Press, 1968), 45–63.

15 Beckett sent another set of revisions to Richard Seaver at Grove Press on June 20, 1968, in anticipation of the book publication of *Play*. Except for the reduction of "Pardon" to "-don" (p. 20, l. 10), these same revisions were *not* included in the Faber revised text of 1968, *Play and two short pieces for radio* (originally published 1964), nor in subsequent Faber reprints. They were dutifully incorporated into Grove's *Cascando and Other Short Dramatic Pieces*, 1968. For *The Collected Shorter Plays* (1984) and *Complete Dramatic Works* (1986), the changes were made save the requested cut of the paragraph in the section entitled "Urns," that is paragraph 2, from "Should traps" to "Should conform."

16 They do appear in the text that critic Breon Mitchell edited and published in the journal *Modern Drama* in 1976, but that text introduces additional and unnecessary variants. See Breon Mitchell, "Art in Microcosm: The Manuscript Stages of Beckett's *Come and Go*," *Modern Drama* XIX.3 (1976): 245–60.

17 For additional details on the texts of *Footfalls* see "Texts and Pre-texts in Samuel Beckett's *Footfalls*," *Papers of the Bibliographical Society of America* LXXVII.2 (1983): 191–5.

18 "Blin on Beckett," *On Beckett: Essays and Criticism*, ed. and with an Introduction by S. E. Gontarski (Grove Press, Inc. 1986), 233.

19 Alec Reid makes something of the same point in the posthumous "Impact and Parable in Beckett: A First Encounter with *Not I*" published in a tribute issue of *Hermathena*, CXLI (1986), ed. Terence Brown and Nicholas Grene: Beckett "will speak of the first run-through with actors as the 'realization' of the play and when it has been performed publicly, he will say that it has been 'created'" (12). Delivering the first Annenberg Lecture at the University of Reading's Beckett Archive in May of 1993, Billie Whitelaw made the following observation of *Not I*: "I very much had the feeling that it was a work in progress" (author in attendance).

20 For further details see "De-theatricalizing Theater: The Post-*Play* Plays," p. xv–xxix.

21  For a fuller discussion of these revisions, see my "What Where II: Revision as Re-creation," *The Review of Contemporary Fiction* 7.2 (summer 1987): 120–3, as well as the *What Where* portion of the *Theatrical Notebooks of Samuel Beckett, Volume IV: The Shorter Plays*, and Martha Fehsenfeld, "Beckett's Reshaping of *What Where* for Television," *Modern Drama* XXIX.2 (June 1986): 236. See also "*What Where*: The Revised Text," ed. and with Textual Notes by S. E. Gontarski, *Journal of Beckett Studies* (New Series) 2.1 (autumn 1992): 1–25.

22  S. B. letter to S. E. Gontarski, July 24, 1983.

23  See *Theatrical Notebooks of Samuel Beckett, Volume I: Waiting for Godot*, ed. James Knowlson and Dougald McMillan (Grove Press, 1994).

# 8

# Beckett's Keyhole Art: Voyeurism, *Schaulust*, and the Perversions of Theater

A relatively minor motif that resonates through Samuel Beckett's early fiction, voyeurism or scopophilia (Freud's *Schaulust,* "pleasure in looking," or what Freud calls "the looking perversion" [Freud 1938, 593]), is detailed most prominently in Samuel Beckett's short story "Walking Out," where bride-to-be Lucy wonders if her dear Bel, one Belacqua Shuah, could be "a creepy-crawly" (Beckett 1972, 116), that is, a pervert. Indeed the name "Shuah," family name of the central figure in Beckett's series of connected stories, *More Pricks than Kicks*, suggests "low-lying" in Hebrew and bears something of an echo of *Schaulust*. Belacqua delights not only in the solitary pleasures of observing couples copulating in "[peeping?] Tom's Wood" but in finding that Lucy has secretly spied on him, too. The pleasure in watching (Freud's *Schaulust* is a minor drive that exists independent of the erotogenic zones) the young German girl and her Harold's Cross Tanzherr is foreshortened as Belacqua himself is discovered mid-indulgence and soundly thrashed (Harold's Cross is a decidedly rough area of south Dublin, near Donnybrook).[1] Fortunately, at least for the maintenance of his spiritual union and his sublimated sexuality, Bel's lovely Lucy suffers a terrible accident, so the couple can be happily married and never consummate their relationship and never allude to the past. That is, Bel's voyeurism is part of the motif of spiritual, ghostly, or other-worldly union, its undercurrent the "noli me tangere" of Christ's resurrection (that is, John 20: 11–15 where Jesus says to Mary Magdalene, "Touch me not; for I am not yet ascended to my Father"). In *That Time*, for instance, narrator B returns to the theme: "no sight of the face or any other part never turned to her not she to you [...] never turned to each other [...] no touching or anything of that nature always space between if only an inch no pawing in the manner of flesh and blood" (Beckett 1986, 391). For Freud, scopophilia is abnormal, a neurosis, if it replaces traditional or "normal" sexuality.[2] Voyeurism, scopophilia, or *Schaulust* for Freud was a duality as well in that it had two forms, one inexorably linked to exhibitionism (see, for example, *Three Essays on the Theory of Sexuality*), and the interplay of the two runs through Beckett's late "closed space" fictions and the late theater, not infrequently called "keyhole" or "peephole drama."

In the prequel to "Walking Out," the aborted novel *Dream of Fair to Middling Women*, Belacqua is called a "hedgecreeper" (Beckett 1972, 72), and similar activities are outlined. The Schule Dunkelbrau (and here Beckett is playfully substituting the dark beer for the Schule Hellerau, the lightness of Hellerau replaced by the darkness of Dunkelbrau), for example, is on the fringe of a park, "more beautiful and tangled far than the Bois de Boulogne or any other multis latebra opportuna [that is, many a secret opportunity] than it is possible to imagine" (Beckett 1972, 13); this gives the Viennese "swells" the chance to watch: "The Dunkelbrau gals were very Evite and nudist [...]. In the summer they lay on the roof and bronzed their bottoms and impudenda" (Beckett 1972, 13). The Latin phrase, *multis latebra opportune*, "many a secret opportunity," derives from Book 3 of Ovid's *Metamorphoses* (III, 443), the words of Narcissus to the woods about him as he pines away for self-love. The phrase simultaneously suggests some of the author's own literary exhibitionism, his flouting of esoteric learning. In *Beckett's Dream Notebook*, where he recorded and translated numerous quotations from Ovid, this is cited with a cryptic "Bois de Vincennes"; that Paris park evidently is the complementary other to the Bois de Boulogne, the one as good as the other it seems for what Beckett calls a "looking place" (160). Ovid's phrase is repeated in *Murphy*, Chapter 5, where it refers to Market Road Gardens, which is "opportune for many" (Beckett 1957b, 74), with similar intonations, but there the allusion is treated more frivolously, with the exception of the distinction between a voyeur and a voyant

(Beckett 1957b, 90), which reflects Rimbaud's desire to be a seer. Wylie in the aforementioned novel, moreover, has also worshipped Miss Counihan from afar, "all last June, through Zeiss glasses, at a watering place" (Beckett 1957b, 60). The scene is echoed in *How It Is* where the narrator's sense of "life in the light" is reflected in the first image of another creature: "I watched him after my fashion from afar through my spy-glass sidelong in mirrors through windows at night" (Beckett 1964, 9).

Miss Carriage has hopes, doomed to frustration, as she watches through the keyhole as Cooper prepares for bed (Beckett 1957b, 256). Moran's son instinctively imitates his father by spying upon him: "I caught a glimpse of my son spying on us from behind a bush. ... Peeping and prying were part of my profession. My son imitated me instinctively" (Beckett 1955, 94).

If *Dream* asserts that the author and so the reader peep and creep and otherwise eavesdrop on private lives, particularly when characters are dressing (Beckett 1993, 207), later works are less overtly concerned with such matters, but related themes of concealed perception and the pleasure of being secretly perceived persist. The "shuttered judas" in the padded cells of the inmates at the MMM in *Murphy* permits the custodian to observe the lunatic secretly (Beckett 1957b, 181). That padded, monadic space excludes all the world, except the prying, spying eye that observes unobserved the inmates' nakedness. In addition to approximating the little world to which Murphy aspires, the padded cell anticipates the intimate performance space of Beckett's late theater, and Murphy projects himself as both the voyeur and voyant.

In the theater then voyeurism is the artistic experience. In *Endgame*, Clov takes up the telescope to spy through the frame of the windows for signs of life, the window a metatheatrical echo of the framed theatrical space. And the play ends with the voyeurism game, Clov apparently unobserved, but observed by the audience, observing Hamm. In *Film*, which opens with a close-up of a reptilian eye, the voyeur E (for eye) is again the protagonist as O is the object of E's prying eye, the camera eye peeping as the audience shares the eavesdropping, as it does in *Film*'s sequel, *Eh Joe*. This is Berkeleyan, of course, as any number of critics have pointed out, *esse est percipi*, but it is Freudian as well and so identical to the sense that the characters have in *Waiting for Godot* and elsewhere (*Texts for Nothing, Happy Days*) that they are being watched, witnessed if not spied upon. Character M in *Play* suggests the central dramatic, ontological, and sexual problem in that play when he asks, "Am I as much as being seen?" His comment is, of course, self-reflexive, implying that theater is inherently a voyeuristic medium, the audience from the safety of the dark spying on the "life [so called] in the light." But in "Walking Out," an Hiberno-English description of courtship, Belacqua experiences a reciprocal seduction, one passive, his voyeurism, one active, his exhibitionism, the one generating as much libidinous energy and frisson as the other.

The audience may grow increasingly complicit in the acts of voyeurism it witnesses and its attraction to what Freud called the "phanic drive," or exhibitionism, in particular that of the author's virtuosity. If, as Freud asserts, the "visual impressions remain the most frequent pathway along which libidinal excitation is aroused," and are the means by which these impressions might be sublimated; that sublimation is the equivalent of the "phanic drive." The two drives (or instincts), "a mania for looking [and] exhibitionism," are corollaries of one another. Freud outlines the relationship most directly in *Three Contributions to the Theory of Sex* (also *Three Essays on the Theory of Sexuality*):

> The little child is, above all, shameless, and during his early years, he evinces definite pleasure in displaying his body and specially his sex organs. A counterpart to this pervasive desire, the curiosity to see other persons' genitals, probably appears first in the later years of childhood when the hindrance of the feeling of shame has already reached a certain development. Under the influence of seduction, the looking perversion may attain great importance for the sexual life of the child. Still, from my investigation of the childhood years of normal and neurotic patients, I must conclude that the impulse for looking can appear in the child as a spontaneous sexual manifestation. Small children, whose attention has once been directed to their own genitals—usually by masturbation—are wont to progress in this direction without outside interference and to develop a vivid interest in the genitals of their playmates. As the occasion for the gratification of such curiosity is generally afforded during the gratification of both excrementitious needs, such children become *voyeurs* and are zealous spectators at the voiding of urine and feces of others. After this tendency has been repressed, the curiosity to see the

genitals of others (one's own or those of the other sex) remains as a tormenting desire which in some neurotic cases, furnishes the strongest motive-power for the formation of symptoms. (Freud 1938, 593)

But the inquiry into concealed meanings that Freud sees as almost exclusively sexual is the heart of theoretical inquiry as well. In his essay "Science and Reflection," Martin Heiddeger reflects on the origins of the word "theory" in the Greek *theoria*, which derives from *theorein* (to look) and evokes *thea*, the root of theater. The "theater of vision" is thus the drive for the knowable or the known, a scopophilic drive. Both theory and theater constitute the drive toward knowledge that informs science and philosophy as well. Heidegger goes on to link the drive to the goddess Thea and its pursuit that of truth. Herbert Blau takes "scopophilic desire" as the central metaphor for theater in his collection of meditations on performance, *The Eye of Prey: Subversions of the Postmodern*: "'the scopic drive,' the desire to see, to see what maybe should not be seen, the intensely specular consciousness which, in refusing that prohibition, is another obsession of the theory that seems to be thinking about itself" (Blau 1987, xxii),[3] that is, theater. Blau's image of seeing is the aggressive, devouring eye, the "eye of prey," the image borrowed from Beckett's *Imagination Dead Imagine* (Beckett 1996, 185), and Blau concludes, "In Beckett we are always looking at what, perhaps, should not be looked at" (Blau 1987, 78). Such seeing "is the hauntedness of being," for Blau,

the *being-perceived* in the beginning which is in Artaud—whom Derrida has studied as a mirror of thought [Blau's sense of spectrality]—the reason for madness. It is also the ontological basis of what for Artaud is Original Sin, the idea of an *audience*, that specular entity whose name suggests the Word, the thing *heard*. The Audience—*the ones who look*—is the look of the Law. It is the audited reflection or originary division and primal separation. [...] it is in this thievish space of private being that, in the very deepest sense, the spectator is constituted and—for Beckett as well as Artaud—the theater gives birth to its Double, the self reflexive subject of thought, the thinking subject stealing thought away, eye of flesh, eye of prey, bringing death to the bloody show. (Blau 1987, 79–80)

Vladimir: A charnal house! A charnal house!
Estragon: You don't have to look.
Estragon: You can't help looking. (Beckett 1954, 41)

And "looking at what, perhaps, should not be looked at" is
the core of at least the dumb show that opens *Endgame*, followed
shortly thereafter by Hamm's interrogation:

> HAMM: Did you ever have the curiosity, while I was sleeping, to
>         take off my glasses and look at my eyes?
> CLOV: Pulling back the lids? (*Pause.*) No.
> HAMM: One of these days I'll show them to you.

And of *Godot*'s prequel, *Eleutheria*, Blau, writing before the play
was published, suggests that

> [...] for the bourgeois audience, gazing on death, is written
> on the price of its ticket. Victor [Krap] has defined liberty
> as 'seeing yourself dead,' there is a final curtain in which,
> reconciled neither to the Krapp [*recte* Krap] family romance
> nor to suicide, he lies down on his bed after looking long at
> the audience, ['He looks perversely at the audience' (Beckett
> 1995a, 191)] 'his thin back turned on humanity' ['his scrawny
> back turned on mankind' (Beckett 1995a, 191)]. As for seeing
> yourself dead, that's the problem of representation that
> plagues Artaud and deconstructionist thought. 'You can't see
> yourself dead,' as Victor says. 'That's playacting' ['One cannot
> see oneself dead. It's theatrics' (Beckett 1995a, 168)] Which is
> the vice of representation in the dominion of death, that death
> can only be represented. Which is to say it can only be theater,
> falsifying theater, that repeats it over and over, an interior
> duplication of the division, the sparagmos, the originary
> bloody show in which we must have thought a little at the
> very beginning to make a charnel house that seems without
> end. (Blau 2000, 91–2)

Almost concurrently, as Beckett is thinking through
"renunciation" in the work of the painter Tal Coat, he wrote to
Georges Duthuit on June 9, 1949, "To want it to be, to work at
making it be, to give it the appearance of being, is to fall back into

the same old plethora, the same old play-acting," "dans la meme comedie" (Beckett *Letters* 2011, 166).

Beckett's theater (and much of his fiction we might add) explores the complementary drives of voyeurism and exhibitionism, even as all literature may involve some degree of invasion of privacy. The looking, in Blau's words, "is compulsive and unrelieved," and so theater is, finally, as much concerned with concealment as revelation. As we peer at partially lit images in the dark, we may yearn for more exposure, more disclosures, but much is suppressed, repressed, more reveiled than revealed. Beckett's theater remains a site of resistance and concealment as well. Victor Krap refuses to tell his story frustrating family, friends, and spectators (one of whom attacks the actors over the issue), and Godot (apparently), stubbornly, refuses to disclose himself. And what Hamm yearns for most persistently is for some light. The interplay of light and dark, Hellerau and Dunkelbrau, disclosure and concealment, is the dominant trope of Beckett's theater from *Krapp's Last Tape* onward, as we watch an old man perform nearly lewd acts with a banana and overindulge his senses with spirits. We come closer to witnessing the forbidden in *Eh, Joe,* as Joe goes through his evening routine to eliminate perceivers, voyeurs, seers of any sort, as he prepares for bed. The almost useless Auditor of *Not I*, who apparently signifies something like "helpless compassion," at least according to stage directions, is more important as a witness, an apparently unobserved spectator, than as a participant. When the BBC filmed the stage play for television, Auditor was eliminated not only to maintain a tight, close-up image of Billie Whitelaw's spittle-stained lips, but because the television camera became the voyeur, the unobserved observer. All the better as more than a few critics commented on the possibility that the central image was vaginal. And the altered perspective of *That Time* may suggest that we are observing a bedded patient in his death throes. The stunning, mannerist theatrical device is Listener's face, slightly off-center, a disembodied head ten feet above the stage, listening to three voices (recorded, not performed) coming from the dark as aspects of his past. The stage image is an exercise in perspective, the head with hair flared as if seen from above, the audience presumably below the feet like the illusionistic *di sotto in sù* technique in Andrea Mantegna's *Foreshortened Christ*. The image of life in its dying moments was all the more poignant when the role was played by Julian Beck as he was dying from cancer. As Blau suggests,

> For there is always the liability—whose irony enlivens the drama from Aeschylus to O'Neill—that meaning is being concealed in the very act of uncovering it, as the repose of becoming is disturbed by the movement of meaning itself. [...] we are inevitably drawn into the dialectical wordplay between the visible and the invisible, where in the very sinews of perception the spectacle appears as a trace or decoy, the ghostly, reverberant surface of the seen. Theater is made from this play of meaning in a structure of becoming, the passing from an invisible force, where we lose meaning by finding it, and there is always something repressed. (Blau 1990, 56–70)

Most of Beckett's late plays, plays at least from *Play* onward, say, are enhanced by viewing them in terms of the voyeuristic imperative of theater or at least the interplay between voyeurism and exhibitionism, but the most curious example is the one play treated by its producers in the most overtly voyeuristic way; that is, Beckett's shortest (roughly 25 seconds) and arguably his most "popular" play, "Breath." The play is simplicity itself, an anonymous life cycle reduced to its fundamental sounds: a debris-littered stage with "[n]o verticals," a brief cry and inspiration as lights fade up for ten seconds and hold for five; then expiration and slow fade-down of light and "immediately cry as before." The two recorded cries, of vagitus and of a death rattle, are identical, as is the lighting on fade-up and fade-down. The symmetrical simplicity recalls Pozzo's poignant comment: "They give birth astride of a grave, the light gleams an instant, then it's night once more" (Beckett 1954, 57b). Blau would see such compacted imagery as a signature of theater:

> Someone is dying before your eyes. That is another universal of performance. There are, to be sure, a myriad of ways in which the history of performance has been able to disguise or displace that elemental fact. You can joke about it, you can laugh it off, you can perform great feats of physical skill, but the image of it is before your eyes all the more because you are looking, even if the space is empty. You can't escape that look even if you close your eyes. (Blau 1990b, 267)

Although Beckett called it a "farce in five acts," "Breath" is something less than a full evening's theater. Its most dynamic performance was as "Prelude" to Jacques Levy and Kenneth Tynan's sextravaganza, *Oh Calcutta*, the title a sexual pun on the French, "O quel cul t'as." John Calder has insisted that Tynan commissioned the work directly for the revue, but Ruby Cohn disputes that provenance, noting that in conversation Beckett had recited it to her years before, and that what Calder published was only a fair copy but not the original, which Beckett had written for Calder on the paper tablecloth of a café [Cohn in conversation with the author]. The prescient Tynan understood the voyeuristic appeal of theater and so added a line to Beckett's opening tableau; to Beckett's "Faint light on stage littered with miscellaneous rubbish," Tynan added three words, "including naked people." The review, and so presumably Beckett's little, if not slight, play, enjoyed enormous, unprecedented success. After an unusually high number of previews, thirty-nine, a precaution to test the mettle of official local censors, the play moved to Broadway on February 26, 1971, and ran until August 6, 1989. Eighty-five million people saw 1,314 performances, making it easily Samuel Beckett's most viewed, and perhaps most celebrated play, a record unlikely to be broken.

Beckett was not exactly complicit in the "sextravaganza" and was finally appalled by Tynan's alteration, but his contract forbade interference. Worse, Barney Rosset, Beckett's American publisher, included the excrescence in an illustrated book version of the play, publishing photographs of Tynan's revised imagery and attributing the work as printed, that is with Tynan's alterations, to Beckett (Beckett 1969, 8–9). The infamous association with *Oh Calcutta* is generally seen as an aberration in Beckett's theater, the association acknowledged officially only in *Collected Shorter Plays* (1984) and *Complete Dramatic Works* (1986). As aberrant as it admittedly was, Tynan's production may suggest something about the appeal to Beckett's late drama and even something of possible future stagings.

A Coda

Offered the opportunity to direct the play, I wanted to explore not only the play's avant-garde potential, its power to shock, subvert, and to defy conventions and expectations, but I wanted to foreground the voyeuristic appeal of Beckett's play and also of theater itself. For such a performance I needed something other than a traditional theatrical venue. The opportunity presented itself in December of 1992 when I was invited to participate in an evening of art, theater and readings at the Florida State University Gallery and Museum. The evening would be built around the electronic satellite reception of a piece of hypertext, *Agrippa (A Book of the Dead)* from novelist William Gibson. The Gibson piece was scheduled for simultaneous broadcast to nine sites around the world, immediately after which the piece would be distorted and destroyed by its own viruses. The overall plan for the evening was to use the gallery as a decentered theater space so that performances would be staged in several venues in the gallery simultaneously, and the audience would drift from exhibit to exhibit. Rather than follow the structure of an outdoor fair where simultaneous performances are offered to an audience free to move about at will, the gallery evening would offer sequential performances without overlap but at a variety of venues to which the audience would be guided by lighting cues. The evening then would entail readings, theatrical performances, and environments to explore among the gallery's various rooms.

I began to plan the production with voyeuristic imagery in mind. Since, like all of Beckett's short plays, "Breath" was not designed for an open space and needed a frame of some sort, and since the traditional proscenium arch was unavailable in the gallery, I would have to create my own frame, that is, a structure through which the audience could peer. Rather than build a proscenium arch, however, I built a huge television screen, behind which "Breath" would be performed "live," or at least the pile of "miscellaneous rubbish" was physically present in the gallery. In the printed program I called the performance "A Simulated Television Production." But the heap of "miscellaneous rubbish" was of a piece with other installations in the gallery so that Beckett's "play" was for many indistinguishable from other art objects on display (or from the gallery's refuse outside the service entrance, for that matter). Mine, or rather Beckett's, was simply framed by a simulated television screen.

With that oversized, simulated television screen, I thought to merge the detachment of television with the intimacy of live theater, that is, I could offer hot and cold media simultaneously and to merge theater with sculpture. The performance of "Breath," as opposed to the gallery's other sculptures, would be "announced" by the light's fading up on the set, that is, on the heap of rubbish some ten feet behind the television screen, as the gallery lights simultaneously dimmed. The brief (birth) cry and amplified inspiration would sound for some ten seconds, and after the prescribed five-second pause, the expiration and identical cry for some ten seconds. Fade down the stage; fade up the gallery.

The performance was repeated several times during the evening, interspersed amid other performances. Since I had deliberately chosen to associate Beckett's "play" with sculpture by the very fact of offering the performance in an art gallery, I was not surprised that the audience never seemed to understand that it was watching live theater since the performance lacked, after all, what had heretofore been an essential ingredient of live theater, live actors. The audience, deprived of its standard ambience and cultural signals for theater, failed to applaud at the fade-down, but neither did its members applaud the viewing of other sculptures, even when the gallery lights dimmed as they did to announce another performance. And, of course, there was no curtain call for "Breath." Who would appear? In part I took that lack of response to the performance as a measure of the success of this production which had blurred the distinction among artistic forms, even as I may have inadvertently linked the performance to a neo-Dadaist revival of found sculpture. Most encouraging, however, was the audience sneaking looks at the tangle of materials between performances, unsure of whether or not it was permissible to peer behind the curtain into the darkness through what, on one level, looked merely like a covered hole in a wall. I thought for a time of putting up a sign between performances that said "No peeking," but then the hanging and removing of the sign would become an added signal that something was about to occur or that something had just been completed. And finally I liked the peeking since it confirmed this integral conjunction of theater and human desire, the drive to see what is forbidden, the Bearded Lady or the Pigman in their dressing rooms preparing for performance, the impulses that Freud, Beckett, and Blau had explored in such depth.

# Notes

1 Many of these details to the stories of *More Pricks than Kicks* derive from and expand the work outlined in that entry for the *Grove Companion to Samuel Beckett* (Ackerley and Gontarski 2004, 381, and cross-references to individual stories).

2 See, for example, *The Standard Edition of the Complete Psychological Works of Sigmund Freud (S.E.)*, volume 7, 56–7.

3 For more on Beckett, Blau, and Artaud, see Chapter 10 "Theatrical and Theoretical Intersections: Samuel Beckett, Herbert Blau, Civil Rights and the Politics of *Godot*."

# 9

# "He wants to know if it hurts!": The Body as Text in Samuel Beckett's Theater

*When I think of it ... all these years ... but for me ... where would you be ... (Decisively.) You'd be nothing more than a little heap of bones at the present minute, no doubt about it. Vladimir,* Waiting for Godot, Act I

What drove (or lured) Samuel Beckett to theater—as a retreat, a haven, or even a sanctuary—was the body, the shape or form that text takes in performance; that is, onstage the body itself, whole or in part, damaged, otherwise restricted, or fully functional, as material object, shade, specter, or voice, is or becomes a, if not the, performative text, and Beckett's theater of what Ruby Cohn has called "afflicted bodies"[1] or what might be deemed spectacles of pain has attracted actors to explore the body's functionality in performance, especially actors with certain limitations on that functionality, actors with forms of physical dysfunction or degenerations, an ill Julian Beck performing *That Time* (1985), for instance, or a failing Harold Pinter's performing *Krapp's Last Tape* in a wheelchair (2006), both actors dying of cancer as they performed. Bodily issues come to the fore as well in "The *Endgame* Project" performed by Dan Moran and Chris Jones, both actors with Parkinson's disease, while "neuro diverse" performances of *Not I* feature Jess Thom of Touretteshero. Such productions by performers whose bodies may be damaged or miswired do not suggest that Beckett was writing for dysfunctional bodies per se but that his creatures themselves tend to be afflicted in one way or another, and so his theater can and has refocused attention on issues of theatrical embodiment with performances that can recalibrate theatrical affect. As Anna McMullan put it, Beckett's drama "provokes modes of perceiving, conceiving and experiencing embodiment that address wider preoccupations with corporeality, technology and systems of power" (McMullan 2010, 2). For the fully able actors, Beckett himself has placed unprecedented restrictions on their performability, limiting movement, posture, expression, and the vocal repertoire, thereby, in some senses, handicapping them, limiting their abilities and functionality. Billie Whitelaw and Lisa Dwan's discussions of performing *Not I* at Beckett's designated pace and amid necessary technical restrictions are particularly apposite here, furthermore.

The author, on the other hand, has famously commented to Deirdre Bair, among others, that he needed something physical and substantial to counteract the writing of what became the three French novels he produced in a white heat in post–Second World War Paris, and he turned to theater amid the interstices, producing one he, finally, rejected, *Eleutheria*, and one on which his international reputation (and his income, as it turned out) would be founded, *En attendant Godot* (*Waiting for Godot*). Much of what we loosely call Samuel Beckett's innovation in the theater, his experimentalism or avant-gardism, his contribution to the Modernist or late Modernist stage, has thus grown out of considering the body textually, the body in performance. As he developed as a playwright his theater was often based on dissatisfaction and so constituted an assault not only on that body but on its platform, the boards, the theater in which he sought and found refuge. Most of these theatrical experiments, then, foregrounded embodiment, or are at least riffs on sets of inherited performative conventions, just as his innovation in fiction constituted an assault on narrative tradition and convention as his characters, for one, became more and more ethereal, less and less substantially recognizable, or at least they were less discretely defined, from *Murphy* to *Watt* to *Molloy* and, most famously, to *The Unnamable* and its residua, in something of a dematerialization if not a degeneration. In those assaults, he has shorn the novel of story and the theater of entertainment value, has reintroduced metaphysics and indeterminacy into the confident, plastic arts of theater and performance, dispersed the idea of literary character and of discreet embodiment into something like disembodied voices, exploring thus the possibilities and limits of character fragmentation and disembodiment to the point of disappearance ("Breathe" most obviously, for instance), to the point of indistinguish-ability ("Quad" most obviously, for instance) while reasserting the primacy of image and pattern on stage. Even language, narrative, and poetry, when they were not abandoned (the "Acts without Words" most obviously, for instance), emerged as material, substance, the book itself part of the theatrical image (*Ohio Impromptu* most obviously, for instance). Even as the capacities of writer, narrative, and language were all diminished and subverted, and while theatrical images too were reduced, they nonetheless dominated performance, the body among them, to the near exclusion of story itself. Theater would be an especially tempting target for Beckett's theatrical revisionings since it is the one literary genre not only mediated by the body but impossible without it (dance, say, would be its wordless equivalent)—or so we thought ("Breath" most obviously, for instance). Theater's "ineluctable modality of the visible" opened imaginative possibilities for Beckett, but possibilities of subversion and diminution of such ineluctability in favor of metonymic, dematerialized images of bodies, often approaching inertia.

The move against an inherited sense of theater is oft discussed in the critical discourse surrounding *Waiting for Godot*. Less celebrated is the innovation inherent in Beckett's second produced play, *Endgame*, which opens with protracted silence, an extended mime, and develops (if that's the word) a world in which bodies are restricted or incapacitated, such incapacity at very least a parallel, nonverbal text to the play's fragmentary narrative threads, to which Hamm calls attention repeatedly: "There's English for you." When George Devine thought that the one-act of *Endgame* needed another to fill out a theatrical evening, Beckett went wordless, returning to the idea of pure bodily movement where *Endgame* began, and he wrote "Act without Words." Once he had written another of the same title, he thought to number them, I and II, but they might have been II and III since preliminary to *Endgame* Beckett had written "Mime du rêveur," an incomplete, four-page typescript now at Dartmouth College, which has strong links to *Fin de partie/ Endgame* and *Krapp's Last Tape*; other scholars have connected the unfinished mime with *Film* and *Nacht und Träume* as well.

*Endgame*, like *All That Fall*, Beckett's first excursion into disembodied voice, is one of the few works of Beckett that explores something like overt codependency, or at least Clov as caregiver seems as reliant on the object of his care, Hamm, as Hamm is on Clov. Neither seems functional without the other, a relationship implied in *Waiting for Godot* but not fully foregrounded as it is in *Endgame*. An early fragment, *Avant Fin de partie*, already contains an embedded narrative (or wild fantasy) of a dutiful son as caregiver to, in this case, a mother, who dies in the course of the narration. In the radio drama of the same period, *All That Fall*, Beckett explores codependency with Maddy and Dan Rooney, another Beckettian odd couple with less than fully enabled bodies who continue their progressive deterioration, the blind Dan, like Hamm, all but incapable of movement without assistance from Maddy, or the unseen child whose life Dan may have terminated amid his frustrations.

Some of Beckett's most profound generic assaults, then, have extended to what we have traditionally called character in literature and its representations in the theater through the body. Such rethinking simultaneously constitutes an exploration of the limits of representation itself. The paradox of the body, visible or invisible, on or off stage, corporeal or incorporeal, and in the later teleplays, live or pixilated, is thus explored from his first, still unproduced play, *Eleutheria,* where the assault on convention may have been too overt and hence too obvious as Beckett returned to it later in life, to his final teleplays where bodily disappearances and erasures could be more easily effected and manipulated electronically through a ghost in the machine, and so his receptiveness if not attraction to filming even some works written originally for stage, Billie Whitelaw's performance in *Not I* (1973, aired on BBC II on April 17, 1977), and Beckett's final directorial and theatrical effort, *Was Wo* (*What Where*, broadcast on June 13, 1986, by Süddeutscher Rundfunk ["Südfunk" or SDR for short]), most prominently.

Beckett's most original literary characters, Godot, for instance, or the boys in *Endgame* and *All That Fall*, remain un-embodied yet forcefully present, driving what action there is and exercising a stranglehold on other embodied characters to whom they are, apparently, tied. That irony was not lost on Beckett who, on the one hand, relished and was even comforted by the very concreteness, the physicality, the thereness of theater, even as he continually worked to undermine and to erode it. Michael Haerdter, Beckett's directorial assistant at the 1967 Schiller-Theater *Endspiel* (*Endgame*), reported Beckett's musing that "Theater for me is first of all recreation [recreation?] from work on fiction. We are dealing with a given space and with people in that space. That is relaxing" (Beckett 1992c, xiii). The phrase "people in that space," however, is nothing if not disingenuous, for at least part of Beckett's fascination with theater has been to play against the very concreteness he seemed to embrace and find "relaxing," to sustain as much epistemological and phenomenal uncertainty and ambiguity as the sign systems and the corporeality of theater would allow. Often, in fact, he has subverted the very senses with which we confirm theater's concreteness, the thereness of character, by having the audience question what it thinks it sees, as he offers us figures, creatures, images who are likely not there, like the boy Clov claims to have sighted in *Endgame*, who remains dis- or un-embodied, the pacing May of *Footfalls*, whose pretense of embodiment is eradicated in the very short fourth part or act of the play, the Voice in *Eh Joe*, Bam in *What Where*, and Godot himself.

   When French novelist and filmmaker Alain Robbe-Grillet observed early on of *Godot* that the two tramps "do nothing [...] say virtually nothing and [...] have no other quality than to be present" (Robbe-Grillet 1965, 111), he is dead-on. He further puts the issue in phenomenological terms, foregrounding something of bodily presence: "The human condition, Heidegger says, is *to be there*. Probably it is the theatre, more than any other mode of representing reality, which reproduced this situation most naturally. The dramatic character *is on stage*, that is his primary quality: he is *there*" (Robbe-Grillet 1965, 111). For Didi and Gogo, the problem most often is their being there, but in which "there" are they situated: the near empty space of the stage, Beckett's anticipated empty theaters or the vast empty spaces of the universe. And yet what is easily overlooked in Robbe-Grillet's compelling assessment of *Godot* and much of Beckett's later drama is "the dramatic character" who is not "*on stage*" at all, or rather not as a corporeal entity, not phenomenally, there only by or as a reflection, a linguistic construct, a spectral image. Even the two characters, the two witnesses to Godot's absence, "who have no other quality than to be present," say, have serious doubts about their own corporeality or presence and fear their not being entities in a phenomenal world, fear their *not* being there at all. In Act II Gogo insists, "We weren't here" yesterday. And Didi shouts at Godot's youthful messenger, doubting his own corporeality, "You're sure you saw me, you won't come and tell me to-morrow that you never saw me!" (Beckett 1954, 59). If theater is in the seeing, this doubt of being seen doubles as a doubt of being itself and of theater itself.

By 1964 Beckett's assault on theatrical presence, or character presence, was redoubled with the imposition of unprecedented bodily restriction. *Play* seems in many respects an assault on itself, on theater—as *Eleuthéria* and *Godot* had been a decade earlier—drama playing against itself, theater playing against the very idea of theater. If *Godot* eliminated "action" from the stage, *Play* all but eliminated motion. If *Godot* eliminated intelligible causality, *Play* all but eliminated intelligibility itself, as the words were to be uttered at machinegun-like speed according to Beckett's instructions. If *Godot* detailed the power of the offstage, the power of the incorporeal, *Play* moved the power source to center stage, the monologues orchestrated by a Godot-like entity wielding, or represented as, a torturous light. The character M reminds us of the central dramatic and ontological problem when he asks, "Am I as much as being seen?" (Beckett 1984b, 157).

The following year a disembodied "Voice" entered Beckett's performance pieces through his first teleplay, *Eh Joe*, written in 1965 and broadcast on the BBC on July 4, 1966. The woman's "Voice" that assails Joe seems a representation, an exteriorization of Joe's internal conflict. After completing the writing of *Film* about May of 1963 (the completion date of the earliest holograph version), Beckett began in late August a series of exploratory monologues, which he worked on for the remainder of that year and called, collectively, "Kilcool." Although "Kilcool" developed some nine years later directly into the metonymical *Not I*, it also contains excerpts that connect it to *Film* and *Eh Joe*. In "Kilcool" the female narrator speaks of the joy of being unseen and introduces the theme of psychological duality or alternate personalities: "Someone in me trying to get out, saying let me out." Joe too seems to have some sort of undeveloped or unborn opposite within him. As we know Beckett had been preoccupied with Jung's theory of multiple personalities, often manifest as voices, since he attended at least one of Jung's

Tavistock Clinic lectures in London in the fall of 1935, a lecture about the lack of unity to consciousness. Aspects of consciousness, according to Jung, can become almost independent personalities and might even "become visible or audible. They appear as visions, they speak in voices which are like the voices of definite people" (Jung 1968, 80). In the late summer of 1976 Beckett recalled this Jungian experience in Berlin to actress Hildegard Schmahl, who was preparing the role of May in *Footfalls* under Beckett's direction. "In the thirties," he told her, "C. G. Jung, the psychologist, once gave a lecture in London and told of a female patient who was being treated by him. Jung said he wasn't able to help this patient and for this, according to Beckett, he gave an astonishing explanation. The girl wasn't living. She existed but didn't actually live" (qtd. in Beckett 1992c, 338). This was in part Beckett's explanation for his character, the incompletely developed May, who hears (or creates) her mother's voice, or is created by her mother's narrative and presumably writes plays herself. Joe too seems to be such an incompletely created being or personality. The theatrical problem that would preoccupy Beckett for the remainder of his career was how to represent in language and stage images the incomplete being, the *être manqué*. The solution was already present in *Endgame*: the part is already the whole (for details, see Chapter 6).

The narrator in "Kilcool" also hopes for peace when memory fails and voices no longer assail her, a hope that suggests the sort of integration of personality Krapp longed for as well. Joe, we are told, on the other hand, has developed the means to still these voices in his head, at least some of them. But in *Eh Joe* Voice is not only the voice of memory, even memory rearranged or juxtaposed, but at least creative if not created memory, that is, memory leeching into imagination or creativity. These voices, which Jung associated with the creative act and which Beckett's characters at times try to quell but as often embrace, are already echoes of or at least in the subconscious, and stilling them is Beckett's famous pursuit of silence, an artistic suicide. Unlike the young Beckett, who could say in *Proust* that "art is the apotheosis of solitude" (Beckett 1957c, 47), Joe is more ambivalent toward the possibility of silence, for, as the devisor of *Company* knows, that voice, internal or external, echo of himself or of others, is also company: "Devisor of the voice and of its hearer and of himself. Devisor of himself for company. [...] Himself he devises too for company" (Beckett 1980, 26).

Such an image of the creator creating himself, presumably from the outside, is almost a verbal Escher drawing or an extension of Lacan's dictum that the unconscious is structured like a language to the notion that self itself (or each "self") is a verbal construct and hence not a substance, not a body, which was much of the point in, say, *The Unnamable*. In *Eh Joe*, the body of the woman, say, or the bodies of the women, exist only in the body of the text.

In 2007 JoAnne Akalaitis revisioned Beckett in a quirky evening of shorts with a consistent actor and set, but a decision to cover the stage with some six inches of sand made sense only for the first of the four plays, "Act without Words, I." The sand made stage movement all but impossible for the three subsequent plays, and perhaps this was part of Akalaitis's point, to echo Winnie's observations in *Happy Days*, "what a curse mobility." The setting at very least handicapped the motion of actors themselves (or himself in this case) already suffering under physical handicap. The wheelchair of "Rough for Theatre, I," for example, was immobilized in the sand. Most at issue was the eponymous Joe of *Eh Joe* who could hardly shuffle about the room in his paranoid mime or ballet to shut out prying eyes, real or imagined. But in her revisioning Akalaitis made something of a virtue of that handicap. Joe's movement was filmed and projected as a set of multiple images on a series of screens in a variety of sizes. In fact, this hybrid genre, live theater, film, and "live" film, a technique Atom Egoyan had used for his staging of *Eh Joe* in 2006, was a central feature to all four plays, used not only to great effect individually but as a thread among the plays: multiple projected images and hence multiple simultaneous perspectives. Less successful, or perhaps the production's fatal flaw, was the decision to take the action outside what the woman's voice calls that "penny farthing hell you call your mind" (Beckett 1984b, 202) and to embody Joe's re-imaginings as a spot-lit woman. A visible, present Karen Kandel spoke the lines of the text, assailing Joe, recounting a story not of her own rejection but that of another spurned lover. Mercifully, the taunting suicide itself was neither filmed nor re-enacted. Such decisions and the addition of music by Philip Glass were the sort of theatrical latitude that caused such a fuss with Akalaitis's 1984 *Endgame*.

By 1976 Beckett continued his ontological exploration of being in narrative and finally being as narrative, producing in the body of the text the text as body. The thought-tormented body we see pacing before us in *Footfalls* is not there, or rather she exists only within the embedded narratives of the play. The subject of these late plays, as in the late narratives, is less the secret recesses of the repressed subconscious or the imagination valorized by Romantic poets and painters than the dispersed, post-Freudian ego or Jungian consciousness, voice as alien other. As the narrator of *Fizzle 2*, "Horn Came Always," suggests, "It is in the outer space, not to be confused with the other [that is, the inner space or the Other?], that such images develop" (Beckett 1996, 230).

In the third act of *Footfalls*, May, who herself seems to be narrated, narrates a semblance of what we see on stage. May's anagrammatic character, Amy, is represented in a dialogue with her mother, Mrs. Winter, concerning the former's attendance at an Evensong service: "Amy, did you observe anything ... strange at Evensong? [...] Amy: I mean, Mother, that to say I observed nothing ... strange is indeed to put it mildly. For I observed nothing of any kind, strange or otherwise. I saw nothing, heard nothing, of any kind. I was not there" (Beckett 1984b, 243). By the crucial short fourth act of *Footfalls*, an act too often swallowed by applause in performance, we find for ten seconds "No trace of May" (Beckett 1984b, 243), a reminder that May was always "not there," or there only as spirit or trace.

By 1981 Beckett produced his most overtly formal, geometric, and symmetrical work and with it Beckett returned to mime in this "Ballet for four people," written directly for television and produced as *Quadrat 1 + 2* by Süddeutscher Rundfunk (SDR), broadcast on October 8, 1981, directed by Beckett with the assistance of Walter Asmus, with Helfried Foron, Juerg Hummel, Claudia Knujpfer, and Susanne Rehe as the dancers. The first English broadcast of the SDR production (no translation required, of course) was by the BBC 2 on December 16, 1982. One, then two, then three, then four figures, each in pastel djellabas, appear in succession to trace the figure of a quadrangle to a rapid, polyrhythmic, percussion beat, then depart in reverse sequence. Each figure describes half the *Quad*, tracing the incommensurability of side and diagonal, and, each abruptly avoids the center, making a jerky turn to his or her left as a diversion away from it. It may first appear that "they were avoiding one another, but gradually one realized they were avoiding the center. There was something terrifying about it ... It was danger." The action at first appears comic, almost slapstick, as characters rush toward an apparent central collision, but collision is avoided by the aforementioned abrupt turns. The pattern is repeated, from one to four participants, then back to one then to none in an oscillation, a crescendo and diminuendo of movement which shatters whatever comic possibilities were present initially. The final effect is one of prescribed, determined, enforced motion. One is reminded again of Winnie's assessment: "What a curse mobility (Beckett 1986, 158)."

*Quad* was not Becktt's sole venture at staging geometry, of course. The thought dates at least from 1963 or so, when, in the same notebook that contains the precursor to *Not I*, "Kilcool," Beckett began a mime for Jack MacGowran, tentatively entitled "J. M. Mime." In that work two pairs, son and father and son and mother (Beckett even entertained the possibility of "one carrying the other"), try to describe the greatest number of paths along quarters of a square to arrive back at center, 0. "Starting from 0 return to 0 by greatest number of paths" is Beckett's description of the action. The pattern of composition in "J. M. Mime" is toward greater and greater complexity, an impulse that does not carry over to the revived notion. In *Quad* Beckett enlarged the triangles and added rhythm. And the theme is reversed as the center is avoided not sought, and the oppression of mobility was reinforced by sinister turns.

Near the end of the taping, Beckett created what amounted to an unplanned second act for the play. When he saw the color production of *Quad* rebroadcast on a black-and-white monitor, he decided instantly to create *Quad II*. Beckett's printed text (in any language) was, however, never revised to acknowledge this remarkable revision of the work's fundamental structure. No printed version of the play bears the title of the production, and so no accurate version, one that includes Beckett's revisions, exists in print. The collected editions of Beckett's plays, (*CDW*) and (*CSP*), however, carry five notes on what became *Quad II,* beginning with: "The original scenario (*Quad I*) was followed in the Stuttgart production by a variation (*Quad II*) (5) (Beckett 1984b, 293). This afterthought to the text of *Quad* has a parenthetical five at the end of the first note (as above), which may be a corrupt version of the "5'," the suggested duration of *Quad II* designated in the second note. More likely it is a designation that these postproduction notes are the fifth element in this script since four other designations are apparent, at least sections numbered 2–4, but those numbers themselves seem arbitrary and have no clear or parallel point of origination, no clear "1." Beckett's own videotaped German production, thus, remains the only "final" text for *Quad*. In the 1980s Beckett began *What Where* with a dimly lit megaphone (at least in the original, unrevised text) that speaks first, announcing images of the last five beings, "In the present as were we still" (Beckett 1984b, 310). The voice of Bam, represented on stage as a megaphone or later as a shimmery light or hologram, is already a voice from beyond the grave, according to Beckett. Four characters, Bam, Bom, Bim, and Bem (the fifth unseen, incorporeal player or vowel mentioned (perhaps Bum) is already in the process of being "worked over" as the play opens), are nearly identical in appearance, even their names are differentiated only by a single, central vowel (an echo of Rimbaud's sonnet, "Voyelles") and are represented as if they existed.[2] Bam's voice (V) controls the action, switching light (of memory and imagination) on and off the playing area, or the space of memory, to initiate action. In recasting the play for television, Beckett drastically altered the visual imagery of his first version and simplified dialogue and action, trimming the false starts, that is, revising away much of the metatheatrical, internal revisions of the original. In Stuttgart the speaking voice became a huge, distorted face of Bam, refracted, diffuse, and dominating half the television screen. In his Stuttgart notebook Beckett wrote that "S (Stimme [Voice]) = mirror reflection of Bam's face." This enlarged and distorted death mask replaced the suspended "small megaphone at head level" of the original publication. As Beckett wrote in his Stuttgart notebook, "Loudspeaker out" (qtd. in Beckett 1999, 451). The image that now intrigued him was that of the hooded "statue of John Donne in St. Patrick's Cathedral in London," according to his cameraman, Jim Lewis (Fehsenfeld 1986, 232). One assumes that Lewis has misremembered his London monuments and that he must mean the 1631 statue of Donne by Nicholas Stone in the east end of the Chancel of St. Paul's Cathedral in London, where Donne is buried. The shrouded Dean of St. Paul's (a post Donne held for the last decade of his life) looks very spectral in this sculptured rendering. This new image finally represented, according to Lewis, "The image of Bam in the beyond or beyond the grave or whatever you want to call it—the death mask thing that wasn't originally planned at all. [...] That was the problem almost up to the end until I came up with this idea of enlarging the death mask [...]" (qtd. in Fehsenfeld 1986, 236). The two Bams, two stage or video representations, and two voices are not one and the same. Because of technical difficulties, the French stage production replaced the enlarged and distorted reflection of Bam's face with a halo, a ring of diffuse light. Pierre Chabert's production note is as follows: "*rond lumineux* = source de Voix" (qtd. in Beckett 1999, 451). For the English stage première, however, Beckett suggested a return to a hologram of the distorted face of Bam.

In the Stuttgart television production the difference between the two Bams was achieved mechanically. "There was a slightly higher frequency in [the voice] of the younger Bam, and a lower, deeper effect in the older Bam," according to Lewis (qtd. in Fehsenfeld 1986, 237). In both French and English stage productions that followed Beckett's full revisioning of the text, the difference in voice was similarly achieved by recording and altering V to create, as Walter Asmus suggests, "the ghost Bam, dead Bam, distorted image of a face in a grave, somewhere not in this world any longer, imagining that he comes back to life in the world, dreaming and seeing himself as a little face on the screen" (qtd. in Fehsenfeld 1986, 238). In the Stuttgart notebook Beckett wrote, "S's voice prerecorded. Bam's, but changed." And shortly thereafter he added, "Bam's voice in dialogue with some colour. S [Stimme, i.e., Voice] colourless" (qtd. in Beckett 1999, 451).

Instead of players in long gray gowns, even there their corporeality suspect, the four figures of the revised *What Where* now appeared as floating faces dissolving in and out as the TV screen itself became the field of memory to replace the lighted rectangle of the stage. In either version, the figures of *What Where* are disembodied, all the more so as they are represented by the patterns of dots on the television screen.

Such an overview suggests not only the extraordinary diversity of Samuel Beckett's theater and televisual works and his concomitant direct work with performance in the theater and on the sound stage, but one finds, if not a consistency at least a series of threads that continually lead to the body in performance, a textual manifestation unique to performing arts. If Beckett was not always happy working in so public an environment, he was always energized and intrigued with its possibilities that performance provided, and that creative space of performance proved to be an heuristic that continued to generate creative possibilities late into his life and even to the end of his own corporeal presence.

# Notes

1 Cohn, Ruby. *A Beckett Canon* (Ann Arbor: University of Michigan Press, 2001), 165, and "'It hurts?': Afflicted Bodies in the Plays of Samuel Beckett." *Peering Behind the Curtain: Disability, Illness and the Extraordinary Body in Contemporary Theatre*, ed. Thomas Fahy and Kimball King (London: Routledge, 2002).

2 See "Beckett's Production Notebook for *Was Wo* (*What Where*) at the Studios of Süddeutscher Rundfunk, Stuttgart, June 1985," reprinted in facsimile with transcription in Gontarski, 1999, 421–47. All the following quotes from this notebook are taken from these pages.

# PART THREE

# A Philosophical Life

# 10

## Theoretical and Theatrical Intersections: Samuel Beckett, Herbert Blau, Civil Rights, and the Politics of *Godot*

*The notion of entertainment is anti-theatrical.*
*Ionesco*, Improvisation, or The Shepherd Chameleon
(Impromptu d'Alma, *1956*).

*For Beckett, irrelevance is next to godliness. Herbert*
*Blau, 1957*

*We propose to establish a theater in the deep South*
*[...] A combination of art and social awareness [...]*
*Through theater, we think to open a new area of*
*protest. (Gilbert Moses, Free Southern Theater, 1963)*

Samuel Beckett could not have emerged as a man of the theater at a more propitious moment, as the staid 1950s were developing into the politically vibrant, active, if finally disappointing 1960s, a time when a literary movement loosely called Modernism was refreshed and took a decidedly political turn, a time when Artaud intersected with Brecht. The timing was, for the most part, accidental for Beckett, unplanned at least, except that, as Martin Esslin has posited in his highly influential study, *The Theatre of the Absurd* (1961), the post–Second World War era generated a wave of cultural change that similarly marked the First World War era, with Surrealism serving as something of a link or bridge. He called this second wave of artistic rejection and experiment absurd, after Albert Camus's critique of futility in *The Myth of Sisyphus* (1942), and since its dominant manifestation seemed to be in postwar performance, perhaps its most direct connection to Surrealism, it became for Esslin "the theatre of the absurd." The phrase became something of a catchphrase to explain (and so, sadly, to domesticate) the dislocations, fragmentation, uncertainties, and irresolutions that characterized the work of certain dominantly European, avant-garde writers, Samuel Beckett among them, even as the designation has subsequently come to be seen as an ill fit, at least for Beckett's literary experiments, as differences between his enterprise and those of others in Esslin's category—say, Eugene Ionesco, Arthur Adamov, or Boris Vian—seem to outweigh similarities. Yet, while Esslin's emphasis on the absurd may have outlived its usefulness, at least for Beckett's work, his book opened by detailing an extraordinary staging of his most famous play, *Waiting for Godot*, performed by the San Francisco Actor's Workshop before 650 inmates of San Quentin Prison in 1957. After the play's failures in preview in Miami, Florida, in January 1956, and its lackluster Broadway debut that April, the San Quentin production served as a revitalization, a validation of the play's visceral power, and it suggested something of a political edge to Beckett's first produced play, as the act of waiting became less an intellectual abstraction or a philosophical conundrum than a realistic depiction of a social group, many of whom were overtly "condemned to life."

By 1957 political undercurrents of this play, seemingly about nothing, had already been established and explored with Broadway's second production from producer Michael Myerberg and his replacement director (for Alan Schneider who staged the Miami tryout) Herbert Berghof (who directed the Broadway premiere some nine months earlier) with, this time, an all African-American cast: Mantan Moreland (of the Charlie Chan films and "Duffy's

Tavern" radio fame) as Estragon and Earle Hyman as Vladimir, with dancer Geoffrey Holder as Lucky and Rex Ingram as Pozzo. Bert Chamberlain made his Broadway debut as the Boy. Producer Myerberg had approached Beckett about the *Godot* revival with, if Bert Lahr were not available, an all African-American cast with some reservation, as Beckett wrote his American publisher on August 30, 1956: "I spent a rather dismal evening with Myerberg (nice man) and his lady friend. I mentioned to him that Godot [*sic*] by an all-negro cast would be interesting. He said he had had the same idea but was nervous about telling me, fearing I wd not like it. [...] I had a letter from him some days ago in which he says that [Bert] Lahr is not available and that he is getting going with preparations for performance with all negro cast. This pleases me, rightly or wrongly, much" (Beckett *Letters* 2011, 647). The revival opened at the Ethel Barrymore Theatre on January 21, 1957. After dismal reviews, however, some charging that the production was under-rehearsed, the play closed after only six performances, making the fifty-nine performances of the original Broadway production at the John Golden Theatre seem the more impressive.[1]

The productions of *Waiting for Godot* that followed the world premiere, then, were politically tinged without being overtly political, but the foregrounding of a racial cast to essentially a white Broadway audience and the prison production of the play, both in 1957, paralleled the hectic, early days of the American Civil Rights movement, and such a connection grew explicit with the start of the Free Southern Theater, which was formed in September of 1963 by activists already engaged in what was then simply called "The Movement." Gilbert Moses was a journalist for the *Mississippi Free Press* and John O'Neal was a leader in SNCC, the Student Non-Violent Coordinating Committee that was founded in 1960 by students from Shaw University, and the FST was rethinking theater as well as advocating a new social order: "we are seeking a new kind of liberation from old forms of theatre, old techniques and ideas. A freedom to find new forms of theatrical expression and to find expression in people who have never expressed themselves in theatre before" (Schechner 1964, 65); "other reasons for getting involved in the FST: a personal commitment to theatre, a belief that the theatre is the most universal of the arts" (Schechner 1964, 66).[2] The project and its goals might have been taken as something of a direct gloss on Beckett's *Waiting for Godot*, and, unsurprisingly, one of the first plays that FST chose to perform was indeed *Waiting for Godot*. While Michael Myerberg famously called for 70,000 New York intellectuals to support the play in its New York debut, FST's audiences were dominantly sharecroppers, and the political climate was explosive: "The church we played in had been shot into the week before we came with *Purlie Victorious* [by Ossie Davis] and *Waiting for Godot*. There were bullet holes above the door. Yet when we played, they all came out" (Schechner, 1964, 64). Knowing very little about the American South, Beckett had a vision of the play's landscape, political, and terrestrial, that was, nonetheless, not far from that in which the FST was working. Writing to art critic Georges Duthuit on January 3, 1951 (as it turns out exactly two years before the world premiere), Beckett explained that he was seeking a "sordidly abstract" form of nature, "a place of suffering, sweaty and fishy, where sometimes a turnip grows." Beckett suggested no bullet holes as part of the décor, but his is a landscape where "a ditch opens up" (Beckett *Letters* 2011, 218).[3]

Midway through one of the FST's tours of the South, director and white actor James Cromwell had fellow actors apply whiteface or blackface, which "immediately stopped that first black-white reaction and forced the audience to deal with something else," and so the performance deflected "the image of a white man holding a rope around a Negro's neck" (King 2012, 71). What the FST was offering, then, was not only protest or politics but new ways of seeing in place of what might be or have become agitprop political performance. Their focus was as theoretical as immediately activist, and so their performances stood at the intersection of Modernist ideology: "The theatre is also at the intersection between political and artistic forces. Its forms, from the Greeks on, have been concerned with the community in conflict. And here [during the Civil Rights movement] we had a situation which suited those old forms" (Schechner 1964, 66). In 2012, playing Pozzo in a Los Angeles revival of the play,[4] Cromwell reflected on his earliest experiences with *Godot* and the FST: "I tried to deal with the race issue in the play. I was white and Lucky was black. The slave relationship [of Pozzo and Lucky], which they understood all too well, was represented. I put on blackface and the black actors put on whiteface" (McNutley 2012). Such an emphasis seemed to echo or respond to Herbert Blau's San Quentin production with his San Francisco Actor's Workshop and his subsequent call for something of a politically charged, activist theater. When he came to write what amounted to a manifesto for America's regional theaters, *The Impossible Theatre*, he noted overtly, "Throughout the book, I shall be using theater as an image of the Cold War and the Cold War as an image of the theater" (Blau 1964a, 21). That Cold War politics surfaced overtly when Blau's production of *Godot* was chosen to represent American theater at Expo 1958, the Brussels World's Fair. The tour was threatened by the U.S. State Department's barring several members of the troupe from international travel because of their leftist political affiliations. In another high-profile performance, the production was reprised at the Century 21 Exposition, the Seattle World's Fair in 1962. Prison productions of Beckett's first produced play, moreover, would become, if not the norm, at least periodically recurrent, as with director Jan Jonson's return to San Quentin Prison in 1988, the production featuring former prisoner Spoon Jackson (himself a prisoner for thirty-eight years) as Pozzo.[5]

Fearing perhaps the assimilation of theater's political edge by a work's aesthetics or, on the contrary, its aesthetic qualities growing subservient to social and political goals, Blau famously turned his back on theater itself, rejected a theater of representation, a decision through which he announced that collaboration with actors, the performance of simulations, the staging of illusions, what he called, after Beckett, "just play" or the whole bloody mimetic show, could go no further and that playing in theatrical space was far less imaginative and less creative, less politically charged than *playing* in what the Surrealists often thought of as "the theater of mind," which was a richer and more resonant chamber than any external or material space. (See, for example, Salvador Dali's theatrical maquette, the spectral, illusionistic *The Little Theater* of 1934.) It was a space into which Beckett would move as well with his late plays of inaction, seriality, specularity, and inarticulation. Blau's decision was also something of a milestone in the development of performance, performance theory, and Modernism itself, which in general had been shy or suspicious of theater and performance. Blau's shift of venues was certainly precipitated by his engagement with critical theory that launched, or paralleled, or confirmed his quest for the sources of performance, that ever-receding ghost of a wellhead, a glimpse of which Beckett, rather Words, searched out as well in *Words an Music*.

What Blau abandoned at first was mimetic or illusionistic theater, even in its nonmimetic, avant-garde guise, to pursue the traces of theatrical thought back through the laminations of the performing subconscious to the primal force that generated theater itself—a quest, in short, for what Blau, citing Artaud, has called "the nonrepresentable origin of performance" (Blau 1987, 166–7), a quest not dissimilar from that of the FST. Much of Blau's theoretics was already at the fore in his earliest productions, however, intuited through the nerve ends. In an unsigned program note to his Actor's Workshop's 1957 production of *Waiting for Godot* called "Who Is Godot?," Blau (unmistakably he, even as the Workshop was founded on ensemble principles)[6] first dismissed the question, then turned it inwards: "But if you must have questions, there are better ones. Who am I? What am I doing here? 'You do see me, don't you,' cries [Vladimir,] one of Beckett's heroes to Godot's angelic messenger. 'You're sure you saw me, you won't come and tell me to-morrow that you never saw me!'" (Beckett 1954, 59). In his second staging of *Waiting for Godot*, after its Miami fiasco, Alan Schneider, who would finally become Beckett's principal theatrical director in the United States, asked to use Blau's original *Godot* program note for his 1959 regional revival at Nina Vance's Alley Theater in Houston, and, in preparation for the Seattle World's Fair, Blau reprised the note again for his *Godot redux* in 1962, some five years after his original 1957 production and just a year before the FST's formation, with an added proviso: "The performance changes, the avant-garde play becomes a classic, the dilemma remains" (Blau 2000, 16). In his memoire, Blau recalled the first cold reading of *Godot* with his tentative cast in his San Francisco home thus: "Many years later, with the figure in the urn of *Play*—'all this,' and enduring pain, could it have been 'just play?'—there's that '*closing repeat*' without closure: 'Am I as much as being seen?' Being *seen* or seen as *being*: either way, no being without being seen" (Blau 2012a, 225). This is a theater *To All Appearances*, as he titled his 1992 critique, subtitling it with the overt declaration of his critical dossier, "Ideology and Performance"—in that order. The decision by James Cromwell to blacken his face and whiten those of his African-American cast, too, was an attempt to destabilize identity and to rethink what is being seen. Cromwell's Black cast, too, might have wondered: "Am I as much as being seen?" Even with its evocation of minstrelsy, the cross-racial makeup can shock audiences into recognition, into rethinking visibility and appearances.[7]

As early as *The Impossible Theater* (1964), then, particularly in the "Notes from the Underground" chapter on his first encounters with Beckett and his critique of theater and the Cold War, Blau was already fully immersed theoretically and politically, thinking through theory and ideology, not only through Freud and Stanislavski, performance "*as if for the first time*" (Blau 2012a, 227), say, but through and beyond Artaud: "In my own theater, under the influence of Artaud, we have experimented with a Theater of Cruelty" (Blau 1964a, 21). That experiment endured, became, finally, a lifelong preoccupation, in relation to which he saw Beckett as well:

> According to Beckett (though, of what I know of [Roger] Blin [Beckett's first French director], this is not quite accurate), Blin considered himself a disciple of Artaud, who—having observed that Western actors have forgotten how to scream—denounced the theater as we know it because it could never be cruel enough. Whether or not it was sufficient became a subject of disagreement between the two [...] when Blin later directed *Endgame* [...]. Certainly Blin admired Artaud, and so did Beckett, though he didn't approve of the enraptured ethic of ritual violence, with its sacrificial actor signaling through the flames, as if the apotheosis of theater—its naked, sonorous, streaming realization, reimagined from the Orphic mysteries—were nothing but a scream. (Blau 2000, 14)

Such a scream is how Blau saw Beckett's theater. He quotes an anecdote from Beckett's meeting with Harold Pinter; Beckett told the English playwright about a visit to a cancer ward and a man dying from throat cancer: "I could hear his screams continually in the night [...]. That's the only kind of form my work has" (Blau 2000, 14), and that apparently is sufficient.

By 1982 in the "Foreword" to his collection of essays, *Blooded Thought: Occasions of Theater*, Stanislavski well behind him, Blau outlined the failures of traditional theater and the ideology which sustains it: "I will not have much to say of the old social occasions of theater when people gathered (so we are told) as a community to remember, through the enactment of a dramatic narrative, the maybe half-forgotten signals of a common set of values and the venerable features of a collective fate" (xi). *Blooded Thought* was a book that signaled Blau's overt shift to the performing self on the *mise en scène* of the page. The shift of playing space from the boards to what Blau calls "the chamber drama of the *mise en scène* of the unconscious" (Blau 1982b, 180) was driven by his assessment "that there is no contemporary theater of any consequence which is conceived for the gathering of an audience with such expectations," that is, "of a common set of values and [...] of a collective fate" (Blau 1982b, xi).

From Roland Barthes, particularly from *The Pleasures of the Text*, then, Blau adopted the notion of writing as performance, and from Jacques Derrida, particularly from his essay on Artaud, he adopted the paradigm of the intertextual weave of discourse laminated so deeply in the spectral subconscious and manifest in traces which remain perpetually at their vanishing points, originless specters of specters, ghosts of thought. In his 1987 essay collection, *The Eye of Prey: Subversions of the Postmodern*, Blau detailed his original attractions as a practical theater man to Derridean theory:

> I began to realize that in the very *difficulty* of his writing he [Derrida] was theorizing the theater work which I had been doing in the seventies. That might be described as a deviation from Brecht to Beckett into a highly allusive, refractory, intensely self-reflexive, ideographically charged process in which we were trying to understand, *to think through*, at the very quick of thought—words, words, words, unspeakably in the body— the metabolism of perception in the (de)materialization of the text. There was also in that process—as there is in the art of acting: *how do I do it? Where does it come from? what is IT?* — something of an obsession with the indeterminacy of origin, and the impact of volition on origin, and whether the thought of it comes before it does, whatever it is, or whether it couldn't be thought without it. (Blau 1987, xxv–xxvi)

Blau's model for theater had generally been psychoanalytic, theater as "that peculiar construct of reflected thought," but his pursuit of the Derridean trace to "the very quick of thought" (Blau 1987, xxv) led to a self-reflexivity which eroded the distance between actor and character, and which in the very impossibility of the pursuit of origination led to a paralysis, something of a solipsistic impasse. That assault against mimesis in the name of desublimated sixties activism, a projection of Artaud's desire to eliminate the remnants of the membrane separating art from life, the elimination, in short, of representation, realized for a time— he thought—by groups like the Living Theater, led, according to Blau, to a theatricalization of culture and "the diffusion of theater into fashion, therapy, politics, education and everyday life" (xvii). In his quest for "Universals in Performance," Blau notes, "The central figure of this critique, as in the most important theatrical experiments of the last generation, is Artaud, whose Theater of Cruelty is not a form of New Theater waiting to be born, but a primordial and juridicial power whose urge, as Derrida shows, is the abolition of representation" (Blau 1987, 166; Blau 1990b, 254). That is, not only "No More Masterpieces," but no more simulations, no more play. In Blau's assessment of theater history, sixties activism, including work by groups like the FST, that most powerful exemplum of street theater, has enjoyed a resurgence in the theater of theory. He notes,

> What I am suggesting, too, is that when the radical activism of the sixties abated or went underground it surfaced again in *theory* as a new erotics of discourse. [And here Blau is again thinking through at least Roland Barthes's *The Pleasures of the Text*.] The lifestyle desires and the polymorphous perversity which were celebrated at Woodstock and seemed to be savaged at Altamont also went under, retreating across the Atlantic, and entered the high intellectual traditions of continental thought, given the *ideology* they were charged with *not* having in the sixties, and are being recycled, biodegradably, as an assault on the phallogocentric structure of bourgeois power, with its invisible ideology. (Blau 1987, 7)

Blau's historiography above may be open to some question since the Frankfurt School, for one, was publishing in the 1940s, but in his version of a theater of theory or theory as theater, he finally found the space for his theatricalized pursuit of self, a specular theater with the self as subject and object of its own reflections (in both senses of that term). But in *The Eye of Prey*, the image gleaned from Beckett's *Imagination Dead Imagine*, Blau situates himself somewhere between (or beyond or behind) Artaud's assault on representation and the theorists' "apotheosis of play" (Blau 1987,

xviii) to reassert the very primacy or at least the inescapability of representation, if only amid the intricacies of language.

Before his full rejection of theater, Blau would launch a Grotowski-like theatrical phase with the touring theater group, KRAKEN, in 1971, a period when he was still concerned with the training of actors and whose protracted periods of rehearsals seemed to grow out of Blau's work on *Endgame*: "Finished, it's finished, nearly finished, it must be nearly finished" (Beckett 1986, 93), which, according to Blau, "became the methodological grounding of the KRAKEN group, where the work was not finished until it was finished, or we'd exhausted everything we could think about it—which usually took more than a year" (Blau 2012a, 249). The details of this work with KRAKEN make up much of the text of his second book, *Take up the Bodies: Theater at the Vanishing Point* (1982). With KRAKEN, text became a performative pretext, but Blau's emphasis was still on psychological acting and the specular self, even as the grounding of that method, a coherent, stable, knowable ego, was disintegrating in post-Freudian psychoanalytic theory. What Blau finally objected to in his repudiation of psychological acting was "the disguise of performance [...] which pretends that it is not performing" (Blau 1987, 181).

The sixties' desublimation of theater coincided with the theatricalization of politics, and so the decade's great drama was less the FST's *Godot* in Mississippi, dangerous and political as that was, than the street violence surrounding the Chicago Democratic Convention in August of 1968 and the subsequent conspiracy trial of the Chicago 8 in the fall of 1969, events of such significance and theatrical magnitude that they dwarfed stage play, even—or especially—re-presentations or simulations of such events (see, for example, the highly dramatized TV "docudrama," *Conspiracy: Trial of the Chicago 8* [1987]). Theater had indeed broken down the walls of its privileged playing space as audiences often found more theater once they left the music halls and confronted the polymorphous play on the streets of Broadway and 42nd Street, or in the streets of Paris in 1968, or in American courtrooms. Artaud had apparently won.

One response to such theatricalization of culture was the detheatricalization of theater itself, versions of something like anti-drama, as in the minimalism of Samuel Beckett's late work and the serialism and inarticulation of some of the Mabou Mines experiments like *Send Receive Send*, remnants of what Walter Gropius called *Total Theater*, the theater he planned for Erwin Piscator in Berlin in the mid-1920s. That concept of theater, a director's theater where the entire theatrical experience took precedence over anything like a (pre)text, was then developed in post–Second World War France by the likes of Jean-Louis Barrault, who had two theatrical models on display at the entrance to his Théâtre du Rond-Point, Antonin Artaud and Samuel Beckett. American versions of Total Theater develop, according to Blau, both "the desire for more theater and the desire for less theater" (Blau 1987, 162); that is, both minimalist theater and that devaluation of text and exaltation of pure play of the anti-verbal experiments of the sixties dubbed "image theater."

What began to suggest itself as futile to Blau as a theatrical director was the precise determination, the origin of voice, of thought, and of authentic being in performance. Who speaks in the theater: the playwright, the director, the actor, history, or simply— or not so simply—text, that is, language itself, inscribed on the page or in the body? Much theatrical squabbling derives, we know, from the internecine battles of apportionment of credit for the voice of theatrical thought, and the conflict is institutionalized in the foundation of "playwright's theaters," as opposed to "actor's theaters (or workshops)," as opposed to "director's theaters"—each asserting its own hegemony. Once we assume that language itself (and I take language here in its broadest, semiotic, psychoanalytic, theatrical sense to suggest all the sign systems converging in theater, or what Blau calls, borrowing from Brecht, "the social" or "theatrical *gestus*, the signifying element of theatre") or voice (which is decidedly not what we have traditionally called "character") speaks, theater becomes the performative mode of discourse, and performance is equally possible on the page and stage (Blau 1987, 165; 1990, 254). The enigma of staging, for Blau, validated a Derridean theory of discourse, as Blau noted:

> It was the precise indeterminacy of the *thing* in all its semantic ghostliness which gave us a method we called *ghosting*. It was an idea of performance concerned, like Derridean theory, with appearance and disappearance [that is, *Theater at the Vanishing Point*] and the following of a trace which is the origin of memory through which it appears. (Blau 1987, xxvi)

If theatrical character and theatrical thought are then spectral, and the performers likewise, where can the quest for authentic theater go but into theoretical multiplicities of difference? For Blau, "The *substance* of the theatrical in the idea of performance is the critical question in the act of performance" (Blau 1987, 166).

In *The Eye of Prey*, however, Blau examines not versions but *Subversions of the Postmodern*, which is, in some senses, Blau's exploration of the limits of theory, and his entrée into the topic is through a reassessment of the sixties, "it is the unfinished agenda of the sixties," he notes, "which infuses the state of mind not only of these essays but of the newer critical thought" (Blau 1987, xv). The nature of Blau's *Subversions of the Postmodern* is a return to the inevitability of representation, in theater manifest most essentially in the consciousness of performance itself in both performer and audience. Such consciousness of repeated or repeating action and the self-consciousness of performance is the essence of representation. This self-consciousness of one's actions—which suggests that one's gestures are always repetitions and hence re-presentations—is what makes theater *theater*, performance *performance*, even according to Derrida in his essays on Artaud.

Blau then became increasingly skeptical of what he calls Grotowski's "paratheatrical enterprise"—"the somewhat utopian desire to replace the illusions of Total Theater with the promise of Total Life" (Blau 1987, 162).[8] Even the studies of performance in primitive cultures, the emphasis on what Richard Schechner calls "actuals,"[9] Blau found, finally, have been misdirected and suspect since, "In the studies of aboriginal cultures, we have been made aware of the accretions of everyday life which become, with inflexions of ceremony but no clear demarcation from just living, occasions of performance" (Blau 1987, 163). For Blau, then, members of that culture are "*performing* those functions of just living," and, finally, "what makes theater theater is our ability to discern it as such" (Blau 1987, 162). Current performance theory, for Blau, too often "obscures the ontological gap between the actuality of everyday life and the actuality of performance" (Blau 1987, 162), a position with which Schechner (one of the early supporters and sponsors of the FST when he was at Tulane) is far less suspicious. The difference in theater is between "just being or being some*one*, the presentation [or re-presentation] of a self" (Blau 1987, 162). There is always that split, that doubling in theater, a repetition, a seeming to be. "There is nothing more illusory in performance," notes

Blau, "than the illusion of the unmediated. It can be a very powerful illusion in the theater, but it *is* theater, it is *theater*, the truth of illusion, which haunts all performance whether or not it occurs in the theater" (Blau 1987, 164–5).

Blau's rethinking of postmodern or late modern performance is not so much a reversal or reaction to developments in theater and theory as a swerve, as Beckett's late theater is not a repudiation of *Godot* but a swerve from it. Blau's is not a call for a return to logocentric discourse, to the dominance of the text in theater, or to the rebirth of the author, or to the ego in character, but a reassertion of the dialectics of betweenness. Blau still nods assent to Derridian dialectics where "Representation mingles with what it represents" (Blau 1987, 165–6). But Blau finds that

> There is something in the theater itself which recoils from its own image as appropriating the world and insists, at the uttermost extremity of performance, when it seems to be overtaking or overtaken by life, upon remaining the illusion which it *is, as theater*, which is only inseparable from theory (they share a lexical root) when it sustains its critical and alienating (originary) distance from life. (Blau 1987, 7–8)

In *The Eye of Prey*, then, Blau takes his most decided stand against Artaud, whose "theater is not a representation"; on the other hand, Blau is equally dissatisfied with the "pure play" of Literary or Performance Theory and what he calls "the solipsism and domesticated shamanism of postmodern performance" (Blau 1987, 178), that is, "just play." He may have found something of a balance, rather not an equilibrium but a fluctuating betweenness, with Gilles Deleuze, or rather with the work of Deleuze and his collaborator Felix Guattari in *Anti-Oedipus*, which appeared in English in 1977. There was play in the anti-Freudianism of *Anti-Oedipus*, but not *just* play, with Blau picking up from the doubleness (in all senses of that term, as he was fond of saying) of Deleuze and Guattari in their critique "of the aura of deconstruction and its behavioral implications," and the fact that "they are particularly suspicious of what is most attractive: the apotheosis of play [...]" (Blau 1987, xviii); there was play, of course, but as process, thought as performance (to follow up Barthes's writing as performance) and toward revolutionary goals of constant becoming and so an ontological play rather than solely linguistic play.

Blau saw Beckett amid such theorizing of play as well, and so,

> Outside ideology, and a marginal figure in the evolution of the modern [...], Beckett surfaced in the fifties when the modern seemed to be running out of desire [...] and entropically winding down [...]; he was a touchstone after the sixties, with the Movement disillusioned and the projects incomplete, for releasing into the postmodern the flow-producing aporias of unfinished forms. (Blau 1987, xix)

Such a touchstone would propel groups like the Free Southern Theater as well.

As early as 1964, Blau noted a suspicion of "just play" in a piece he wrote for *Saturday Review* (vol. 47) entitled "I Don't Wanna Play" (Blau 1964b, 32, 39). "The sixties," after all, as Blau saw those years amid the political disillusionment of New York, "led through the licensing of Love's Body to the apotheosis in theory of the inflated currency of play" (Blau 1987, 12). Much of Blau's personal conclusion is thus not news: "No performance," he notes, "is either all happening or all appearance" (Blau 1987, 178). What is worthy of reflection, however, is Blau's discussion of theatrical universals, especially that possibility that theater is always a repetition, which entails the absence or impossibility of origin; that is, there is no first time to the action or thought represented, even as theater creates the illusion that this is all happening for the first time. Little wonder, then, of Blau's sustained attraction to, even preoccupation with Samuel Beckett's metatheatrical masterpiece, *Endgame*, in which the voice we first hear and which we call Clov is ventriloquized by Hamm: "Grain upon Grain, one by one, and one day, suddenly, there's a heap, a little heap, the impossible heap" (Beckett 1986, 93). "It was with *Endgame*, however," Blau notes, "that I started asking that series of questions, act *how*, act *why*, act *where*? And what do we *mean* by acting?" (Blau 2012a, 249). Yes, this is warmed over Stanislavski but refocused and reemphasized: "But like no other play we'd done, the issue of subjectivity in the art of the actor seemed to be there in the bloodstream, with doubt in the marrow bone" (Blau 2012a, 251). And it was that subjectivity, being dissolved as it was accessed or approached, receding at each approach, recovering with each uncovering, or "unveiling," as Beckett termed the opening dumb show of *Endgame* (Beckett 1992c, 45n17), being become becoming that would preoccupy Blau for the remainder of his career, but, in place of the stage, on the *mise en scène* of the page.

Blau's recollections upon the shifting emphasis of his thought form part of the final chapter, "Dark Energy," of the first volume of his autobiography. His *Endgame* was a punishing, cruel, nearly four-hour performance that seemed to horrify even Beckett: "When I told him about it in Paris, he had to measure his disturbance against the *Endgame* pictures I'd sent, not at all what he'd imagined [...] though he was clearly quite impressed" (Blau 2012a, 250). It was such cruelty that Blau brought to San Francisco, to San Quentin Prison, to New York, and to university faculties and classrooms, and, although it was often unsustainable (as in New York, say), Blau's thought was nourished by such tensions, a perpetual betweenness or neitherness of aesthetics and ideology that groups like the Free Southern Theater tried to maintain. This was a "Dark Energy" that he managed to sustain through to his own endgame, his perpetual rethinking of the modern, the theatrical, and, like Beckett, committed to change and to rethinking theater even as it is performed in churches or in the streets. Blau would work to overcome the anti-theatrical tradition of theory embedded in its history, and both figures would explore ways of moving beyond the limitations of the stage, beyond the conventions of theater, offering performances against the expectations of theater, to create performances central to Modernist thought, Blau toward the performance of thought on the page, Beckett with a series of theatrical reconceptions that would undervalue story and thematics with a theater at the limits of thought, at the limits of comprehension, a theater of affective lyricism.

# Notes

1  For further details, see Kronenberger, Louis, ed. (1957). *The Best Plays of 1956–1957 (The Burns Mantle Yearbook)*. New York: Dodd, Mead & Co., p. 350.

2  Ruby Cohn (1967) includes short excerpts about both the FST and the San Quentin *Godot*s in her excellent, if underappreciated, *Casebook on "Waiting for Godot."* New York: Grove Press, pp. 79–89.

3 For more on this image, see my "'A Mixed Choir' from The Ditch of Astonishment: An Introduction." *Creative Involution: Bergson, Beckett, Deleuze* (2015). Edinburgh: Edinburgh University Press, pp. 2–30.

4 This revival featured Beckett stalwarts Barry McGovern and Alan Mandel as Didi and Gogo, respectively. (See http://latimesblogs. latimes.com/culturemonster/2012/03/theater-review-waiting-for-godot-at-the-mark-taper-forum.html). See also Minor, W. F. and Larocco, Christina, "'COFO Is Not Godot' The Free Southern Theater, the Black Freedom Movement, and the Search for a Usable Aesthetic." *Cultural and Social History*, XII.4 (2015): 509–26.

5 For further details, see Rosset 2016, 450–7. Jan Jonson also directed the play in Stockholm in April 1986 with "five inmates of the country's top maximum security jail." See also Beckett *Letters* 2016, 716 n.3).

6 "Who Is Godot" is reprinted as the opening chapter to *Sails of the Herring Fleet: Essays on Beckett* (2000). Ann Arbor: University of Michigan Press, pp. 21–2.

7 This is, of course, the great theme of Ralph Ellison's superb 1952 novel *The Invisible Man* (New York: Random House).

8 For a discussion of this phase of Jerzy Grotowski's work, see the 1981 Louis Malle film, with Wallace Shawn and André Gregory, *My Dinner with André*

9 This is a whole category in Schechner's highly influential *Performance Theory*, second edition, New York and London: Routledge, 1988, then as a Routledge Classic in 2003.

# 11

# Beckett and the Revisioning of Modernism(s): *Molloy*

*Extraordinary how everything ends like a fairytale or
can be made to, even the most unsanitary episodes.*
(Dream of Fair to Middling Women, 98)

*I am not ashamed to stutter like this with you who are
used to my wild way of failing to say what I imagine
I want to say and who understand that until the gag
is chewed fit to swallow or spit out the mouth must
stutter or rest.* (SB to Tom MacGreevy, 1932)

Within the ideology of Modernism, Samuel Beckett was always an uneasy and anxious ally, with all the apprehension and hesitancy of a latecomer. Early on he distanced himself from the Realists and Naturalists who, he complained, attributed "absolute value to one system of reference and point of view,"[1] that is, they privileged a stable world that was apprehensible and representable empirically and accepted the duality of an objective language expressing accurately or copying a stable, knowable reality. Balzac was singled out for particular scorn in *Dream of Fair to Middling Women* (1932) because he was "absolute master of his material," the creator of "clockwork cabbages" (Beckett 1992a, 106, 107). Against the narrative, psychological, and philosophical simplicity of Balzac,

Beckett posited the complexity of his fellow countryman, James Joyce, with whom, for a time, he avidly associated himself. For the contributor's page of the *European Caravan: An Anthology of the New Spirit in European Literature* (London: Brewer, Warren & Putnam, 1931), edited by Samuel Putnam, for instance, Beckett could proclaim his Irishness unabashedly, say of himself that "S Beckett is the most interesting of the younger Irish writers" and speak freely of "influence," allying himself with his countryman, noting further that he "has adapted the Joyce method to his poetry with original results. His impulse is lyric, but has been deepened through this influence and the influence of Proust and the historic method," the last presumably a reference to the historicity of Giambattista Vico. In *T.C.D.: A College Miscellany* the previous year, moreover, Beckett's story "The Possessed" was associated with *transition* magazine and was called, in a subsequent editorial, a "Joyceian medley" (Harrington 1991, 10). Yet such alliances were always tentative, the influence anxious, marked by the simultaneous identification with and disaffiliation from Joyce, and so characterized by a general uneasiness with Modernism itself. Beckett's early comments are those of a writer paying homage to literary forebears and yet uneasy with the possibility of repetition—a debutant poet making room for himself, insisting on his separate identity, emphasizing his "original results." For much of his early artistic career, then, Beckett was caught in the aesthetic tension of repeating yet revising Joyce and, more broadly, proclaiming and denouncing those writers, principally European, we generally call Modernists.

The issues of aesthetic and ideological ambivalence were similar with Beckett's associations with the Surrealists. Although André Breton's first *Manifesto of Surrealism* appeared in the autumn of 1924, followed in December by the first number of Breton's journal, *The Surrealist Revolution*, the English-speaking world was essentially introduced to the movement with the Surrealist issue of Edward Titus's journal, *This Quarter,* in September of 1932, which was guest edited by Breton. Much of the translation for that issue was done by Beckett, and his contribution to the issue was substantial enough that general editor Edward Titus could say, writing in a preface he called "Editorially," "We shall not speak of the difficulties experienced putting the material placed at our disposal [by André Breton] into English, but we cannot refrain from singling out Mr. Samuel Beckett's work for special acknowledgment.

His rendering of the [Paul] Eluard and [André] Breton poems in particular is characterizable only in superlatives" (6). More important and much less discussed in the critical discourse are the experiments in prose that Beckett was "rendering" for the issue, as he says to Tom MacGreevy on February 6, 1936, recollecting the work, "I came across all the 'Surrealism and Madness' texts [these excerpts from Breton's writings, including 'The Treatment of Mental Disease and Surrealism' (113–17), apparently not translated by Beckett, although the attributions seem inconsistent] I translated for Titus and sent them to him with the Eluard and Breton *Essais de Simulation* ... perhaps they were too much for him" (Beckett *Letters* 2009, 311); these included the pieces that Beckett was acknowledged to have translated: "The Posessions" (119–20), "Simulation of Mental Debility Essayed"(121–2), "Simulation of General Paralysis Essayed" (123–5), "Simulation of Delirium of Interpretation Essayed" (126–8), all, like the poems, "Rendered into English by Samuel Beckett" (128), and René Crevel's "Simulation of General Paralysis Essayed" (Beckett *Letters* 2009, 314n3). In "The Treatment of Mental Disease and Surrealism," Breton quotes Henri Baranger writing in 1931 thus: "Surrealism now aims at 're-creating' a condition which will be in no way inferior to mental derangement.' Its ambition is to lead us to the edge of madness and make us feel what is going on in the magnificently disordered minds of those whom the community shuts up in asylums" (117–18). This is exactly the sort of creative upheaval that Max Nordau would have called "degeneration" (for more on which, see also the Introduction), and the thread seems a continuation of Beckett's translating "some Breton and Eluard MSS [for Nancy Cunard]. I wrote saying it was always a pleasure to translate Eluard and Breton," in this case "Murderous Humanism," one of nineteen essays he translated for Cunard's *Negro, An Anthology* (1934, 574–5, see also Friedman) (Beckett *Letters* 2009, 134, 137n11). These translations, particularly of *Essais de Simulation*, were done as Beckett was completing *Murphy* (i.e., final typescript, June 1936). Yet the associations with Surrealism seem also to have been tentative, much of the work done for economic rather than aesthetic or ideological motives. That is, Beckett soon distanced himself from these translations by refusing to translate other Eluard for George Reavey and to allow only those Eluard poems already published to appear in *Thorns of Thunder: Selected Poems* in 1936, the volume edited by Reavey, his sometime literary agent but with whom he was piqued at the time over the delays with the publication of *Echo's Bones and Other Precipitates* (1935), for which Beckett had paid a £20 subvention that he could ill afford to lose: "I am bitterly disappointed that my book should be delayed again & again" (Beckett *Letters* 2009, 323n2). By June 9, 1936, Beckett was also furious with Reavey's handling of the Eluard translations, particularly the publicity campaign for it: "I object to my name appearing near such an abomination. I object to Mr. [Herbert] Read's bloody preface [the longer 'Foreword' by Reavey, however]. I object to the suggestion conveyed in the blurb that I am *performing* [i.e., reading his translations] at the new Burlington BAVE [International Surrealist Exhibition at the New Burlington Galleries] (Beckett *Letters* 2009, 342n5, emphasis added)]. I was not consulted about any of these matters" (Beckett *Letters* 2009, 340). Beckett reported the follow-up to MacGreevy on June 27, 1936, as he completed *Murphy*: "Reavey wrote angrily in reply to my angry letter. He is (1) A liar (2) A Clumsy Sophist (3) An Illiterate. He spells emmerder en merder" (Beckett *Letters* 2009, 345 [see Redshaw for further details]).

By 1956, all three of what will become three French novels and *Godot* behind him and in print and only *The Unnamable* left to be translated into English, Beckett's ambivalence toward writers of the period, both Irish and Continental, abated some and he could divorce himself with some confidence from two "Apollonian" (Beckett's term) Modernist authors. Of Kafka he noted,

> I've only read Kafka in German—serious reading—except for a few things in French and English—only The Castle in German. I must say it was difficult to get to the end. The Kafka hero has a coherence of purpose. He's lost but he's not spiritually precarious, he's not falling to bits. My people seem to be falling to bits. Another difference. You notice how Kafka's form is classic, it goes on like a steamroller—almost serene. It *seems* to be threatened the whole time—but the consternation is in the form. In my work there is consternation behind the form, not in the form. (Israel Shenker in *The New York Times*, May 5, 1956, Section II, 1, 3)[2]

His corresponding separation from Joyce at this same time is phrased in the language of control reminiscent of his attack on Balzac some twenty-five years earlier: "Joyce was a superb manipulator of material," says Beckett, "perhaps the greatest [...] The more Joyce knew the more he could" (Federman and Graver 1997, 148).[3] Whether or not Beckett's literary criticism is accurate here, that is, whether or not Joyce's work reflects the degree of artistic control Beckett attributed to it (*Finnegans Wake* seems particularly problematic), or whether or not the Kafka hero demonstrates the sort of "coherence of purpose" Beckett finds in his work, is at least open to question if not, finally, irrelevant to an assessment of those authors. More germane here is what such comments signify about Beckett and his desire to distance himself from those literary forebears, as earlier he could embrace Proust only by rewriting him, by careful selection and revisioning. In the "Foreword" to his 1931 study of Proust, Beckett writes, "There is no allusion in this book [*Proust*] to the legendary life and death of Marcel Proust, nor to the garrulous old dowager of the Letters, nor to the poet, nor to the author of the Essays, nor to the Eau de Selzian correlative of Carlyle's 'beautiful bottle of soda-water'" (*recte* "a bottle of beautiful *soda water*," thus Carlyle's comment about the overly effusive John Ruskin) (Carlyle 1904, 177, letter 274). For Beckett's Proust, Beckett's revisioning of Proust, he emphasizes the most aleatory elements of Proust's aesthetics, as would Joyce in his comments to Jacques Mercanton: "Chance furnishes me what I need. I am like a man who stumbles along; my foot strikes something; I bend over, and it is exactly what I want" ("The Hours of James Joyce," 213). In Beckett's hands in 1931 the chronicler of *la belle epoque* is molded into a late Modernist, in fulfillment, almost, of Jorge Luis Borges's comment in his essay on Kafka, who, amid his reflections on Zeno's paradoxes of motion and Kierkegaard's *North Pole* and counterfeiter parables, offers what is generally called the Borgesian conundrum:

> If I am not mistaken, the heterogeneous pieces I have enumerated resemble Kafka; if I am not mistaken, not all of them resemble each other. The second fact is the more significant. In each of these texts we find Kafka's idiosyncrasy to a greater or lesser degree, but if Kafka had never written a line, we would not perceive this quality; in other words, it would not exist. The poem "Fears and Scruples" by Browning foretells Kafka's work, but our reading of Kafka perceptibly sharpens and deflects our

reading of the poem. Browning did not read it as we do now. In the critic's vocabulary, the word "precursor" is indispensable, but it should be cleansed of all connotations of polemic or rivalry. The fact is that every writer *creates* his own precursors. His work modifies our conception of the past, as it will modify the future. ("Kafka y sus precursores" ["Kafka and His Precursors"], *Other Inquisitions 1937–1952*)

By 1956 Beckett is undoing, re-creating, and revisioning his own "precursors," Joyce, Proust, Kafka, and even Eliot. That is, Borges's aesthetics is a prominent feature of T. S. Eliot's "Tradition and the Individual Talent" and equally important for Kafka and Joyce. Beckett's undoing and revisioning of such precursors is finally a positive aesthetic and psychological step for the late-blooming artist. Harold Bloom would rephrase Borges's conundrum and reintroduce "rivalry" into the equation as he describes an "anxiety of influence" as follows: "Conceptually the central problem for the latecomer necessarily is repetition, for repetition dialectically raised to recreation is the *ephebe*'s [the young poet's] road to excess, leading away from the horror of finding himself to be only a copy or a replica" (Bloom 1973, 80). Embedded in Beckett's comments on Joyce and Kafka, then, is a stealth aesthetics which rejects the teleology, the overall, all-embracing, unifying metaphors characteristic of Modernism, be they id, ego, memory, or any version of a unified personality or being, or the temporal metaphor of the single day or the passing seasons (although *Molloy* features a subverted version of this final trope), or the grand, unifying myth.

*Molloy* is Beckett's most deliberate undoing of the potential or perceived replication of Joyce in particular and of the Modernist text in general as it demarks a post-Joycean aesthetics. And one term of such creative tension is *destruction, obliteration*: "you would do better," writes Beckett, rather observes Molloy early in the novel, "at least no worse, to obliterate texts than to blacken margins [with notes, presumably], to fill in the holes of words till all is blank and flat and the whole ghastly business looks like what it is, senseless, speechless, issueless misery [...] but then the murmurs began again" (Beckett 1965a, 13). The narrator, who has evidently annotated many a margin in his day, betrays himself and fails to follow his own prescription and issues, fathers, say, a readable text, which, while it obliterates the tradition of the novel, simultaneously reiterates or reinscribes that tradition, returning to and reasserting the most fundamental structures in the history of narrative art. Entailed in the displacement of the conventions of fiction is a corresponding and simultaneous re-placement, or what I am calling a revisioning, of those conventions as they reassert themselves, particularly (1) the literature of quest or journey, from the Homeric voyage and medieval Romance, through Chaucer and Boccaccio, to the picaresque novel; (2) the detective story or procedural, not the tale of, ratiocination developed in the nineteenth century by Edgar Allen Poe, Arthur Conan Doyle, and G. K. Chesterton, but the archetypal detective story of self-discovery, of the man who discovers the cause of the plague on the city of Thebes; and (3) the oral tale from Homer to folk and fairy tales, at least in their recorded forms. Obliterating the novel is a means of denying one's progenitors, while reiterating it is a means of giving birth to one's creative self.

Repeatedly, the narrative or thematic pattern in Beckett's work is the journey, the out and inevitable return, the going and coming. In Molloy's case, the journey, the quest is for his mother, which we learn from the novel's first page, has already been, more or less successfully, accomplished. And, as previous critics have noted, that quest is overtly Oedipal, at least in its overall pattern, a union with the mother. The narrator suggests of his mother that "She never called me son, fortunately, I couldn't have borne it, but Dan, I don't know why, my name is not Dan. Dan was my father's name perhaps, yes, perhaps she took me for my father. I took her for my mother and she took me for my father" (Beckett 1965a, 17). The sexual fantasy here, however, also suggests an autoeroticism since the narrator has "taken her place" (Beckett 1965a, 7). Such replacement of father and mother is an obliteration of progenitors, a denial of lineage with an emphasis on self-creation, a trope for Beckett's dissociation from Modernism, his insistence on a separate identity and aesthetics. Molloy's journey—like all Oedipal activity—is a quest for sources, origins, true literary parents, which quest finally returns him to himself.

The circularity of the journey is reinforced structurally in both parts of Molloy, where each tale ends at its beginning, that is, returns us to its (narratological) origins. The Molloy section opens with Molloy's having completed the journey he is about to embark on, having not so much discovered his mother as replaced or recreated her, become his own mother—and so Oedipal and Narcissistic impulses merge. The Moran section opens with the report that Moran begins writing at the end of the novel: "It is midnight. The wind is beating on the windows. It was not midnight. It was not raining" (Beckett 1965a, 176). Moran's report which we have just completed as he begins writing, which we finish as he begins it, is, of course, a lie, a fiction, as he admits, and so true, at least by virtue of his admission. The novel is Beckett's literary version of the paradox of the Cretan. Since the narrator insists that his fictions lie, he is telling the truth; therefore, he is lying; therefore, he is telling the truth; therefore, he is lying, etc. The more he undercuts the veracity of his text, the more he asserts its veracity. Such is the Vico road. Molloy admits at the opening of his section, "Perhaps I'm inventing a little, perhaps embellishing, but on the whole that's the way it was" (Beckett 1965a, 8). And Moran later admits, "it would not surprise me if I deviated in the pages to follow from the true and exact succession of events" (Beckett 1965a, 133). Such subversion of the veracity of the text is an assault not only on the tradition of verisimilitude established by DeFoe and Richardson but on the aesthetics of Joyce as well.

And so within this fictive journey, or these fictive journeys, Moran not so much becomes Molloy, and so chronologically the second half of the novel ought to precede the first (an elementary narrative ploy), but Molloy was always part of Moran as were Gaber (for the angel, Gabriel, perhaps) and Youdi (for Yaweh), both agents of some sort of power, the superego even, the embodiment of the voice of the father: "For who could have spoken to me of Molloy if not myself and to whom if not to myself could I have spoken of him" (Beckett 1965a, 112). What we might have in the Moran section, and this is why it follows the Molloy section when chronologically it *might* very well precede it and why the novel is called *Molloy*, is a fiction written by Molloy of Molloy as Moran discovering Molloy.

But the journey or quest (in Beckett's subverted version) is not the only culturally coded form reiterated or reinscribed in *Molloy*. The novel, especially the Moran section, is structured like a detective story, an attempt to discover a hidden truth (if a hidden crime, then perhaps the crime is birth) except in this case the hidden truth is that there is no truth to discover, save perhaps that our journey has been verbal and hence a fictive one. Oedipus does discover the horrible truth, like Moran's discovery of Molloy, or Molloy's discovery of the Moran who discovers Molloy, that he himself is the criminal he seeks. Beckett's characters suffer—if *suffer* is the word—less from the Oedipal desire to know than from the anti-Oedipal Davus complex. In the appendix of his novel *Watt*, for instance, Beckett notes of his hero, "Watt's Davus complex," and then defines it in parentheses, "morbid dread of sphinxes" (Beckett 1959, 251). The allusion is to the Terence play *Andria* (l. 194), where the character Davus says, "Davos sum, non Oedipus." The remark is famous enough to be listed in *Bartlett's Familiar Quotations*. If sphinxes have reason to dread Oedipus, they might snuggle up to Davus/Watt/Molloy/Moran. And so Molloy takes comfort in the insoluble enigma. Contemplating an object he has pilfered from the house of Lousse, Molloy delights in the fact that he "could never understand what possible purpose it could serve, nor to contrive the faintest hypothesis on the subject." It is an object over which he could "puzzle ... without the least risk [of solving the problem]. For to know nothing is nothing, not to want to know anything likewise, but to be beyond knowing anything, to know that you are beyond knowing anything, that is when peace enters in, to the soul of the incurious seeker." Likewise when Moran studies the dance of the bees, he could say "with rapture, Here is something I can study all my life and never understand" (Beckett 1965a, 169), or "[...] to see yourself endlessly doing the same thing endlessly over and over again [like Sisyphus] fills you with satisfaction" (Beckett 1965a, 133).

When Sigmund Freud turned his attention to describing the psychosexual development of human beings and used as his model the famous play of Sophocles, he argued that all males (females had their own problems with the Electra Complex) at one stage of their development want to destroy the competition for the sexual gratification with the mother, namely they desire the father's death. But the pursuit of mother is only the most notorious element of the Oedipal paradigm. What the child learns during the Oedipal stage, according to Freud, is the "Reality Principle," to accept limitations on his sex drive or risk punishment—in Freudian terms the fear of castration forces the son to accept the taboo against sex with the mother. That acceptance of the taboo is the acceptance of the law of the father, the prohibitions of society. It is one way through which culture is transmitted. Moran, recalling or more likely projecting the

Primal Scene, says of his son, for example, "He would doubtless at that moment with pleasure have cut my throat, with the selfsame knife I was putting so placidly in my pocket" (Beckett 1965a, 131). The Moran section of *Molloy* develops this element of the Oedipal model, Moran struggling to force his son to accept the taboo, the law of the father, as Moran had accepted the law of the church fathers. But accepting the law, social restriction, does not destroy the sex drive; it merely represses it. The libidinal, anti-Oedipal, Dionysian element— Molloy, say, with no sense of order or organization, or Jacques the potential parricide—lurks within. Both halves of the novel, then, explore facets of the Oedipal paradigm, the Molloy section with maternal and the Moran section with paternal emphases.

Tropologically, the Oedipal conflict suggests the artist's tension with his literary culture, embodied in a literary father, and the relationship between writing and literary repression. The most dominant literary force in Beckett's life was James Joyce. Beckett's relationship with Joyce was in many ways Oedipal or at least Lacanian. Joyce was the law, the transmitter of cultural/literary heritage, the phallus, the embodiment of language. Beckett's swerve (Harold Bloom's term would also be *clinamen*) from the language of the Father is a means of his making room for himself as an artist. The three postwar French novels, if not overtly an attempt to revise, rewrite, or recast Modernism in general and the Joycean legacy in particular, certainly suggest that after the war, after the death of Joyce (whose postmortem presence, however, remains potent, especially for Irish writers), Beckett was free enough of parental control to choose or create his own literary forebears, to choose not from classical myths as Joyce or T. S. Eliot used them, but from the popular forms of narrative like the detective story, the fairy tale, and the vaudeville skit, and finally to triumph where Joyce failed, in the theater as an offshoot of the music hall (at least at first). After the Second World War, Beckett could misread Joyce sufficiently to develop his own voice. "To live," writes Harold Bloom, "the poet must *misinterpret* the father, by the crucial act of misprision, which is the re-writing of the father" (Bloom 1975, 19).

In his attempt to define what for a time was called, too glibly perhaps, Post-Modernism, Leslie Fiedler suggested that one of the characteristics of the new post–Second World War art would be to "Cross the Border—Close the Gap" with pop culture, through which one might "invent a New New Criticism, a Post-Modernist criticism appropriate to Post-Modernist fiction or verse" (Fiedler 1977, 271). The aesthetic shift in Beckett's post–Second World War writing, while not invoking pop culture overtly, nonetheless moves toward closing such a gap, between at least high and low culture. Yet artistic deviation is not accomplished without at least the anxiety of potential punishment for paternal disobedience, even from a deceased parent, or the anxiety of separation from the mother's body, which is the original lost object, according to Jacques Lacan (hence the *Molloy* text is also a search for a lost one). The pursuit of the mother is the pursuit of a lost wholeness which also characterizes at least the subtext of *Krapp's Last Tape*, *Film*, *Footfalls* and *Rockaby*. "All our lives long," writes Bloom, "we search in vain, unknowingly, for the lost object when even that objet was a *clinamen* away from our true aim" (Bloom 1982, 70). Yet that quest for reunion, for wholeness, the quest for the lost one, which is a quest for self, is doomed, is always illusive since that wholeness, that recognition of unity with the mother, was always a misrecognition. The literature of impotence, Beckett's own description of his work, is perhaps the only literature a punished son could write.

The third narrative structure which Beckett reiterates in *Molloy* is the oral tale with as much emphasis on the teller as the tale. Beckett's teller, however, is not the neutral ancient historian, but the compulsive, reluctant repeater of tales, driven perhaps by Gaber and Youdi, as is Moran, or by the person who comes to pick up the pages from Molloy. In *Beyond the Pleasure Principle* Freud moves away from the pleasure principle and discusses the problem of repeating unpleasant, traumatic events in order to gain mastery over them, if only linguistically, as his grandson did with the *fort/da* game or as any patient does in psychoanalysis itself. Freud links this "repetition compulsion" to a new principle—not the pleasure principle, through which one sought gratification, vitality, life, but its opposite, the tendency of animate matter to return to its original inorganic state, a death instinct. The goal of all life, Freud argued, is its cessation, death, an end desired by Murphy and Molloy. Not strange, then, that the method of narration of this repeater of painful tales in Molloy is not affirmation, but denial, paradox, obliteration. The goal of speaking is to end speaking; the goal of writing to end writing; the goal of life, death.

Such an aesthetics of reiteration or of revisioning—a means of separating oneself from the literary past while reinscribing it in reconstituted form—has become one of the characteristics of much late Modern, self-referential, American fiction. The list of major post–Second World War experimental American fiction is dominated by works which break with the traditions of at least early Modernism, a tradition which John Barth would call "exhausted," by reiterating, reinterpreting, and revisioning the most fundamental patterns in the history of narrative: Donald's Barthelme's novel *Snow White* and innumerable stories like "Grandmother's House"; Robert Coover's stories in *Pricksongs & Descants*, especially "The Door: A Prologue of Sorts," "The Magic Poker," "The Gingerbread House," and even the note or "story" on the book's dust jacket which begins "Once, some time ago and in a distant land," and his plays like "Rip Awake" and "The Kid" as well; John Barth's collected tales, *Lost in the Funhouse* and *Chimera* (the first story of the former, "Frame-Tale," is designed to be cut from the book so that the word literally leaves the page, twisted [trope, I'm sure, intended] and the ends taped together in a Möbius strip. I quote the tale in its entirety: "Once upon a time there was a story that began," which end finally returns us to the beginning); J. P. Donleavey's *A Fairy Tale of New York*; and perhaps the most anti-Oedipal of American prose works, Thomas Pynchon's *The Crying of Lot 49* whose quasi-mythical heroine, Oedipa Maas, is a would-be riddle solver who learns finally that the Davus complex has much to offer. Writers like Barth and Pynchon are not so much continuing a mythic or archetypal tradition as subverting, recasting, and revisioning it. Like Joyce, Barth may be working within the outlines of ancient myth in everyday life, but myth's purpose, as it is in Beckett's work, is dispersive rather than cohesive. Barth sees Greek myths, or the stories and narrative situation of *A Thousand and One Nights*, or fairy tales in general, not as stable, overriding master narratives suggestive of an archetypal unity of human experience but as historical narratives open to the plenitude of interpretation written for the Davuses among us. And Barth has gone on to reiterate other narrative patterns such as the epistolary novel in *Letters*, as Robert Coover has reiterated the father of modern prose narratives *Don Quixote* in tales like "Seven Exemplary Fictions" with its "*Dedicatoria y Prologo a don Miguel de Cervantes Saavedra*." Even mainstream Post-Modern American fiction reiterates elaborated versions of such popular narrative genres as science fiction and the pornographic novel. I am thinking here particularly of Mason Hoffenberg and Terry Southern, and even some of the work of William Burroughs.

In Borges's "Pierre Menard, Author of Don Quixote" the French Symbolist Menard reiterates *Don Quixote*—verbatim. And yet it is Borges who in such denial of the possibilities of originality, a denial guaranteed by the books already housed in the "Library at Babel," asserts an originality by what John Barth calls "ironic intent": "I mentioned earlier that if Beethoven's Sixth were composed today, it would be an embarrassment; but clearly it wouldn't be, necessarily, if done with ironic intent by a composer quite aware of where we've been and where we are" (Barth, 1977). The literary fathers of these American writers are not the dominant American Modernists like Hemingway, Faulkner, Fitzgerald, Dreiser, Steinbeck, or James, but these writers have created their own parentage, their own precursors: Homer, Cervantes, Scheherazade. The late Modern American novel might well be termed the "Reiterated Novel" and its roots, its precursors, are in the swerve from Modernism that Beckett takes in *Molloy* and the other two French novels.

# Notes

1  From a notebook kept by one of Beckett's students, Rachel Burrows, during Michaelmas term in 1931.

2  Beckett translated Arthur Rimbaud's poem "Le Bateau ivre" for a subsequent issue of *This Quarter* but the journal suspended publication before Beckett's translation could appear and all copies of the work were presumed lost. Once rediscovered in the mid-seventies, Beckett allowed its publication by the University of Reading: *Drunken Boat: A Translation of Arthur Rimbaud's Poem "Le Bateau ivre"* (Reading: Whiteknights Press, 1976), the Preface to which, by James Knowlson, details the translation, loss, and rediscovery.

3  Originally in Shenker, Israel. "A Portrait of Samuel Beckett, the Author of the Puzzling *Waiting for Godot*," *New York Times*, May 6, 1956, Section 2, pp. 1, 3. Reprinted in *Samuel Beckett: The Critical Heritage*, ed. Lawrence Graver and Raymond Federman (London: Routledge & Kegan Paul, 1979), 146–9. (See also Macklin.)

# 12

# A Sense of Unending:
# Fictions for the End of Time

*Perhaps there is no whole, before you're dead.*
(Molloy)

*[S]he is not subject to time.* Dream of Fair to Middling
Women.

*[...] now as always time was never and time is over.*
(Endgame)

In his metatextual "Studies in the Theory of Fiction," Frank Kermode
proffers a paradigm for literature based on apocalypse. Literature is
driven, he notes, by *the sense of an ending*, which in turn presupposes
and is dependent on a beginning, and that to speak of ends, as writers
increasingly have done during the turbulent twentieth century
(a period we often loosely call Modern or Modernist), is already
to assume, even tacitly, limits, origins. The fill, the link between
the two, Kermode calls "fictive concords," narratives that "give
meaning to lives and to poems" (Kermode 1967, 7). To fictionalize
time itself is something of a human trait, Kermode proposes: "At
some very low level we all share certain fictions about time, and
they testify to the continuity of what is called human nature [...]"
(Kermode 1967, 43–4). Despite the near-universal praise that
greeted the work's publication in 1967, Kermode's paradigm may
seem decidedly anachronistic in this twenty-first century, little more

than a prop for faltering humanism (see Walker, for instance, who calls Kermode's clerical insights "apocalyptic fantasies"). It remains, however, a useful point of entry (or departure) into a literature of perpetual crisis which dominates the twentieth century, a literature teetering on the brink of oblivion, which, in fact, threatens to effect its own demise, which stands as testimony to its own irrelevance, and Samuel Beckett's *art* (if that is the word) is among the century's (and Kermode's) test cases. Beginning with that post–Second World War creative burst that Beckett memorably dubbed the "siege in the room" (Bair, 346–80), his work took an overt turn toward the apocalyptic and the eschatological. Beckett's sensibility remained riven between an inherently classical temperament that dominated much "High Modernism" in the first half of the twentieth century (and much of his own early work) and the spirit of postwar annihilation that dominated the second half of the century (as well as the latter half of his *oeuvre*). The impact of the Second World War on human consciousness is still being assessed, but it was clear by 1945 that whatever vestiges of cultural assumptions survived the First World War, whatever shards of humanism persisted, they were obliterated by images from a liberated Auschwitz, Dachau, and Buchenwald, by the obscenely aesthetic mushroom clouds hanging over Hiroshima and Nagasaki irradiating civilians. Language itself seemed to fail before such grotesqueries. Not even the denotative precision of numbers could communicate the horrors. Thus more than a war ended in 1945, and philosophers like Theodor Adorno would even proclaim, at least for a time, that poetry, or more broadly the idea of art itself, after Auschwitz was obscene (Rothberg 2000, 29–30, *passim*); George Steiner, in *Language and Silence: Essays on Language, Literature, and the Inhuman* (1967), indicted the German language for its complicity in such dehumanization (the "Inhuman" of his subtitle), such obscenity (cited in Rothberg 2000, 30), but language itself seemed complicitous. And yet somehow something persisted, something went on. The composer Olivier Messiaen, for example, a member of the French forces, was captured in the summer of 1940 and imprisoned in Gorlitz, Silesia, where he composed at first a trio for the only musical instruments available in the camp: violin, cello, and clarinet. He later added a piano not available in the camp, to create the *Quatour pour la fin du temps*. The trio premiered in the camp on January 15, 1941, and, as Messiaen later recalled, "Never have I been heard with as much attention and understanding" (centenary concert program notes). Its apocalyptic imagery announced, "The End of Time," but with a transcendent, consoling religious mysticism, apocalyptic teleology as divine conquest. Its seventh movement (after the seventh angel of the "Book of Revelation," chapter 10) is called *A mingling of rainbows for the Angel who announces the end of Time* (i.e., "that there should be time no longer").

Between Adorno's indictment of language (and art) and Messiaen's transcendence of it lies, on the humanist plane, the apocalyptic rupture or contorted postwar consciousness in response to the Final Solution which Samuel Beckett called *L'Innommable, The Unnamable*. For Beckett those coherent entities that in literature we call story and character ("concord fictions," perhaps) were exposed as frauds for much of the twentieth century, and his French writing, the *Quartre nouvelles*, the three sequential postwar novels, *Molloy, Malone meurt*, and *L'Innomable*, and their residua, *Textes pour rien*, chart the disintegration. After *The Unnamable*, fiction—even Beckett's own—had come to an end, apparently, and yet, paradoxically, it, too, continued, if only to go nowhere. For Beckett what was possible after the war were shards, fragments, *Texts for Nothing*, texts for "The End of Time," without beginnings, middles, ends, or angelic transcendence. What remained were residua, limitations, the necessary incoherence and fragmentation within which the writer was *obliged* to work in the post-Auschwitz era in order to convey something of the lived experience of existence. "I'm here," proclaims the narrating voice of the third text, "that's all I know, and that it's still not me, it's of that the best has to be made" (Beckett 1996, 113). Even the simple "I'm here" would thus undergo serious interrogation.

Yet even at the "end of time," Beckett continued to treat what Hamm in *Fin de partie* (or *Endgame*) called "the old questions." To Clov's comment, "You've asked me these questions millions of times," the blind, moribund Hamm replies with nostalgia, "Ah the old questions, the old answers, there's nothing like them" (Beckett 1958, 38). But how treat them in a world where shared values seem to have collapsed. In the "Moran" section of *Molloy*, Jacques raises a series of questions "of a theological nature" having to do fundamentally with origins and ends. The thirteenth of his questions asks, "What was God doing with himself before creation?" (Beckett 1965a, 167); that is, was the "In the beginning" of Genesis the beginning of anything significant? The question teases the postwar and late Modernist reader toward the central debates about the nature of matter and the creation of the universe that dominated the Middle Ages and the early Renaissance. Could Christianity accommodate the Aristotelian cosmology first posited by Parmenides that *ex nihilo nihil fit*? Or as the Roman poet Lucretius suggests in his *De Rerum Natura* ("On the Nature of Things"), that nature's "first principle" is "that nothing's brought/ Forth by any supernatural power out of nought" (lines 149–50). If so, the world, that is, matter of some sort, would have to be eternal, that is, with neither beginning nor end? Such a logical contradiction posed difficulties for medieval theologians since biblically the world is said to have been created presumably *ex nihilo*, out of nothing. In Christian theology/philosophy, then, no matter existed before the creation narratives of "Genesis," so Moran's question is decidedly pointed as it evokes issues of beginnings and ends, and, of course, of time and eternity since "Genesis" was not only the beginning of matter but the invention of time as well. In the fifth century, St. Augustine struggled to resolve the contradictions about beginnings and ends with a "concord fiction" about time, essentially, or timelessness, inchoate or formless matter, an intermediary, perhaps atomic soup, some state between something and nothing. Descartes found in him a meeting of minds, attracted to the Saint's rejection of the evidence of the senses in favor of the principle of thought. Beckett's reading of Augustine focused particularly upon *The Confessions*, from which he took extensive notes, which were in turn worked into the early fiction. Beckett's most celebrated evocation of the Saint is his statement about "the shape of ideas," which he attributes to Augustine. The renewed challenge of Aristotle in the thirteenth century revived the issues and led to a solution by St. Thomas Aquinas, who offered another concord fiction, defining matter as pure potentiality.

In our skeptical age, Kermode admits, "there is a correlation between the subtlety and variety of our fictions and the remoteness and doubtfulness about ends and origins" (Kermode 1967, 67). Such skepticism suggests Samuel Beckett's own overt turn toward the apocalyptic and eschatological, most explicitly in his third full-length French play, *Fin de partie,* which was for Beckett in 1957 a turning point, a new beginning for talking about the old ends. Unlike *En attendant Godot* which came to Beckett almost whole—a first draft in under three months, between October 1948 and January 1949, albeit some of the way having been paved by work on the incomplete and then rejected French novel *Mercier et Camier* in 1946—what became *Fin de partie*, or *Endgame*, emerged only after a turbulent creative process that may have begun as early as 1954 and that was not completed until 1957—that is, in four years rather than the four months of *Godot*. Much of the writing was precipitated by personal tragedy, the unexpected ending of his brother Frank's life on September 13, 1954. And so even the title of the new play proclaimed Beckett's overt preoccupation with eschatology, endings, final things, and the narratives that lead up to, shape, and explain them. In *Endgame* Hamm suffers from teleological anxiety and is narcissistically obsessed with his own senescence as he struggles to make of his imminent, quite common and ordinary end something uncommon and extraordinary. "Can there be misery loftier than mine" (Endgame 1958, 2), he intones in his opening monologue. What will redeem the degradations of the natural process of aging, the "something" that "is taking its course," is a narrative of tragic dignity, as opposed to the comic bathos that characterizes daily life in the shelter. Not surprisingly, Hamm is equally obsessed with origins, the Noah story in particular, even in its corrupt versions like the discovery of the flea on Clov's person, the reported persistence of a rat in the kitchen, or finally the sighting of a boy amid the waste outside the shelter. Continued or renewed life suggests that the apocalyptic imagery that dominates the play, that is, the sense of an ending, may have to be refigured, since what appears to be an ending may be less linear decline than a cyclical, recurring strange loop. That is, Clov's climactic, if unverified, sighting of the boy near the play's end suggests that the calculus of apocalypse may have to be recalculated, yet again, and so the linear drive or slide toward ending may turn out to be yet another loop in a Möbius strip of existence, and so of narrative itself, as the overt circular structure of *Waiting for Godot* is folded into *Endgame* without repeating its symmetries.

Indeed, in Beckett's world, birth, creation, and breath itself are punishments. Stunningly fresh in Beckett's work, the theme is, however, one of the "old questions." In his study of the development of drama, *The Birth of Tragedy from the Spirit of Music*, Friedrich Nietzsche traced the suppression of what he called the pessimistic Dionysian spirit in Western civilization to the emergence of the more optimistic Apollonian. The Dionysian truths represented the dark side of Greek mythology: Titanic wars and heroes, the agonies of Prometheus, Oedipus, Orestes, and the definitive wisdom of Silenus, satyr companion to Dionysus, who, when asked by King Midas what humanity most desires replied, "Oh, wretched ephemeral race, children of chance and misery, why do ye compel me to tell you what it were most expedient for you not to hear? What is best of all is beyond your reach forever: not to be born, not to be, to be nothing. But the second best for you—is quickly to die" (Nietzsche 1995, 42), that is, the "defunctus," ending, or completion that Hamm is denied. Nietzsche's source, as well as Beckett's, was doubtless Schopenhauer, Nietzsche's early mentor, in whose *The World as Will and Idea* the sentiment was axiomatic. The thought is echoed in Freud's *Jokes and Their Relation to the Unconscious* as well: "Never to have been born would be best for mortal man." "But," adds the philosophical comment in the *Fliegende Blätter* (a well-known comic weekly), "this happens to scarcely one person in a hundred thousand" (Freud 2000, 57). For Beckett, Silenus's Dionysian wisdom constitutes not only an apposite description of the human condition but a definition of modern tragedy as well. As Beckett put the matter in *Proust*,

> tragedy is not concerned with human justice. Tragedy is the statement of an expiation, but not the miserable expiation of a codified breach of a local arrangement, organized by the knaves for the fools. The tragic figure represents the expiation of original sin, of the original and eternal sin of him and all his "soci malorum," the sin of having been born. (Beckett 1957c, 49)

Beckett follows the comment in *Proust* with a quotation from Calderón's *La vida es sueño*, "Pues el delito mayor del hombre es haber nacido" ["For the greatest crime of man is to have been born"] (Beckett 1957c, 49). That spirit is evoked by Neary in *Murphy* in terms of both the womb and the asylum: "back to the cell, blood heat, next best thing to never being born" (Beckett 1957b, 44), and it permeates Beckett's work. *The Unnamable* improves on it: "ah, you can't deny it, some people are lucky, born of a wet dream and dead before morning" (Beckett 1965a, 379–80). In *Embers* Henry recalls his father's last words, describing him as a washout, as he recalls "Wish to Christ she had" [that is, washed him out, douched after sex so that he never was born] (Beckett

1984b, 96). In *Endgame* Hamm reminds us, "The end is in the beginning," (Beckett 1958, 69), which echoes blind Pozzo's lament in *Godot*, "They give birth astride of a grave" (Beckett 1954, 57b). The protagonist of *From an Abandoned Work* notes, "No, I regret nothing, all I regret is having been born" (Beckett 1995c, 158). A *Piece of Monologue* opens with the words, "Birth was the death of him" (Beckett 1984b, 265), and that phrase is repeated throughout the play. In *Fizzle 3*, "Afar a Bird," the theme is varied only slightly, "I gave up [...] I gave up before birth" (Beckett 1976b, 25; 1995c, 232); the refrain, then, links *Fizzle 3* with *Fizzle 4* in which the phrase is used to open the narrative.

The calculated, apocalyptic ending of *Endgame* remains deferred and the origins of life in the shelter lost to memory. Hamm struggles to reconstitute life in the shelter with a series of narratives— fragmented, incomplete, unending, and not specifically referential. Failing either to connect beginnings to ends or to give meaning to the lives they lead, these narratives provide less concord than discord. Hamm begins a tale of concord, "Imagine if a rational being came back to earth, wouldn't he be liable to get ideas into his head if he observed us long enough. (*Voice of rational being.* [that is, another imbedded performance]) Ah, good, now I see what it is, yes, now I understand what they're at!" (Beckett 1958a, 33). But the narrative breaks down and is broken off, the story remaining unended.

Hamm, then, is Samuel Beckett's first dramatic character struggling to connect ends to origins, making sense, like his fictive avatars, through narratives of a lost, forgotten past, struggling (and failing since all narratives fail) to create continuities between origins and endings, which would give meaning to the middle, the present. As a schematic then, Samuel Beckett's fictions become fictions of discord rather than concord, assaults on the mythologies of origins, of ends, and of everything in between. What remains are fragments of memory, history, imagination, forgotten, reimagined, forgotten again. The dominant trope of these narratives is their sense of unending, which manifests itself formally in fragmentation, caesura, and incompletion. And the final *Fizzle 8* evokes overtly the repetitiousness of endings, "For to end yet again" (Beckett 1995c, 243). What appears to be an end, then, may be in fact only a pause before a reboot.

Between fictive, mythologized beginnings and inaccessible ends lies unrelieved travail, borne through the fiction of punishment, life as pensum, Samuel Beckett's metaphor for the "task" that damns the life of the body, as defined in Schopenhauer's remarks "On the Suffering of the World"[1]: "Das Leben ist ein Pensum zum Arbeiten: in diesem Sinne is defunctus ein schšner Ausdruck" ("life is a task to be worked off: in this sense defunctus is a fine expression") (*Parerga und Paralipomena* [that is, Appendices and Omissions, Beckett referencing the second volume, that of *Paralipomena,* things left out of the main body of Schopenhauer's oeuvre, the Omissions] II.xii section 157, see O'Hara 1997, 27; see also *Letters* 2009, 38n10) "Pensum" and "defunctus" meaning, respectively, a task done as a punishment and its completion, rather ending. Beckett ends *Proust* with an evocation of this passage from Schopenhauer: "the aesthetic vision that damns the life of the body on earth as a pensum and reveals the meaning of the word: 'defunctus'" (Beckett 1957c, 93). Beckett was fascinated with Schopenhauer's intellectual justification of unhappiness (one that Freud would share as well). Writing to his confidant Thomas MacGreevy in July 1930, Beckett commented, "I am reading Schopenhauer. Everyone laughs at that. [Jean] Beaufret & Alfy [Alfred Péron] etc. But I am not reading philosophy, nor caring whether he is right or wrong or a good or worthless metaphysician. An intellectual justification of unhappiness—the greatest that has ever been attempted—is worth the examination of one who is interested in Leopardi & Proust rather than Carducci & Barrès" (*Letters* 2009, 32–3, see also Feldman 2006, 48). In the next letter, he added, with direct reference to the end of his own essay on Proust and endings in general: "Schopenhauer says 'defunctus' is a beautiful word—as long as one does not suicide. He may be right" (*Letters* 2009, 36): that is, "defunctus" as death, but not self-inflicted.

Schopenhauer stayed with Beckett. In a like vein, then, Molloy laments, "You invent nothing, you think you are inventing, you think you are escaping, and all you do is stammer out your lesson, the remnants of a pensum got one day by heart and long forgotten, life without tears, as it is wept" (Beckett 1965a, 32). His cry is repeated by the Unnamable, in a sustained metaphor which defines his relationship to the Master, in terms of the need for punishment, which implies fixation, order, somebody or something inflicting this: "I was given a pensum, at birth perhaps, as a punishment for having been born perhaps, or for no particular reason, because they dislike me, and I've forgotten what it is" (Beckett 1965a, 310–11). In *Texts for Nothing* 7, the setting is a "Terminus," the third-class waiting room of the "Slow and Easy," and the pensum that of waiting among the dead, for a train that will never come, in a city that is not eternal (Beckett 1995c, 129). As Francis Doherty comments, "Man needs the fiction of punishment for a crime uncommitted in order that he bear up under the burden of an emptiness and isolation which are unbearable but must be borne" (Doherty 1971, 43).

One recurrent motif Beckett has deployed to accommodate the pensum is the traditional trope of the journey, but by the mid-1960s, Beckett essentially abandoned stories featuring the compulsion to (and so solace in) movement, in favor of stories featuring stillness or some barely perceptible movement, at times just the breathing of a body or the trembling of a hand. I have elsewhere called these late tales "closed space" stories, and they often entail little more than the perception of a figure in various and alternate postures, like an exercise in human origami. The journey theme had been a mainstay of Beckett's fiction from *Murphy* and *Watt*, and its motion offered Beckett's *omnidolent* creatures a degree of solace: "As long as I kept walking I didn't hear [the cries] because of the footsteps" (Beckett 1995c, 45), the narrator of *First Love* reminds us. But it was the fact of journey, the act of movement rather than any particular goal or ending that consoled, as the narrator of *From an Abandoned Work* overtly reminds us: "I have never in my life been on my way anywhere, but simply on my way" (Beckett 1995c, 156). The shift from journeys, the comings and goings, movement from and return to some place or space, to the "closed space" tales is announced in a series of fragments and faux départs that Beckett eventually published as *All Strange Away* (1963–4) and its sibling *Imagination Dead Imagine* (1965): "Out the door and down the road in the old hat and coat like after the war, no not that again" (Beckett 1995c, 169). The alternative now was: "A closed space five foot square by six high, try for him there" (Beckett 1995c, 272). The change necessitated the creation of a new character or a new conception of character as well, a nameless "him," who became Beckett's second major fictional innovation. The first was "voice," that progressive disintegration of "literary character" which dominated the journey fictions from *Molloy* through *From an Abandoned Work* and included most of Beckett's major novels—and was occasionally reprised in "closed space" tales like *Company* and *Ill Seen Ill Said*, for instance. In the drama the journey motif was transformed as overt repetition. In *Play* (1964), for example, Beckett launched a parallel assault on literature with a plot remarkable for its banality, as language or meaning was devalued from the opening "largely unintelligible" fragments of chorus, and with an assault against the very idea of resolution, ending, and so completion with, at least as originally written, overt repetition. The play's *da capo* structure, even as revised in rehearsals into a subtle decline, suggests that these figures are trapped not only in urns but in an unending series of discordant narratives, in an endless, eternal cycle, a Möbius strip of narrative that offers no explanation of beginnings, no solace of ends, no justification for the pensum. Beckett would visually recast these images of unending nearly a decade later in the pacing figure of *Footfalls*, then again in the ballet, *Quad*. Circularity and repetition were, of course, already implicit in the structure of *Waiting for Godot, Endgame*, and *Happy Days*, but with *Play* the repetition grew even more sinister, more punishing (especially for the performers); the characters became less corporeal, more dehumanized than in anything Beckett had heretofore written for the stage. Moreover, the visual image of *Play* suggests that Beckett had turned to his fiction for tropes, as the stage iconography echoed less that of his earlier drama than that of his more disembodied prose narratives, the voice. One of the narratological voices of *The Unnamable*, for example, notes, "a collar, fixed to the mouth of the jar, now encircled my neck. And my lips which used to be hidden ... can now be seen by all and sundry" (Beckett 1965a, 332). *Play* and *Not I* may emerge from the same jar. In these plays, then, the journey motif was transformed into a looping, unending cycle.

Beckett's second major character development, then, was the pronominal "him," or on occasion "her," "one," or "it," objects of the narrator's perception, memory, or imagination, the narrator himself often only part of a series or multiplicity of replications, a creation, "devised," a "him" to someone else's imaginings. These "closed space" tales not infrequently resulted in intractable creative difficulties, literary cul-de-sacs into which Beckett had written himself or progressions that could not be ended, and so they were more often than not abandoned. As often, however, they were unabandoned, resuscitated, revived, and revised as Beckett periodically returned to his "trunk manuscripts," and that hesitating, stuttering creative process of experiment and impasse, breakthrough and breakdown became the subject of the narratives themselves. These are tales designed to fail; that is, they were continued until they broke down, and then continued a bit more. As these stories were begun, abandoned, recommenced, and ended yet again, they often existed in multiple, connected versions most of which were, at one time or another, published, like the triptych of mid-seventies stories: "Still," "Sounds," and "Still 3." "Still" became one of the *Fizzles*, while "Still 3" and "Sounds" were fizzles of fizzles. These stories featured a narrative consciousness straining to see and hear images which may have come from within or without, often from both simultaneously, resulting in what the narrator of *Ill Seen Ill Said* calls the confusion of "That old tandem": "the confusion now between real and—how say its contrary? No matter. That old tandem. Such now the confusion between them once so twain" (Beckett 1981, 40). That exploration of "the confusion between them once so twain" is one of the old questions, the realm of what Leibniz or Kant would call "apperception," but today we might call cognition, cognitive science, or cognitive psychology, the exploration of the function of mind or intelligence, the interaction of reason, perception, memory, and language. For Leibniz, Kant, and even Schopenhauer, apperception was the active process of the mind's reflecting upon itself, the mind's perception of itself as a conscious agent, the consciousness of being conscious. The concept was of particular importance to Kant, whose teachings are predicated on replacing the Platonic notion of transcendence with a rigorously defined sense of the synthetic unity of consciousness. The word is used by Beckett in such early works as *Dream* and *Murphy* to delineate the mental territory he would explore for the rest of his life, even as his distrust grew of the synthetic unity of the perceiving subject, the "I" to whom the field of immanence is ascribed. The endeavor perhaps culminates in *Film* with O's "flight from extraneous perception breaking down in inescapability of self-perception." Many of Beckett's later "closed space" stories feature the act of perception in terms of unconscious inferences from uncertain stimuli. This is not the world of behaviorist psychology, whose literary equivalent Beckett ridiculed as early as 1932 in his unfinished novel *Dream of Fair to Middling Women* by calling Balzac's characters "clockwork cabbages." In the "closed space" stories we watch the process of meaning creation, the process of cognition as an active process, a becoming, the activity of the stories, plot, say, as opposed to the passive nature of behaviorism.

In "Afar a Bird," "*Fizzle* 3" of the 1976 *Fizzles*, Beckett's translation (begun Paris, March 28, 1975) of the sixth of the *Foirades*, "Au loin un oiseau," features an "I," some sort of consciousness, memory, or, more broadly, mind within or part of a moribund "he": "it was he, I was inside" (Beckett 1994c, 232). The "he" slowly treads a "ruinstrewn land," on perhaps his last journey, stopping every ten or so paces to rest, "one on top of the other the hands weigh on the stick, the head weighs on the hands" (Beckett 1994c, 232). The "I" evaluates the relationship between the two, "it was he had a life, I didn't have a life, a life not worth having, because of me." Within mind an external reality is affirmed with the titular phrase, "afar a bird," but the complications within mind suggest interminable complexity: "someone divines me, divines us." In the novel *Company* some five years later, such apperception or cognition will be expressed with the image of a "devised devisor." The "I" then feeds the "he" images: "I'll put faces in his head, names, places, churn them all up together." Potentially sentimental, such images of haunting faces, remnants of love lost, have driven much of Beckett's late work, particularly the drama, from *Krapp's Last Tape*, through the radio play *Words and Music* to the television plays. In "Afar a Bird" the "I" will supply images that feed the cycle of loss: the "he" "may love again, lose again" (Beckett 1994c, 233).

Another unabandonment is *Bing*, written in French in 1966, published by Minuit that same year, and then translated into English as *Ping*. The text was composed at first in columns entitled "corps," "endroit," "divers" (the last finally deleted). The column structure allowed Beckett to arrange and observe his material in sequence, through which he was able to trace and place themes and variations. *Bing* derives from Beckett's struggles with *Le Dépleupleur, The Lost Ones*, though markedly dissimilar in length, style, tone, and content. In a note accompanying the French manuscript of *Bing*, translated into English first as "Pfft" but quickly revised to the equally onomatopoeic "Ping," for example, Beckett noted, "'Bing' may be regarded as the result or miniaturization of *Le Dépeupleur* abandoned because of its intractable complexities" (Reading University Library, Samuel Beckett Archive, Ms 1535/1–7).

The figure described, the narrator hints, is "perhaps not alone," and so the possibility exists of others, whose perceptions fail as well. Although the story lines of the late tales are fairly simple, narratologically they are considerably more complex. The reader's focus is not only on a figure in a closed space, but on another figure and a narrator imagining them. We have then not just the psychologically complex but narratologically transparent image of an apperceptive self, but an apperceptive self imagining itself apperceiving, often suspecting that it, too, is being imagined and perceived.

The theme is treated more expansively in Beckett's last novel, *Worstward Ho*. As Beckett outlined its themes in the early drafts it was clear that in addition to the "pained body" and "combined image of man and child," we have "The perceiving head or skull. 'Germ of All.'" But the term "All" already contains a paradox which threatens to become a narratological impasse. Can the skull be "Germ of All," even of itself, the narrator asks: "If of all of it too?" (Beckett 1983, 18). Can it then perceive itself if there is, to adapt Jacques Derrida, no outside the skull. From what perspective, from what grounding could it be perceived? If "All" happens inside the skull, is skull inside the skull as well? Such paradoxes shift the narratological focus to language and its complicity in the act of representation to a cyclical unending series. If the pivotal word, what in *A Piece of Monologue* is called "the rip word," in *Ill Seen Ill Said* is "less," in *Worstward Ho*, like *Company*, it is "gone": "Gnawing to be gone. Less no good. Worse no good. Only one good. Gone. Gone for good. Till then gnaw on. All gnaw on. To be gone" (Beckett 1996, 41–2). But to be gone is impossible. What remains is a sense of unending since even denial re-invokes, reconstitutes the image or the world, the gone always a going, the end an ending. Beckett summarized the paradox in the title of one of the best of the late prose fragments, *Imagination Dead Imagine*. Writing about absence reifies that absence, makes of it a presence, as writing about the impossibility of writing about absence is not the creation of silences but its representation. Beckett's silences have always been very wordy. As the image shifts in *Worstward Ho* from the skull, "Germ of All" (Beckett 1996, 91), to the language representing it, the narrator tries to imagine the end of words, for which, then, he substitutes the word "blanks"—still, however, a word—and then simply a dash, "—" (Beckett 1996, 105–6). But the dash too is representation as it recalls the conventions of referring to proper names in nineteenth-century Russian fiction. The closer we come to emptying the void, of man, boy, woman, skull, the closer void itself comes to being an entity imagined in language, the more void is less absence than plenum. The desire to worsen language and its images generates an expansion of imaginative activity in its attempt to order experience. The drive worstward is, thus, doomed to failure, and so all an artist can do, Beckett has been telling us, is to "Try again. Fail again. Fail better" (Beckett 1996, 89).

With his late "closed space" fictions, Beckett has managed to reduce (but not end) narrative time nearly to points of space, pensum to punctum. With the development of the "closed space" images in the mid-1960s, Beckett broke with his own early narrative tradition, which relied heavily on a pastiche of the Western literary and philosophical canon. But he retained even in the fragmentary minimalism of his late work his preoccupation with the old questions, with beginnings and endings, matter and its origins, its perception and representations. Questions of cosmic creation were redirected to matters of literary creation, *ex nihilo* or from some eternal, inchoate matter which coalesces into temporary shapes through the imagination. Unsurprisingly, then, the final sense of these miniatures is less that of completed tales than a momentary glimpse of an infinite, self-reflexive mosaic of images whose series is unending.

# Note

1   See Arthur Schopenhauer, "On the Suffering of the World," *Studies in Pessimism*, a selection of essays from the *Parerga*, published as an e-book by the University of Adelaide: "Life is a task to be done [the pensum]. It is a fine thing to say *defunctus est*; it means that the man has done his task." https://ebooks.adelaide.edu.au/s/schopenhauer/ arthur/pessimism/contents.html. As a sidebar, we might note that the death of King Edward in the Bayeaux tapestry is described thus: ET HIC DEFUNCTUS EST.

# 13

# The Death of Style: Samuel Beckett's Art of Repetition, Pastiche, and Cutups

Le style c'est l'homme même
*Georges-Louis Le Clerc de Buffon*
Discours sur le style, *1753*

*en français c'est plus facile d'écrire sans style.*
*[ ... in French it is easier to write without style.]*
*SB to Nicholas Gessner, 1956*

Samuel Beckett was among the last European authors, among the last humanist European authors, at least, even as he struggled to disabuse such notions. That humanist idea of authorship that Beckett both epitomized and simultaneously dismantled remained central to his creative makeup and output. He was among the last of the major authors deeply immersed in canonical European literature, and his memory was nearly eidetic. His was an elite, Ascendancy, Anglo-Irish education that even James Joyce envied, one that he continued as an autodidact. He had at his ready command, even in his later years, not only all of Shakespeare, Dante, Milton, Petrarch, The King James *Bible* (not to mention the *Book of Common Prayer*), and much of English and German Romantic Poetry (Goethe, Heine, and Hölderline in particular), Sterne, Defoe, Flaubert, Yeats, as well as Dr. Johnson and his commentators (he owned *The Poetical Works of Samuel Johnson*, 1785, and the 1799 *Dictionary*), but Robert Burton's *The Anatomy of Melancholy* (his a three-volume edition) and St. Augustine's *Confessions* as well. He owned a compact *OED*, which he consulted regularly, and Anne Atik recalls his defense of language some might deem obsolete, like "haught" in *What Where* and "feat" in *Footfalls* (Atik 2005, 25, 56). In 1960 he was "learning Matthias Claudius by heart! 'Friend Death'" (Atik 2005, 65, her translation). The latter would substantially shape his own 1969 and subsequent stagings of *Krapp's Last Tape*.

That education, and its stylistic manifestations, may finally have become a burden to him as the European *eidos* weighed on his consciousness and pen, so much so that he launched an assault not only against a particular style, but against style itself. One plausible explanation for his linguistic shift from English to French, for example, was to evade his cultural history, to write, as he said about the change, without style, a possibility that French seemed to offer him. If style is the man, a version of which Beckett would certainly have encountered in Burton ("It is most true, *stylus virum arguit*, our style bewrays us." [*Anatomy of Melancholy*, "Democritus Junior to the Reader," 107][1]), then Beckett's assault on style was concomitantly an assault on authorship, if not on identity. By 1953 Roland Barthes would elevate such French café chatter to an aesthetics, a theory of literature, and call it "writing degree zero." But Beckett's 1956 comment (to Nicholas Gessner) was itself already a recasting of an aesthetics-in-progress, developed in his first sustained piece of fiction, *Dream of Fair to Middling Women*, a novel with which he struggled through 1931 and completed (at least enough to expose it to English if not Irish publishers) in summer 1932, just after he resigned his teaching post at Trinity College, Dublin. (It was published, however, only in 1992.) The point is made by Beckett's thinly disguised alter ego, Belacqua Shuah, a radical celibate with castration fantasies who is practiced in the rites of that patron saint of Irish birth control, Saint-Onan: "They have no style, they write without style, do they not, they give you the phrase, the sparkle, the precious margaret. Perhaps only the French can do it. Perhaps only the French language can give you the thing you want" (Beckett 2012, 48, cited in Beckett 1984, 47).

Having come of age as a writer amid the stylistic flourishes and excesses of Modernism, Beckett found himself lured for a time to the prison house of style. *Ulysses* had been the forbidden fruit of his early years, and in what must have been as much literary masochism as reverence, he undertook the translation of segments of *Finnegans Wake* into French once he had met Joyce. He read Proust closely enough to write a monograph on the obsessive stylist in his short-lived bid at an academic career ("Don't be too hard on him," pleads *Dream*'s narrator, one "Mr. Beckett," of the poet Belacqua Shuah, "he was studying to be a professor" [Beckett 1992, 48]). And he translated the stylistic excesses of "the Infernal One, the Ailing Seer" (Beckett 1992a, 137), the Rimbaud of *Le Bateau ivre*, into rhetorically equivalent English in *The Drunken Boat*, a fact also acknowledged by *Dream*'s narrator: "Shall he roll his eyes, blush and quote him in translation? You know, of course, didn't you, that he did him pat into English" (Beckett 1992a, 137–8). Editors Eoin O'Brien and Edith Fournier seem to have decided that Beckett's original language wanted improving. Beckett actually wrote, "You know, of course, don't you, that he did him into the eye into English." (For more details on Beckett's own translation of Rimbaud, see Pilling 2004, 238–9.) Linguistic expatriation enabled Beckett to recast his literary lineage, to father himself, as it were, by sloughing the heritage of English style so keenly mimicked by Joyce in the "Oxen of the Sun" chapter of *Ulysses*. But in *Dream* Belacqua fancies he might become "the Cézanne ... of the printed page, very strong on architectonics," that is, very systematic (Beckett 1992a, 178–9; Pilling 2004, 293). It was an aesthetics from which Beckett would soon distance himself. In another jettisoned piece of this period, "Casket of Pralinen for the Daughter of a Dissipated Mandarin" (that daughter being the Smeraldina-Rima of the New Year's Eve debacle treated in *Dream*), Beckett was already repenting the aesthetics of mastery: "Oh I am ashamed/of all the clumsy artistry/I am ashamed of presuming/to arrange words/of everything but the ingenuous fibres/that suffer honestly" (Beckett 2012, 32).

What continues to claw in the late work—even in this age of hypertext, which, like contemporary theater, has valorized spectacle and so returned to the ostentation of Modernism—is not solely the sparseness of narration and dialogue, the textual indeterminacy in contrast to the "architectonics," that is, the rejection of the grandiloquence of Modernism, a rejection of rhetoric and figurativeness, a rejection finally of style. Beckett became astonishingly adept at writing without or beyond style— or at least in the style of stylelessness as the Surrealists wrote in the style of the insane. Much of his early work, apprentice fiction and poetry written under the temporary delusion that he could become James Joyce, charts the disillusionment—with Joyce, with Modernism, and finally with literature, with art itself. Art had become the religion of Modernism, and the task that Beckett finally set for himself was to record what was left once art too had passed, and we were returned to that silence where we have always already struggled to know ourselves. He would finally labor to chart the void art refused to fill, failing at each attempt, but each time failing perhaps better. After the Second World War he would jettison the virtuosity of Modernism (along with the English language, at least for a time), banish its bravado, shun literariness for a linguistic literalness confounding in its simplicity. ("Alas cang of emblem ..." [Beckett 1992a, 188], the narrator alerts the nodding reader in *Dream*, anticipating the "No symbols where none intended" of *Watt* [Beckett 1959, 254].) The shelter of *Endgame* may, finally, resist metaphoricity or symbolization, likewise the road of *Godot*, the cylinder of *The Lost Ones*, the mud of *How It Is*. Sometimes a shelter is just a shelter, a road just a road, mud, mud. The power of these works rests finally with their ruthless, unrelieved abandonment of the literary, with their embrace of "the ingenuous fibers that suffer honestly" (Beckett 2012, 32).

Despite his struggles to free himself from the prison house of style, much of Samuel Beckett's writing is intimately, even inextricably, tied to his reading; that conclusion is one of the seminal developments of recent Beckett criticism and may define Beckett scholarship well into the new century. Much of the direct evidence for such connection emerged after his death in 1989 with the discovery of documents whose existence had previously been unknown: notebooks and chapbooks from the early years, particularly the German diaries of 1936–7 and the *Dream* and *Whoroscope* notebooks of roughly the same period. As James Knowlson explains in his 1996 biography, the more we know about Beckett's reading, matter and method, the more fully we understand his struggles with and against style and so his creativity, much of which developed through what Knowlson calls a "grafting technique," and, moreover, the more

direct resemblance we find to methods of composition employed by
Beckett's fellow Dubliner, James Joyce:

> Certain parallels between Beckett's early methods and those
> of Joyce are fairly obvious. Joyce took particular care with his
> research, reading books primarily for what they could offer
> him for his own writing. (Indeed many people who knew him,
> including Beckett, have claimed he read almost exclusively for
> this purpose.) Though he was inspired more by disinterested
> intellectual and scholarly curiosity than Joyce was, Beckett's
> notebooks show that he too plundered the books he was reading
> or studying for material that he would then incorporate into his
> own writing. Beckett copied out striking, memorable or witty
> sentences or phrases into his notebooks. Such quotations or
> near quotations were then woven into the dense fabric of his
> early prose. It is what could be called a grafting technique, and
> at times it almost runs wild. He even checked off the quotations
> in his private notebooks once they had been incorporated into
> his own work. This technique was not specifically adopted by
> Joyce, but it was very Joycean in its ambition and its impulse.
> (Knowlson 1996, 109)

We have known for some time how heavily Joyce relied on
*The Spiritual Exercises of Saint Ignatius Loyola* for the structure
of Chapter III, the retreat at Belvedere, of *A Portrait of the Artist
as a Young Man*. James R. Thrane has further demonstrated the
scope of Joyce's use of a 1688 text by an Italian Jesuit, Giovanni
Pietro Pinamonti, *Hell Opened to Christians, To Caution Them
from Entering into It* (English translation, Dublin, 1868) in that
same chapter of *Portrait*. James S. Atherton has demonstrated in
notes to his 1964 edition of *Portrait* that all of Stephen Dedalus's
quotations from John Henry Newman derive from a single source,
*Characteristics from the Writings of John Henry Newman* (London,
1875). Atherton also uncovered Joyce's principal sources for the
"Oxen in the Sun" chapter of *Ulysses*: Saintsbury's *History of
English Prose Rhythm* (1912) and Peacock's *English Prose:
Mandeville to Ruskin* (1903).

In Beckett's case whole passages of *Dream of Fair to Middling
Women* came directly from St. Augustine's *Confessions*. Belacqua
Shuah, for instance, describes the Smeraldina-Rima thus:

"Incorruptable, uninjurable, unchangeable. She is, she exists in one and the same way, she is every way like her herself, in no way can she be injured or changed, she is not subject to time, she cannot at one time be other than at another" (Beckett 1992a, 42). Knowlson informs us that "these are *the precise words* that St. Augustine used to define true Being" (Knowlson 1996, 112, emphasis added). It should come as little surprise then, as critics are slowly discovering, that most of *Dream* may indeed be quotation or allusion of one sort or another, what today we would call pastiche. In fact, the development of what might be Samuel Beckett's most distinctive literary creation, the disseminated, sourceless voice of the late fiction and drama, is already anticipated in this first, if incomplete, novel, and its source is also Augustine. *Dream* mocks the voice of "the little poet speaking" (Beckett 1992a, 26), but acknowledges Augustine's sense (*Confessions* 11:6) of that voice: "So shall their voices pass away, begin and end, the syllables sound, sound and pass away, the second after the first, the third after the second, and so forth in order, until the last after the rest, and silence, with a bit of luck, after the last…" (Beckett 1992a, 105, 137). So Beckettian a statement from Augustine found its way into the *Dream Notebook* (Pilling 1999, 27) and was recycled into "Echo's Bones" (Beckett 2015, 6, 15) and *First Love* (Beckett 1995c, 37). It is an early but defining statement of the disjunction between the internal and external, the sourced and sourceless, the eternal and quotidian voice. Similarly, Beckett read Thomas Dekker's *Old Fortunatus* "just before he wrote *Murphy*" (Knowlson 1996, 198), and he copied into the *Whoroscope* Notebook the dilemma of Agripyne that would become the pattern of Neary's yearnings for Miss Counihan and Miss Dwyer, "Whether more torment to love a lady & never enjoy her, or always to enjoy a lady you cannot choose but hate." C. J. Ackerley summarizes the contents of the extraordinary *Dream Notebook* that John Pilling has so ably edited and annotated:

> Its content largely determines the texture of *Dream*, and was primarily compiled for that purpose; but other details made their way into *Murphy, More Pricks than Kicks*, and some of the early poems. There are extensive quotations from Lockhart's *History* and Bourrienne's *Memoirs* of Napoleon, Augustine's *Confessions*, Renard's *Journal intime*, Carlyle's *On Heroes and Hero Worship*, Mario Praz's *The Romantic Agony*, Thomas à Kempis's *De*

*Imitatione Christi*, W. R. Inge's *Christian Mysticism*, Victor Bérard's translation of the *Odyssey*, and Burton's *Anatomy of Melancholy*. Other authors include Rousseau, Stendahl, Rameau, Ovid and the Comtesse d'Aulnoy. There is a chunk of Dante's *Purgatorio*, including the "Sedendo et quiescendo" passage from the Anonimo Fiorentino; odds and ends from Shakespeare, the Bible, Johnson's *Dictionary*, the *Encyclopedia Britannica* and the Dublin *Evening Herald*; and a range of entries upon such diverse matters as flagellation and chastisement (William Cooper), onanism (Pierre Garnier), degeneration (Max Nordau), Chinese music and history (Laloy and Giles), food, difficult words and corsets. [...] The *Dream* Notebook is an invaluable guide to Beckett's early reading, and offers fascinating insights into his creative method at this stage.[2]

Scholars had already begun to connect Beckett's reading and his creative methods before the details in the diaries and chapbooks were available. The received wisdom about *Whoroscope* was that Beckett's primary source was Adrien Baillet's *La vie de Monsieur Des-Cartes* (1691), which Beckett acknowledged having read just before composing the poem. But Francis Doherty has discovered a more immediate source. As he convincingly demonstrates in an essay "Mahaffy's *Whoroscope*," "Some of the footnotes Beckett gave to the poem seem to be drawn, *often verbatim*," from J. P. Mahaffy's *Descartes* (1880, but Doherty cites the 1901 reprint in the "Philosophical Classics for English Readers" series), "and some of the poem's text could well have been generated from the same source" (Doherty 2012, 28, emphasis added). Mahaffy was not only a more current and shorter source for Beckett (Baillet's is a two-volume work), but he had strong ties to Dublin as a Fellow of Trinity College and Professor of Ancient History in the University of Dublin until his death in 1919. In Doherty's detailed comparison he finds Beckett's direct debt to Mahaffy incontestable:

Lieder! Lieder! she bloomed and withered,
a pale abusive parakeet in a mainstreet window.

(*Whoroscope*, ll. 70–1)

In Mahaffy, Doherty discovers most of the source of those lines: "Also on Petit he [Descartes] says, 'I think no more of him than I do of the abuse given to me by a parrot hanging in a window as I pass the street'" (Doherty 2012, 28). And the poem's "Fallor, ergo sum!" (l. 73), attributed directly to St. Augustine in Beckett's own note on that line, seems to have come through Mahaffy as well (Doherty 2012, 28). Even the title *Whoroscope*, Doherty suspects, may have been generated by Mahaffy and Baillet. Beckett's introductory note to the poem is as follows: "He [Descartes] kept his own birthday to himself so that no astrologer could cast his nativity." The following sentence occurs in Mahaffy: "He objected to his birthday being noted under his picture, because it exercised idle people in superstitions about his horoscope" (Doherty 2012, 9). "In Baillet's index," continues Doherty, "the relevant comments are noted under [the rubric] 'Horoscope,' and we can see that Beckett saves the word 'horoscope' for his own poem, and substitutes 'nativity'" (Doherty 2012, 45). "The poem," concludes Doherty, "for all its haste, is a remarkable accomplishment, but it was made all the more possible because of Mahaffy's little book" (Doherty 2012, 46). In C. J. Ackerley's summary, "the 'Whoroscope' poem, as impressive and witty as it is, makes on-going, flagrant use of Mahaffy's short life of Descartes and almost everything in it can be found there" (Ackerley 2004 [1998], xi, see also Feldman 2006, 46).

The essay that follows Doherty's in the same issue of the *Journal of Beckett Studies* is J. D. O'Hara's "Freud and the Narrative of 'Moran'" (47–63). In it O'Hara demonstrated that Beckett's method of relying heavily on sources was not restricted to his earliest work, but carried over into what is generally considered his most important novel, the diptych, *Molloy*. The O'Hara essay on "Moran" was actually the second part of his study of *Molloy*. The first half, "Jung and the Narratives of 'Molloy'" appeared a decade earlier in the *Journal of Beckett Studies*, No. 7 (spring 1982): 19–47, and then in a revised and expanded form as "Jung and the 'Molloy' Narrative" in *The Beckett Studies Reader*. These essays, however, were merely an *aperçu* for O'Hara's 1997 *summa, Hidden Drives: Samuel Beckett's Structural Use of Depth Psychology*. As comprehensive a study of Samuel Beckett's use of source material for *Molloy* as exists in print, *Hidden Drives* focuses particularly on works of Freud and Jung (and their predecessor Schopenhauer), which Beckett used extensively as what O'Hara calls "scaffolding" or "structures of thought that uphold Beckett's literary works." O'Hara's method is to trace Beckett's "use of Freudian psychology, moving from the many specific details in his texts to their actual or probable sources in Freud's writing" (O'Hara, 1). covers not only the whole of *Molloy*, but also the critical work *Proust*, the prose fictions *Murphy, First Love*, and *From an Abandoned Work*, and the radio play *All That Fall*. Such structural emphasis, moreover, confirms at least Beckett's early affinity with the Modernists, but the preoccupation persists as well into his late career as a director of his own plays, where it becomes almost obsessive, what in *Dream* he called, "very strong on architectonics" (Beckett 1992a, 179). What O'Hara details in the parallel readings of *Hidden Drives* is something like Beckett's own "discourse on method," intensely through *Molloy*, and then sporadically to the mid-1950s in the short story, *From an Abandoned Work* (1954–5), and the play, *All That Fall* (1957).

The "*Whoroscope* Notebook" itself (RUL 3000/1), which Beckett began about 1932 and used until 1937, contains the early notes he took from the *Encyclopaedia Britannica* on astrological matters that find their way into *Murphy* (hence John Pilling's preferred designation of it as the "*Murphy* Notebook"). Its great significance is as a guide to Beckett's reading and work habits during this mid-1930s period, and Pilling finds traces of Beckett's composite compositional technique as late as the 1981 novel *Company*:

> The *Murphy* [or "Whoroscope"] notebook was obviously plundered intermittently, or served as *aide-mémoire*, in such diverse cases as the *nouvelles, Premier amour* (the paradoxical two-line epitaph), *Waiting for Godot* ("neither despair nor presume," which Beckett was later to attribute to St. Augustine), the radio play *All that Fall* (whose hinny is revealed here as prompted by reading a passage of Darwin's *Origin of Species*) and—perhaps most remarkable of all—the late fiction *Company*, the Aspirate Aitch section of which was half adumbrated more than forty years earlier by the use of the letter H to designate the persona of the horoscope section of the notebook. (Pilling and Bryden 1992, 6)

This compositional pattern is explored further in Ackerley's *Demented Particulars*, which details the "unacknowledged references," Beckett's graftings, in *Murphy* to an unprecedented degree. The range of allusion, quotation, "distant echo and semi-allusion" (xi) Ackerley discovers and discusses in *Murphy* defies summary here. The very pervasiveness of echo and allusion is testimony not only to Ackerley's scholarly persistence but also to Beckett's determination to situate his work firmly within the complexities of the Western European intellectual tradition. Yet even as he struggled to free himself from just that tradition, he could still dictate to Anne Atik in 1968 from memory long quotations from Boccaccio's lectures on Dante, particularly those on the allegory of the peacock (Atik 2005, 79–81).

Ackerley's demonstration of how thoroughly Beckett's "grafting technique. ... almost runs wild" in *Murphy* suggests that the novel comes close to what today we might call collage or pastiche, but such methodological discoveries have left more than one critic uneasy about their implications for Beckett's "originality." Knowlson for one raises the specter (only to dismiss it, finally) of plagiarism: "It is not that he plagiarizes; he makes no attempt to hide what he is doing. Anyone familiar with Augustine's book would recognize the passages involved" (Knowlson 1996, 112). Ackerley too is sensitive to the issue and argues that Beckett's method is "not so much plagiarism as part of a private dialogue" (Ackerley 2004 [1998], xi). In fact, we might go further to declare that Beckett's technique is the very opposite of plagiary, the intent of which is to conceal and deceive. Beckett's renderings, on the contrary, invoke his sources and are played against them like free translations, their recognition imperative to the full effect of the prose. In the 1930s when Beckett was inventing the technique, in the process of inventing himself as a writer, the critical vocabulary integral to its exegesis was yet to be developed. It would take another generation before Roland Barthes and Jacques Derrida would reconstitute Dada and Surrealist theory to begin celebrating such collage as intertextuality. Beckett's cutting and pasting his reading onto his own stock of prose produced a discourse that Gilles Deleuze might call rhizomatic or a technique Fredric Jameson might call pastiche. That is, these early works are finally assemblages, intertextual layerings, palimpsests, the effect of which is to produce (if not reproduce) multiplicity, of texts and meanings, in a manner that will come to be thought late Modernist in the second half of the twentieth century. Beckett may have dismissed the neo-Dadaist "cut-up" techniques of William Burroughs and Brion Gysin in the 1950s as not writing but plumbing, but Beckett himself seems to have begun artistic life as such a plumber. What

Beckett rejected in both Surrealist and post-Surrealist techniques like that of Burroughs and Gysin is the overtness and exaltation of the method and the reduction if not the destruction of the agency of authorship, even as he worked himself to reduce the idea of such agency. What Beckett missed in both Surrealist methods and the Burroughs/Gysin process was cerebration and deliberation, design. Beckett remained too much the Modernist to abandon authorship (and its ally humanism) entirely, although he dabbled in near-automatic writing himself, courted the aleatory with the short prose pieces like "Lessness."

Beckett's own development of pastiche was, then, less Post-Modernist than extended Modernist, Pastmodernist, perhaps, less a means of destroying the hierarchy of culture, erasing the distinctions between high and low art as it would develop later in the century (as it did in the Pop art of Stuart Davis and Andy Warhol, say), as it was an attempt to obliterate style, that mark of coherent and discrete individuality or ego, as was much Surrealist technique like the *exquisite corpse* experiments. Post-Modern pastiche would suggest that the only style possible in contemporary culture is travesty or mimicry of past styles—quite the opposite of what Beckett was developing. Intertext or assemblage or pastiche allowed Beckett to assault the idea of style and so (or thereby) develop his own, as the rejection of occasion itself becomes a new occasion. The assault on style, then, particularly through the three great French novels of the post–Second World War period made possible Beckett's late minimalist imagism, the complexity of which resides in the rigor with which it eschews complexity.

# Notes

1  One can chart the Burton quotations used in *Dream of Fair to Middling Women* through the Index to Pilling (2004).

2  Ackerley's summary was written for and edited from *The Grove Companion to Samuel Beckett*, New York: Grove Press, 2004, but see also the "Beckett's Reading" from Ackerley 2004, 20–25, and the Preface to the volume, "Reading Beckett's Reading," Gontarski 2004, 6–9.

# BIBLIOGRAPHY

Ackerley, C. J. (2004). *Demented Particulars: The Annotated Murphy.* "Preface" by S. E. Gontarski. Edinburgh: Edinburgh UP (second edition; first edition Tallahassee, FL: Journal of Beckett Studies Books, 1998).

Ackerley, C. J. (2006). "Samuel Beckett and Max Nordau: Degeneration, Sausage Poisoning, the Bloodied Rafflesia, Conaesthesis, and the Not-I." *Beckett after Beckett.* Ed. S. E. Gontarski and Anthony Uhlmann. Gainesville, FL: University Press of Florida, 167–76.

Ackerley, C. J. and S. E. Gontarski (2004b). *The Grove Companion to Samuel Beckett: A Reader's Guide to His Works, Life, and Thought.* New York: Grove Press.

Ackerley, C. J. and S. E. Gontarski (2006). *The Faber Companion to Samuel Beckett: A Reader's Guide to His Works, Life, and Thought.* London: Faber and Faber.

Adorno, Theodor and Max Horkheimer (2002). *Dialectic of Enlightenment: Philosophical Fragments.* Ed. Gunzelin Schmid Noerr. Trans. Edmund Jephcott. Stanford, CA: Stanford University Press. (See also Thompson, Peter [2013].) PDF available at: https://archive.org/stream/pdfy-TJ7HxrAly-MtUP4B/Dialectic%20of%20Enlightenment%20-%20Theodor%20W.%20Adorno,%20Max%20Horkheimer_djvu.txt.

Albery, Donald (1954). Memo to Lord Chamberlain April 26, 1954. Sir Donald Albery Collection. Harry Ransom Humanities Research Center, University of Texas, Austin. Box 526.1. Web exhibition, 2006: "Fathoms from Anywhere: A Samuel Beckett Centenary Exhibition." Web June 11, 2017. http://www.hrc.utexas.edu/exhibitions/web/beckett/career/godot/productions.html.

Asmus, Walter D. (1986). "Rehearsal Notes for the German Première of Beckett's *That Time* and *Footfalls.*" *On Beckett: Essays and Criticism.* Ed. S. E. Gontarski. New York: Grove Press, 335–49. [Second Ed. 2012, London: Anthem Press, 253–64].

Atik (Arikha), Anne (2005). *How It Was: A Memoir of Samuel Beckett.* Berkeley, CA: Counterpoint Press.

Bair, Deirdre (1990). *Samuel Beckett: A Biography.* New York: Summit Books [1978].

Banville, John (2014). "John Banville on Samuel Beckett: A Man of Many Letters." "Culture." *The Irish Times*, 2 October. https://www.irishtimes.com/culture/books/john-banville-on-samuel-beckett-a-man-of-many-letters-1.1949370.

Barron, Stephanie, ed. (1991). *"Degenerate Art": The Fate of the Avant-Garde in Nazi Germany.* New York: Harry N. Abrams.

Barth, John (1977). "The Literature of Exhaustion." *The Novel Today: Contemporary Writers on Modern Fiction.* Ed. Malcolm Bradbury. Manchester: Manchester University Press.

Bataille, Georges (1985). *Visions of Excess: Selected Writings, 1927–1939* (Theory and History of Literature, Vol. 14). Minneapolis: University of Minnesota Press.

Beckett, Samuel (1954). *Waiting for Godot.* New York: Grove Press.

Beckett, Samuel (1955). *Molloy.* New York: Grove Press.

Beckett, Samuel (1956a). *Waiting for Godot.* London: Faber and Faber.

Beckett, Samuel (1956b). *Malone Dies.* New York: Grove Press.

Beckett, Samuel (1957a). *Waiting for Godot.* London: Samuel French Ltd.

Beckett, Samuel (1957b). *Murphy.* New York: Grove Press.

Beckett, Samuel (1957c). *Proust.* New York: Grove Press.

Beckett, Samuel (1958). *Endgame.* New York: Grove Press.

Beckett, Samuel (1959). *Watt.* New York: Grove Press.

Beckett, Samuel (1965a), *Three Novels: Molloy, Malone Dies, The Unnamable.* New York: Grove Press.

Beckett, Samuel(1965b). *Waiting for Godot.* London: Faber and Faber, Ltd.

Beckett, Samuel (1966). *En attendant Godot.* Ed. Colin Duckworth. London: George G. Harrap.

Beckett, Samuel (1971). *Film.* New York: Grove Press.

Beckett, Samuel (1971b). *Fizzles.* New York: Grove Press.

Beckett, Samuel (1980). *Company.* New York: Grove Press.

Beckett, Samuel (1981). *Ill Seen Ill Said. The New Yorker*, October 5: 48–58. https://www.newyorker.com/magazine/1981/10/05/ill-seen-ill-said.

Beckett Samuel (1981). *Ill Seen Ill Said.* New York: Grove Press.

Beckett, Samuel (1983). *Worstward Ho.* New York: Grove Press.

Beckett, Samuel (1984a). *Disjecta.* Ed. Ruby Cohn. New York: Grove Press.

Beckett, Samuel (1984b). *The Collected Shorter Plays of Samuel Beckett.* New York: Grove Press.

Beckett, Samuel (1986). *Samuel Beckett: The Complete Dramatic Works.* London: Faber and Faber, Ltd.

Beckett, Samuel (1992a). *Dream of Fair to Middling Women.* Dublin, New York: Arcade Publishing.

Beckett, Samuel (1992b). *The Theatrical Notebooks of Samuel Beckett, Volume III: "Krapp's Last Tape.* " Ed. James Knowlson. London: Faber and Faber; New York: Grove Press.

Beckett, Samuel (1992c). *The Theatrical Notebooks of Samuel Beckett, Volume II: "Endgame."* Ed. S. E. Gontarski. London: Faber and Faber and New York: Grove Press.

Beckett, Samuel (1994). *The Theatrical Notebooks of Samuel Beckett, Volume I: "Waiting for Godot."* Ed. James Knowlson. London: Faber and Faber and New York: Grove Press.

Beckett, Samuel (1995a). *Eleutheria.* New York: Foxrock, Inc.

Beckett, Samuel (1995b). *Eleuthéria.* Paris: Les Editions de Minuit.

Beckett, Samuel (1995c). *Samuel Beckett: The Complete Short Prose, 1928–1989.* Ed. and with an Introduction and Notes by S. E. Gontarski. New York: Grove Press.

Beckett, Samuel (1996). *Nohow On: Company, Ill Seen Ill Said, Worstward Ho.* New York: Grove Press.

Beckett, Samuel (1999). *The Theatrical Notebooks of Samuel Beckett, Volume IV: "The Shorter Plays."* Ed. S. E. Gontarski. London: Faber and Faber and New York: Grove Press.

Beckett, Samuel (2009a). *Selected Poems: 1930–1989.* Ed. David Wheatley. London: Faber and Faber.

Beckett, Samuel (2009b). *"Krapp's Last Tape" and Other Short Plays.* Ed. and with a "Preface" and notes on the texts by S. E. Gontarski. London: Faber and Faber.

Beckett, Samuel (2009c). *The Letters of Samuel Beckett,* Volume I, 1929–1940. Ed. George Craig et al. Cambridge: Cambridge University Press.

Beckett, Samuel (2010). *Waiting for Godot.* "Preface" by Mary Bryden. London: Faber and Faber.

Beckett, Samuel (2011). *The Letters of Samuel Beckett,* Volume II, 1941–1956. Ed. George Craig et al. Cambridge: Cambridge University Press.

Beckett, Samuel (2012). *The Collected Poems of Samuel Beckett.* Ed. Seán Lawlor and John Pilling. New York: Grove Press.

Beckett, Samuel (2014). *The Letters of Samuel Beckett,* Volume III, 1957–65. Ed. George Craig et al. Cambridge: Cambridge University Press.

Beckett, Samuel (2015). *"Echo's Bones."* Ed. Mark Nixon. New York: Grove Press.

Beckett, Samuel (2016). *The Letters of Samuel Beckett,* Volume IV, 1966–1989. Ed. George Craig et al. Cambridge: Cambridge University Press.

Bishop, Tom (1986, 2014). "Blin on Beckett." *On Beckett: Essays and Criticism.* Ed. and with an Introduction by S. E. Gontarski. New York:

Grove Press. Rpt. in *On Beckett: Essays and Criticism*. Ed. and with an Introduction by S. E. Gontarski. London: Anthem Press, 2012.

Blanchot, Maurice (1982). *The Space of Literature*. Translated and with an Introduction by Ann Smock. Lincoln: University of Nebraska Press, 1982.

Blau, Herbert (1964a). *The Impossible Theater: A Manifesto*. New York: The Macmillan Co.

Blau, Herbert (1964b). "I Don't Wanna Play," "The American Theater '64: Its Problems and Promise," *The Saturday Review*. XLVII.8 (22 February): 32, 39.

Blau, Herbert (1982a). *Take Up the Bodies: Theater at the Vanishing Point*. Urbana: University of Illinois Press.

Blau, Herbert (1982b). *Blooded Thought: Occasions of the Theater*. New York: Performing Arts Journal Publications.

Blau, Herbert(1987). *The Eye of Prey: Subversions of the Postmodern*. Bloomington: Indiana University Press.

Blau, Herbert (1990a). *The Audience*. Baltimore: The John Hopkins UP.

Blau, Herbert (1990b). "*Universals in Performance.*" *By Means of Performance: Intercultural Studies of Theatre and Ritual*. Ed. Richard Schechner and Willa Appel. Cambridge: Cambridge UP.

Blau, Herbert (2000). *Sails of the Herring Fleet: Essays on Beckett*. Ann Arbor, MI: University of Michigan Press.

Blau, Herbert (2012a). *As If: An Autobiography*. Ann Arbor, MI: University of Michigan Press.

Blau, Herbert (2012b). "Notes from the Underground: *Waiting for Godot* and *Endgame.*" *On Beckett: Essays and Criticism* (Anthem Studies in Theater and Performance). Ed. S. E. Gontarski. London: Anthem Press, 189–208.

Blau, Herbert (2013a). *Programming Theater History: The Actor's Workshop of San Francisco*. London: Routledge.

Blau, Herbert (2013b). "The Actor's Workshop." *An Ideal Theater: Founding Visions for a New American Art*. Ed. Todd London. New York: Theater Communications Group, 385–406.

Bloom, Harold (1973). *The Anxiety of Influence: A Theory of Poetry*. London: Oxford UP.

Bloom, Harold (1975). *A Map of Misreading*. (Oxford: Oxford UP).

Borges, Jorge Louis (1972). *Other Inquisitions, 1937–1952*. New York: Touchstone Books (Simon and Schuster).

Bradby, David (2001). "*Waiting for Godot.* "The First Productions in English," 86–105. Cambridge: Cambridge University Press.

Breton, André, ed. (1969). *This Quarter*, September 1932. New York: Arno & *The New York Times*.

Bryden, Mary (2010). "Preface." Beckett, *Godot* [F&F 2010], vii–xviii.

Burton, Robert (1638 [1621]). *The Anatomy of Melancholy*. https://
books.google.com/books?id=cPgveWnCdRcC&printsec=frontcover#v
=onepage&q&f=false.

Carlson, Julia (1990). *Banned in Ireland: Censorship and the Irish*.
Athens, GA: University of Georgia Press, 142–6.

Carlyle, Thomas (1904). *New Letters of Thomas Carlyle*, Volume 2.
Ed. and annotated by Alexander Carlyle with illustrations. London
and New York: John Lane, Bodley Head. https://archive.org/details/
newlettersthoma03carlgoog.

Cohan, William D. (2011). "MoMA's Problematic Provenances," *Art
News*, November 17. http://www.artnews.com/2011/11/17/momas-
problematic-provenances/.

Cohn, Ruby (1980). "The Play That Wasn't Staged: *Eleuthéria*." *Just Play:
Beckett's Theater* (Princeton Legacy Library, 2014). Princeton, NJ:
Princeton UP, 163–72.

Coughlan, Patricia and Alex Davis, eds. (1995). *Modernism and Ireland:
The Poetry of the 1930s*. Cork: Cork UP.

Cronin, Anthony (2003). " 'A Play in Which Nothing Happens, Twice.' "
*The Independent*. January 5.

Cunard, Nancy (1934). *Negro: Anthology Made by Nancy Cunard,
1931–1933*. London: Nancy Cunard at Wishart and Co.

Deleuze, Gilles (1986). *Cinema 1: The Movement Image*. Trans Hugh
Tomlinson and Barbara Habberjam. Minneapolis, MN: University of
Minnesota Press.

Deleuze, Gilles (1989). *Masochism*. New York: Zone Books.

Deleuze, Gilles (1997). "The Greatest Irish Film." *Essays Critical and
Clinical*. Trans. Daniel W. Smith and Michael A. Greco. Minneapolis,
MN: University of Minnesota Press, 23–6.

Dent, Thomas C., Richard Schechner, and Gilbert Moses (1969). *The Free
Southern Theater by The Free Southern Theater: A Documentary of
the South's Radical Black Theater with Journals, Letters, Poetry, and
Essays, and a Play Written By Those Who Built It*. New York: Bobbs-
Merrill.

Dent, Tom and Jerry W. Ward Jr. (1987), "After the Free Southern Theater:
A Dialog." *The Drama Review: TDR*, XXXI.3 (autumn): 120–5.

Diamond, Elin (2000). "Re: Blau, Butler, Beckett, and the Politics of
Seeming," *TDR: The Drama Review* XLIV.4 (winter): 31–43.

Doherty, Francis (1971). *Samuel Beckett*. London: Hutchinson.

Doherty, Francis (2012). "Mahaffy's *Whoroscope*." *The Beckett Critical
Reader: Archives, Theories and Translations*. Ed. S. E. Gontarski.
Edinburgh: Edinburgh UP. [Rpt. from the *Journal of Beckett Studies*
(New Series). 2.1 (autumn 1992): 27–46.]

Douglas, Martin (2013). "Herbert Blau, Pioneering Theater Director, Dies at 87." *The New York Times*, May 7, 2013: A20. http://www.nytimes. com/2013/05/08/theater/herbert-blau-iconoclastic-theater-director-dies-at-87.html?_r=0.

Ó Drisceoil, Donal (2011a). "A Dark Chapter: Censorship and the Irish Writer." *The Oxford History of the Irish Book, 1891–2000*. Ed. Clare Hutton and Patrick Walsh. Oxford: Oxford UP, 285–303.

Ó Drisceoil, Donal (2011b). "Appendix A: Irish Books Banned under the Censorship of Publications Act, 1929–67." *The Oxford History of the Irish Book, 1891–2000*. Ed. Clare Hutton and Patrick Walsh. Oxford: Oxford UP.

Ó Drisceoil, Donal (2017). "The Irish Writers Banned in Their Own Land." *The Irish Examiner*, 20 July. http://www.irishexaminer.com/ lifestyle/artsfilmtv/the-irish-writers-banned-in-their-own-land-455179. html.

Duckworth, Colin (1967). "The Making of *Godot*." *Casebook on* Waiting for Godot. Ed. Ruby Cohn. New York: Grove Press.

Earle, David M. (2003). "Green Eyes, I See You. Fang, I Feel": The Symbol of Absinthe in *Ulysses*." *James* Joyce *Quarterly* XL.4 (summer 2003): 691–709. http://www.jstor.org/stable/25477982.

Eliot, T. S. (1986). "The Use of Poetry and the Use of Criticism" (the 1932–33 Charles Eliot Norton Lectures at Harvard University). *The Use of Poetry and the Use of Criticism: Studies in the Relation of Poetry to Criticism in England*. Cambridge, MA: Harvard UP [1933].

Esslin, Martin (1987). "The Absurdity of the Absurd." *Samuel Beckett's "Waiting for Godot"* (Bloom's Modern Critical Interpretations). Ed. Harold Bloom. Cambridge, MA: Chelsea House Publications, 25–32.

Fallon, Brian (2000). "*The Unfortunate Fursey*, by Mervyn Wall (Wolfhound Press), £8.99." *The Irish Times*, June 17. https://www. irishtimes.com/news/the-unfortunate-fursey-by-mervyn-wall-wolfhound-press-8-99-1.283266.

Federman, Raymond and Lawrence Graver (1997). *Samuel Beckett: The Critical Heritage*. London: Routledge & Kegan Paul.

Fehsenfeld, Martha (1986). "'Everything Out but the Faces': Beckett's Reshaping of *What Where* for Television," *Modern Drama* XXIX.2 (June): 229–40.

Feldman, Matthew (2006). *Beckett's Books: A Cultural History of Samuel Beckett's "Interwar Notes."* London: Continuum.

Fiedler, Leslie (1977). "Cross the Border—Close the Gap," *A Fiedler Reader*. New York: Stein and Day, Publishers, 270–94.

Freud, Sigmund (1938). *The Basic Writings of Sigmund Freud*. Translated and edited, and with an Introduction by A. A. Brill. New York: The Modern Library.

Freud, Sigmund (1953). *Three Essays on the Theory of Sexuality. On Sexuality: "Three Essays on the Theory of Sexuality" and Other Works*. The Pelican Freud Library, V. VII. Trans. James Strachey, ed. Angela Richards. London: Pelican Books [1905].

Freud, Sigmund (1965). *The Interpretation of Dreams*. Trans. and ed. James Strachey. New York: Discus Books/Avon Books. [Strachey's re-trans. (after Brill) is based on the eighth German edition of 1930.]

Freud, Sigmund (1994). *The Standard Edition of the Complete Psychological Works of Sigmund Freud (S.E. )*, V 7. Trans. James Strachey (in collaboration with Anna Freud). London: The Hogarth Press.

Freud, Sigmund (2000). *Jokes and Their Relation to the Unconscious*. Trans. and ed. James Strachey. New York: W. W. Norton & Co.

Friedman, Warren Alan, ed. (2000). *Beckett in Red and Black: The Translations for Nancy Cunard's "Negro" 1934*. Lexington, KY: University of Kentucky Press.

Garbus, Esq., Martin, (1995). "Foreword." *Eleutheria*. New York: Foxrock Books, Inc.

"Gay UK: Love, Law & Liberty" (2017). British Library, June 2 September 19: https://www.bl.uk/events/gay-uk-love-law-liberty. Viewed July 14, 2017.

Gifford, Don and Robert J. Seidman (2008). *"Ulysses" Annotated: Notes for James Joyce's "Ulysses"* (2nd edition). Los Angeles: University of California Press.

Gillis, Alan (2005). "Denis Devlin, Brian Coffey and Samuel Beckett: Across the Tempest of Emblems." *Irish Poetry of the 1930s*. Edinburgh: Edinburgh UP. [Oxford Scholarship On-Line] (September 2007): 96–140. http://www.oxfordscholarship.com/view/10.1093/acprof:o so/9780199277094.001.0001/acprof-9780199277094-chapter-5.]

Gontarski, S. E. (1990a). Guest Editor. *The Review of Contemporary Fiction* (Grove Press Number), 10.3 (fall).

Gontarski, S. E. (1990b). "Dionysis in Publishing: Barney Rosset, Grove Press and the Making of a Counter Canon." *The Review of Contemporary Fiction* 10.3 (fall): 7–19.

Gontarski, S. E. (1992a). "Censorship and the Literary Canon: The Rise and Fall of Grove Press," *The CEA Critic: An Official Journal of the College English Association* (Noncanonical American Literature) 55.1 (fall): 47–58.

Gontarski, S. E., ed. (1992b). "Textual Notes." *Journal of Beckett Studies* (New Series). 2.1 (autumn): 1–10.

Gontarski, S. E., ed. (1992c). "What Where: The Revised Text." *Journal of Beckett Studies* (New Series). 2.1 (autumn): 1–10.

Gontarski, S. E., ed. (1999). *The Beckett Studies Reader*. Gainesville: University Press of Florida.

Gontarski, S. E. (2000). *Modernism, Censorship, and the Politics of Publishing: The Grove Press Legacy*, Chapel Hill (The Hanes Foundation, Rare Book Collection/University Library, The University of North Carolina at Chapel Hill)

Gontarski, S. E., ed. (2001). *The Grove Press Reader, 1951–2001*. New York: Grove Press.

Gontarski, S. E., ed. (2012). "On Stage," *Un tram che si chiama desiderio/A Streetcar Named Desire. Canone teatrale europeo/Canon of European Drama*. No. 7. Pisa, Italia: Editioni ETS.

Gontarski, S. E., (2016a). "A Centenary of Missed Opportunities: Assembling an Accurate Volume of Samuel Beckett's Dramatic 'Shorts.'" *Beckett Matters: Essays on Beckett's Late Modernism*. Edinburgh: Edinburgh University Press, 120–39.

Gontarski, S. E. (2016b). "'I Think This does Call for a Firm Stand': Beckett at the Royal Court." *Staging Beckett in Great Britain*. Ed. David Tucker and Trish McTighe. London: Bloomsbury, 21–36.

Graf, Stephen (2014). "You Call This "Freedom"? The Fight to Publish and Produce Beckett's First Full-length Play." *New England Theatre Journal* XXV (2014): 71–92.

Graver, Lawrence (2004). *Beckett: "Waiting for Godot."* Cambridge: Cambridge University Press.

Groys, Boris (2012). *Introduction to Anti-Philosophy*. Trans. by David Fernbach. London: Verso.

Groys, Boris (2014). *On the New*. Trans. by G. M. Goshgarin. London: Verso.

Gussow, Mel (1994). "A Reading Upsets Beckett Estate." *The New York Times*, September 24.http://www.nytimes.com/1994/09/24/theater/a-reading-upsets-beckett-s-estate.html.

Hall, Peter (1997). "Peter Hall Looks Back at the Original Godot." Web June 11, 2017. http://samuel-beckett.net/PeterHallGodot.html.

Harmon, Maurice, ed. (1998). *"No Author Better Served": The Correspondence of Samuel Beckett & Alan Schneider*. Cambridge, MA: Harvard University Press.

Harrington, John P. (1991). *The Irish Beckett*. New York: Syracuse University Press.

Hoffmann, Theodore (1965). "Who the Hell Is Herbert Blau?: The Road May Be Dead, but Regional Theater Is a Lively Business," *Show: The Magazine of the Arts*, April.

Hope-Wallace, Philip (2017). "*Cat on a Hot Tin Roof* Eludes Censor." *The Guardian*, January 31, 1958: n.pag. Web June 17. https://www.theguardian.com/theguardian/2013/jan/31/tennesseewilliams-theatre.

Horkheimer, Max, see Adorno, Theodor (2002).

James, Henry (1884). "The Art of Fiction." *Longman's Magazine* 4 (September): n.pag. Web June 11, 2017. https://public.wsu.edu/~campbelld/amlit/artfiction.html.

Jones, Jonathan (2004). "André in Wonderland." *The Guardian*, June 16. https://www.theguardian.com/culture/2004/jun/16/1.

Jordan, Ken (1998). "Barney Rosset: The Art of Publishing II" (an interview). *The Paris Review*, 145: 171–215.

Joyce, James. *Ulysses* (1986). Ed. Hans Walter Gabler. New York: Vintage.

Joyce, Trevor (1995). "New Writers' Press." *Modernism and Ireland: The Poetry of the 1930s*. Ed. Patricia Coughlan and Alex Davis. Cork: Cork University Press, 294.

Jung, Carl (1968). *Analytical Psychology: Its Theory and Practice*. New York: Pantheon Books.

Kennedy, Dennis (2010). http://www.denniskennedy.eu/trinityspeechoct2010.htm.

Kennelly, Brendan (1970). *The Penguin Book of Irish Verse*. London: Penguin Books, second, expanded edition 1981.

Kermode, Frank (1967). *The Sense of an Ending: Studies in the Theory of Fiction*. Oxford: Oxford UP.

Kiberd, Declan (1996). *Inventing Ireland: The Literature of a Modern Nation* (Convergences: Inventories of the Present series). New York: Vintage.

King, Susan (2012). "Spotlight: James Cromwell in *Waiting for Godot*." *Los Angeles Times*, March 28 [http://latimesblogs.latimes.com/culturemonster/2012/03/spotlight-james-cromwell-in-waiting-for-godot].

Knowlson James (2004). *Damned to Fame: The Life of Samuel Beckett*. New York: Grove Press.

Kroll, Jeri (1993). "Belacqua as Artist and Lover: 'What a Misfortune.'" *The Beckett Studies Reader*. Ed. S. E. Gontarski. Ganesville, FL: University Press of Florida, 35–63.

Kronenberger, Louis, ed. *The Best Plays of 1956–1957 (The Burns Mantle Yearbook)*. New York: Dodd, Mead & Co., 1957.

Lake, Carlton (1984). *'No Symbols Where None Intended': A Catalogue of Books, Manuscripts, and Other Material Relating to Samuel Beckett in the Collections of the Humanities Research Center*. Selected and Described by Carlton Lake (Austin, TX: Humanities Research Center).

Lindon, Jérôme (1995). "Avertissment." *Eleuthéria*: Paris, Les Editions de Minuit. http://www.leseditionsdeminuit.fr/livre-Eleutheria-1496-1-1-0-1.html

Lodge, David (1968). "Samuel Beckett: Some *Ping* Understood." *Encounter*, February, 85–9. Rpt. in *The Novelist at the Crossroads and Other Essay*. Ithaca, NY: Cornell University Press, 1968, 172–83.

London, Todd. "The Repertory Theater of Lincoln Centre/Founded1965: Jules Irving." *An Ideal Theater: Founding Visions for a New American Art*. Ed. Todd London. New York: Theater Communications Group, 2013, 340–1.

Lord Chamberlain Plays Correspondence. LCP Corr 1954/6597, LCP
    Corr 1964/4604, and LCP Corr 1965/304. British Library, London.
Lord Chamberlain Plays LCP 1954/23, LCP 1964/51, and LCP 1965/47.
    London: British Library.
Lowry, W. McNeil, 2013. "The Ford Foundation Program in the
    Humanities and the Arts [1963]." *An Ideal Theater: Founding Visions
    for a New American Art.* Ed. Todd London. New York: Theater
    Communications Group, 355–60.
Macklin, Gerald M. (2003) "'Drunken Boat': Samuel Beckett's
    Translation of Arthur Rimbaud's 'Le Bateau ivre.'" *Studies in 20th
    Century Literature* 27 (1), Article 7. https://doi.org/10.4148/2334-
    4415.1549.
McMillan, Dougald and Martha Fehsenfeld (1998). *Beckett in the
    Theatre: The Author as Practical Playwright and Director,* Volume I.
    New York: Riverrun Press.
McMullan, Anna (2010). *Performing Embodiment in Samuel Beckett's
    Drama.* London: Routledge.
McMullan, Anna, Trish McTighe, David Pattie, and David Tucker (2014).
    "Staging Beckett: Constructing Histories of Performance." *Journal of
    Beckett Studies* XXIII.1 (April): 11–33.
McNulty, Charles (2012). "Theater Review: *Waiting for Godot* at
    the Mark Tapeer Forum." *Los Angeles Times,* March 22. [http://
    latimesblogs.latimes.com/culturemonster/2012/03/theater-review-
    waiting-for-godot-at-the-mark-taper-forum.html.]
Mahaffy, J. P. [John Pentland] (1880). *Descartes.* Edinburgh and London:
    William Blackwood and Sons. https://babel.hathitrust.org/cgi/
    pt?id=uva.x000359150;view=1up;seq=12.
Mays, J. C. C. (1995). "How Is MacGreevy a Modernist?" *Modernism
    and Ireland: The Poetry of the 1930s.* Ed. Patricia Coughlan and
    Alex Davis. Cork: Cork UP, 103–28. [http://www.macgreevy.org/
    style?style=text&source=crit.cont.009.xml&action=show.]
Menand, Louis (2010). *The Marketplace of Ideas: Reform and Resistance
    in the American University.* New York: W. W. Norton & Co.
Menand, Louis (2016). "Banned Books and Blockbusters: How the
    Publishing Industry Took on the Taboo," *The New Yorker,* December
    12: 78–85.
Minor, W. F. (1965). "They Are 'Waiting for Godot' in Mississippi, Too."
    *The New York Times,* January 31. (http://www.thekingcenter.org/
    archive/document/they-are-waiting-godot-mississippi-too.)
Monnier, Adrienne (1976). *The Very Rich Hours of Adrienne Monnier:
    An Intimate Portrait of the Literary and Artistic Life in Paris Between
    the Wars.* Trans. with an Introduction and Commentaries, by Richard
    McDougal. New York: Charles Scribner's Sons.

Montague, John (1994). "A Few Drinks and a Hymn: My Farewell to Samuel Beckett." *The New York Times*, April 17. http://www.nytimes.com/books/97/08/03/reviews/30107.html?mcubz=0.

Nietzsche, Friedrich (1995). *The Birth of Tragedy out of the Spirit of Music*. Trans. Clifton Fadiman. New York: Dover Thrift Books [1872].

Nixon, Mark (2005). "'A Brief Glow in the Dark': Samuel Beckett's Presence in Modern Irish Poetry." *Yearbook of English Studies*. XXXV: 43–59.

Nordeau, Max (1895). *Degeneration*. "Translated from the Second Edition of the German Work (Third Edition)." New York: D. Appleton and Company.

Nottle, Diane (1994b). "For Ireland's *Book of Kells*, History Repeats." *The New York Times*, January 1. http://www.nytimes.com/1994/01/01/books/for-ireland-s-book-of-kells-history-repeats.html.

Oakes John (1990). "The Last Days of Grove," *The Review of Contemporary Fiction*, (Grove Press Number) S. E. Gontarski, Guest Editor, X.3 (fall): 175–8.

O'Hara, J. D. (1992). "Freud and the Narrative of 'Moran'." *Journal of Beckett Studies* (New Series). 2.1 (autumn): 47–63. Currently available on line: http://www.euppublishing.com/doi/abs/10.3366/jobs.1992.2.1.5?journalCode=jobs.

O'Hara, J. D. (1997). *Hidden Drives: Samuel Beckett's Structural Use of Depth Psychology*. Foreword by S. E. Gontarski. Gainesville, FL: The University Press of Florida.

O'Toole, Fintan (2009). "Oblomov in Dublin," *The New York Review of Books*, August 13. http://www.nybooks.com/articles/2009/08/13/oblomov-in-dublin/.

O'Toole, Fintan (2011). "The Fantastic Flann O'Brien." *The Irish Times*, October 1. http://www.irishtimes.com/culture/books/the-fantastic-flann-o-brien-1.611390.

Pilling, John (1997). *Beckett before "Godot."* Cambridge: Cambridge UP.

Pilling, John, ed. (1999). *Beckett's Dream Notebook*. Edited, annotated, and with an Introductory essay by John Pilling. Reading, UK: Beckett International Foundation.

Pilling, John (2004). *A Companion to "Dream of Fair to Middling Women."* Tallahassee: Journal of Beckett Studies Books.

Pilling, John (2006). *A Samuel Beckett Chronology*. London: Palgrave MacMillan.

Pilling, John and Mary Bryden, eds. (1992), *The Ideal Core of the Onion: Reading Beckett Archive*. Reading, UK: Beckett International Foundation.

Purcell, Siobhán (2015). "BUCKLED DISCOURSES": Disability and Degeneration in Beckett's *More Pricks than Kicks*." *Samuel Beckett Today/Aujourd'hui*. Ed. Conor Carville and Mark Nixon, 27, 29–41.

Rabaté, Jean-Michel (2016). *Think Pig!: Beckett and the Limits of the Human*. New York: Fordham UP.

Redshaw, Thomas Dillon (1995). "'Unificator': George Reavey and the Europa Poets of the 1930s." *Modernism and Ireland: The Poetry of the 1930s*. Ed. Patricia Coughlan and Alex Davis. Cork: Cork UP, 249–71.

Rembar Charles (1968). *The End of Obscenity: The Trials of Lady Chatterley, Tropic of Cancer, and Fanny Hill*. New York: Random House.

Renton, Andrew (1992). "*Worstward Ho* and the Ends of Representation." *The Ideal Core of the Onion*. Ed. John Pilling and Mary Bryden. Reading, UK: Beckett International Foundation, 99–135.

Robbe-Grillet, Alain (1965), "Samuel Beckett, or Presence on the Stage (1953, 1957)." *For a New Novel: Essays on Fiction*. Trans. by Richard Howard. New York: Grove Press.

Rosset, Barney (*c.* 2011). *"The Subject Is Left Handed"* [Unpublished memoir, portions of which have appeared in Rosset 2016]. Cited as Rosset 2011.

Rosset, Barney (2016). *Rosset: My Life in Publishing and How I Fought Censorship*. New York: OR Books.

Rosset, Barney (2017). *Dear Mr. Beckett—Letters from the Publisher: The Samuel Beckett File Correspondence, Interviews, Photos*. Ed. Lois Oppenheim. New York: Opus Books.

Rothberg, Michael (2000). *Traumatic Realism: The Demands of Holocaust Representation*. Minneapolis: University of Minnesota Press.

Seaver, Richard, ed. (1977). *"I Can't Go On, I'll Go On": A Selection from Samuel Beckett's Work*. New York: Grove Press, 87–96.

Seaver, Richard (2001). "The 1960s: Within a Budding Grove." *The Grove Press Reader, 1951–2001*. Ed and with an Introduction by S. E. Gontarski. New York: Grove Press.

Seaver, Richard (2012). *The Tender Hour of Twilight, Paris in the '50s, New York in the '60s: A Memoir of Publishing's Golden Age*. Ed. Jeannette Seaver, Introduction by James Salter. New York: Ferrar, Straus & Giroux.

Schechner, Richard (1964). "Dialogue: The Free Southern Theatre." *Tulane Drama Review* IX.4 (summer): 63–76.

Schneider, Alan (1986). *Entrances: An American Director's Journey*. New York: Viking Press.

Schopenhauer, Arthur (2000). *Parerga and Paralipomena: Short Philosophical Essays*, Volume II. Trans. by E. F. J. Payne. Oxford: Oxford UP, 1974 (reissued, 2000).

Schopenhauer, Arthur (2010). *The World as Will and Representation: Volume I*. Trans. and ed. Judith Norman, Alistair Welchman, and Christopher Janaway, with an Introduction by Christopher Janaway. *The Cambridge Edition of the Works of Schopenhauer*. Gen. ed. Christopher Janaway. Cambridge: Cambridge UP. file:///Users/user/Downloads/Schopenhauer-The-World-as-Will-and-Representation-Volume-1-The-Cambridge-Edition-of-the-Works-of-Schopenhauer.pdf.

Shainberg, Lawrence (1978). *Brain Surgeon: An Intimate Look at His World*. Philadelphia: Lippincott; paperback Greenwich, CT: Fawcett Crest Books, 1980.

Shainberg, Lawrence (1987). "Exorcising Beckett." *Paris Review*. 104 (fall). https://www.theparisreview.org/letters-essays/2632/exorcising-beckett-lawrence-shainberg.

Shakespeare, William (2015). *Macbeth*. Ed. Sandra Clark and Pamela Mason. New York: The Arden Shakespeare (Third Series).

Shakespeare, William (2017). *Cymbeline*. Ed. Valerie Wayne. New York: The Arden Shakespeare (Third Series).

Shenker, Israel (1956). "A Portrait of Samuel Beckett, the Author of the Puzzling *Waiting for Godot*," *New York Times*, May 6, Section 2, pp. 1, 3. Reprinted in *Samuel Beckett: The Critical Heritage*, ed. Lawrence Graver and Raymond.

Soloski, Alexis (2009). "*Godot*'s Return to Broadway Isn't Worth the Wait." *The Guardian*. 5 May. https://www.theguardian.com/culture/2009/may/05/godot-broadway.

*Stanford Encyclopedia of Philosophy*. https://plato.stanford.edu/entries/beauvoir/

Steiner, George (1998). *Language and Silence: Essays on Language, Silence, and the Inhuman*. New Haven: Yale UP.

Stewart. Bruce (2004). "Another Bash in the Tunnel: James Joyce and the *Envoy*." *Studies: An Irish Quarterly Review*. XCIII.370 (summer): 133–45.

Taylor-Batty, Mark, and Juliette Taylor-Batty (2008). *Samuel Beckett's 'Waiting for Godot.'* London: Continuum.

Thomas, Louisa (2012). "The Most Dangerous Man in Publishing." *Newsweek*, February 23. http://www.newsweek.com/most-dangerous-man-publishing-83395.

Thompson, Peter (2013). "The Frankfurt School, Part 3: *Dialectic of Enlightenment*." *The Guardian*, April 8. https://www.theguardian.com/commentisfree/2013/apr/08/frankfurt-school-dialectic-of-enlightenment.

Tucker, David (2011). "Posthumous Controversies: The Publication of Beckett's *Dream of Fair to Middling Women* and *Eleutheria*." *Publishing Samuel Beckett*. Ed. Mark Nixon. London: The British Library, 229–44.

Uhlmann, Anthony (1999). *Samuel Beckett and Poststructuralism*. Cambridge: Cambridge UP.

Uhlmann, Anthony (2006). *Samuel Beckett and the Philosophical Image*. Cambridge: Cambridge UP.

Uhlmann, Anthony (2014). "Beckett, Duthuit, and Ongoing Dialogue." *The Edinburgh Companion to Samuel Beckett and the Arts*. Ed. S. E. Gontarski. Edinburgh: Edinburgh UP, 146–52.

Uhlmann, Anthony (2015). "Ideas in Beckett and Deleuze." *Deleuze and Beckett*. Ed. Stephen Elliot Wilmer and Audrone Zukauskaite. London: Palgrave, 25–35.

"*Waiting for Godot*: Productions" (2006). *Fathoms from Anywhere: A Samuel Beckett Centenary Exhibition*. Harry Ransom Center at the University of Texas at Austin. Web June 11, 2017. http://www.hrc. utexas.edu/exhibitions/web/beckett/career/godot/productions.html.

Wall, Mervyn (1971). "Michael Smith Asks Mervyn Wall Some Questions about The Thirties." *The Lace Curtain*, 4, 77–86.

Webster, Richard (1974). "New Ends for Old: Frank Kermode's *The Sense of an Ending*." *Critical Quarterly* XVI.4 (winter). http://www. richardwebster.net/kermode.html.

Weir, David (1996). *Decadence and the Making of Modernism*. Amherst: The University of Massachusetts Press.

Woolf, Virginia (1925). *Mrs. Dalloway*. New York: Harcourt Brace Jovanovich, Publishers.

*The Yellow Book*: https://en.wikipedia.org/wiki/The_Yellow_Book.

Zarrilli, Philip B. (1997). "Acting 'at the nerve ends': Beckett, Blau, and the Necessary," *Theater Topics* 7.2, 103–16.

Zeigler, Joseph Wesley (1973). *Regional Theater: A Revolutionary Stage*. Minneapolis: University of Minnesota Press.

Zurbrugg, Nicholas (2000). *Critical Vices: The Myths of Postmodern Theory*. Amsterdam: G + B Arts International.

# INDEX